PRAISE FOR *MOVE. THINK. REST.*

"If you're ready to stop grinding yourself into exhaustion and start living with more creativity, energy, and purpose, *Move. Think. Rest.* is your new go-to guide. Natalie Nixon is a visionary, and in this book, she hands you a research-backed framework to break free from the outdated hustle mentality. This isn't just another productivity hack—it's a life-changing operating system for sustainable success. Read this book, implement its wisdom, and watch your potential skyrocket!"

—Mel Robbins, #1 *New York Times* bestselling author
and host of *The Mel Robbins Podcast*

"As a dancer, I've always understood the transformative power of movement, rest, and thoughtful reflection to spark innovation and sustain excellence—it's at the heart of my creative process. Natalie Nixon's *Move. Think. Rest.* is an inspiring guide for embracing wonder and intuition, helping us to unlock our fullest potential with grace and purpose."

—Misty Copeland, *New York Times* bestselling author and
principal dancer with American Ballet Theatre

"Busy is not a strategy. Instead of hustling to please the system, Dr. Nixon helps us see that we can make a difference most effectively when we don't burn out."

—Seth Godin, author of *This Is Strategy*

"MTR is a groundbreaking new framework for conceptualizing creativity and productivity. Using science, storytelling, and practical exercises, Nixon takes us on a journey to discover and redefine how we spend our precious time. Treat this book as a handbook you will return to again and again!"

—Eve Rodsky, author of *Find Your Unicorn Space*

"Dr. Nixon offers a potent prescription for nurturing the workplace's most vital asset: your mental health and capacity to grow. Her MTR framework blends science with actionable practices to foster a more human-centered way of knowing and being. Timely and essential, this work provides a philosophy and practice for building career resilience—just when we need it most."

—John Maeda, VP, Artificial Intelligence, Microsoft

"Natalie Nixon has done the hard work of distilling everything that goes into great work and giving us eight big ideas to internalize and adopt. This is a grounded and deeply useful guide to organizing your emotions and activities around the contributions you hope to make across a lifetime."

—Kelly Corrigan, *New York Times* bestselling author and host of the *Kelly Corrigan Wonders* podcast

"As a culture, we've long equated productivity with output, speed, and constant busyness—but what if that's all wrong? In *Move. Think. Rest.*, Natalie Nixon challenges us to redefine what it means to work well, showing how movement, reflection, and rest are not distractions but essential ingredients for creativity and success. A must-read for anyone looking to reclaim time and unlock their best thinking."

—Jessi Hempel, host of LinkedIn's *Hello Monday*

"This is one of the best books I've read about productivity and leadership. In *Move. Think. Rest.*, Natalie Nixon gifts us with an inspired guide to reimagine what is possible AND essential about our work and organizations."

—Josh Linkner, *New York Times* bestselling author, 5x tech founder/CEO, venture capital investor, jazz guitarist

"Natalie Nixon has long been a trusted guide for leaders who want to think differently and innovate boldly. In *Move. Think. Rest.*, she provides a refreshing antidote to hustle culture, showing that true productivity doesn't come from grinding harder—it comes from allowing space to reset. This book is a game changer for anyone looking to work with more ease and impact."

—Dorie Clark, executive education faculty at Columbia Business School and *Wall Street Journal* bestselling author of *The Long Game*

"Natalie Nixon masterfully redefines productivity in *Move. Think. Rest.*, offering a refreshingly human-centric approach to work and life. This book is a game changer for anyone looking to thrive—not just survive—in the modern world. It's time we embrace a way of working that fuels creativity, innovation, and well-being."

—Lisa Bodell, CEO of FutureThink and author of *Kill the Company* and *Why Simple Wins*

MOVE.
THINK.
REST.

Also by Natalie Nixon, PhD

The Creativity Leap: Unleash Curiosity, Improvisation, and Intuition at Work

Strategic Design Thinking: Innovation in Products, Services, Experiences and Beyond

MOVE.
THINK.
REST.

Redefining Productivity & Our Relationship with Time

NATALIE NIXON, PHD

balance

New York   Boston

Balance

Hachette Book Group

1290 Avenue of the Americas

New York, NY 10104

GCP-Balance.com

@GCPBalance

First Edition: September 2025

Balance is an imprint of Grand Central Publishing. The Balance name and logo are registered trademarks of Hachette Book Group, Inc.

The publisher is not responsible for websites (or their content) that are not owned by the publisher.

The Hachette Speakers Bureau provides a wide range of authors for speaking events. To find out more, go to hachettespeakersbureau.com or email HachetteSpeakers@hbgusa.com.

Balance books may be purchased in bulk for business, educational, or promotional use. For information, please contact your local bookseller or the Hachette Book Group Special Markets Department at special.markets@hbgusa.com.

Print book interior design by Amy Quinn.

Library of Congress Cataloging-in-Publication Data

Names: Nixon, Natalie W. author

Title: Move. Think. Rest. : redefining productivity & our relationship with time / Natalie Nixon.

Description: First edition. | New York, NY : Balance, Hachette Book Group, 2025. | Includes bibliographical references.

Identifiers: LCCN 2025017099 | ISBN 9780306835582 hardcover | ISBN 9780306835605 ebook

Subjects: LCSH: Time management | Creative ability in business | Industrial productivity | Quality of work life

Classification: LCC HD69.T54 N59 2025 | DDC 650.1/1—dc23/eng/20250604

LC record available at https://lccn.loc.gov/2025017099

ISBNs: 9780306835582 (hardcover), 9780306835605 (ebook)

Printed in the United States of America

LSC-H

Printing 1, 2025

To all of us who want to do less, better.

CONTENTS

INTRODUCTION: THE MOST IMPORTANT WORK YOU'VE NEVER SEEN

What is essential is invisible to the eye.

—Antoine de Saint-Exupéry, *The Little Prince*

If you happen to spot me while I'm in the midst of some of my most important work, here's what you'd see: me, gazing out my office window at the chattering birds in my yard. Or taking a leisurely stroll past my neighbors' front stoops. Or maybe sitting quietly by myself, staring into space.

Here's what you won't see: brow-furrowing, shoulder-hunching, emailing, or back-to-back Zoom calls.

In other words, you won't see what we typically think of when we visualize "work." That's the thing: When I'm sitting on my stoop, I'm doing work that doesn't look like work.

There's more to "our best work" than meets the eye. Much more.

Now, if you bristle instinctively at the idea of "best work" being materially the same as "daydreaming" or "wasting time," I get that. I was also skeptical that any true work could be done outside of my conscious thinking. Like a lot of people, I used to assume that I was procrastinating when I stepped away from the desk. (Granted, sometimes, I *was* procrastinating.) But time and again, when I did return to my desk after my "procrastination" was done, I ended up creating some of my best work. To be sure, I could get things done—and did so just fine—without these little sessions of wandering, pondering, and pausing. But the projects or ideas that arose *after* some time away from my desk were just . . . *better.*

Better in the sense that the work felt right, felt more fulfilling, and felt directly tapped into what I, as a human, want my working experience to be, to mean, and to do in the context of my whole life.

In short, I was flourishing.

Work done with these increments of stepping away was helping me to flourish personally, and as a significant by-product, my business was expanding. My client base was growing, and so was my team.

Now, this book is *not* about procrastination. It's about reframing productivity and how we work. But the topic of this book was certainly sparked by my wrestling with my proclivity to quote-unquote procrastinate. It made me wonder.

I wondered: What if we moved away from our dated model of productivity focused on time increments and tangible outputs, on efficiency measured in speed only, and on a micromanagement leadership style?

What if our most productive selves are *not* when we are on Zoom, or churning through email, or at the whiteboard . . . but when we give ourselves the space and time to move, think, and rest? I call this *MTR* (pronounced "motor") activity.

What if when we move, think, and rest, we're not really procrastinating, putting off for tomorrow what we should be doing today?

What if we're just approaching challenges from a different and uniquely human angle?

Move, think, rest: So simple. So needed. Then why don't we do it more regularly and more intentionally?

This book is a provocation to rethink productivity, redesign work, and reframe our relationship with time. You'll walk away with a human-centric operating system to navigate ubiquitous technology, unprecedented burnout, and hybrid work. The goal is to spark social acceptance of creative thinking and intellectual risk-taking in perhaps some nontraditional ways. It's time.

The bad news, perhaps for some of you, is that the way we view work and productivity needs to change. The great news is that we are at a perfect inflection point in history to make this change.

ORGANIZATIONS ARE ORGANISMS

As I write this, I'm on the patio of a condominium complex in Miami Beach, where I am taking a writing sabbatical. A young woman is seated three sofas down to my right on a Zoom call. I am eavesdropping—because I am "procrastinating."

I realize that she is giving a Pilates class. From her laptop. As she sits cross-legged. She looks to be about twenty-five years old. This is a normal workday for her. I overhear her say, encouragingly to the person on the other side of the screen, "Awesome. . . . Now, when you're ready, inhale, push up through your fingertips. Extend your leg, then lower it slowly. . . . Great! Now exhale. . . . Can you try moving your hands a bit more forward? How does that feel?" And on and on her work session goes.

This is work for this young woman. Luckily for her, moving, thinking, and resting are built into the rhythm of her workday. And while hers may not be a typical working day for you, increasingly, the span and scope of work, where we do it, and how we do it are expanding and opening up, offering each of us more opportunities to work in ways that also allow us to flourish.

But my call to action that you move, think, and rest is not just relegated to individuals. Mine is an entreaty to all organizations, from the tiniest mom-and-pop shop to the largest global corporation. Organizations are organisms, consisting of humans who are imperfect, inconsistent, and nonpredictive. In a world where basic tasks are being taken over by automation, artificial intelligence (AI), and robotics, the organizations that can amplify what makes their employees uniquely human will be the ones that will attract and retain the best human talent.

Going forward, integrating more movement, thought, and rest into the workday will be one of the single most effective drivers companies can do to improve their business return on investment (ROI), increase their creative capacity, and innovate consistently. Evidence of MTR activity will be the greatest predictor of a company's success because it activates its more implicit and intangible assets: its people, their creativity and well-being, and their connection to others.

I am admittedly selfishly motivated as I cajole more people to move, think, and rest. As a creativity strategist, my work is about helping businesses connect the dots between creativity and business impact. It turns out that MTR activity is a driver of the two most fundamental elements of creativity as described in my previous book, *The Creativity Leap*: wonder and rigor. In that book, I explained that creativity is our ability to toggle between wonder and rigor to solve problems, produce novel value, and generate meaning. What better way to escape into wonder than a serotonin-induced walk in the woods (movement), spending some time with a good novel (thought), or indulging in some sweet do-nothing moment (rest)? And what better way to get rooted into rigor than the discipline of exercise (movement), the healthy intellectual debate with a colleague (thought), or the commitment to taking ten-minute breaks every couple of hours (rest)?

As I sat with this question, it became clear to me. Now, more than ever, a shift away from old productivity models makes sense for three primary reasons: unprecedented burnout, ubiquitous technology, and hybrid work.

Because we have the technology to replace basic tasks, we have the opportunity to rethink work. What, after all, is the point and purpose of productivity? For me, at the end of the day, it's got to be about flourishing (which is not the same as *thriving*, by the way—I'll explain in the next section). More and more people are demonstrating that they agree with me by embracing flexible work models, taking sabbaticals, and choosing their health and well-being over the 24-7 hustle culture. The old model of productivity saw ROI only through the lens of shareholder value. The new model of productivity I am proposing, what I'm calling *cultivation*, factors in shareholder value as well as stakeholder value, and that liminal space where the most important work that we don't see happens. What it results in is true flourishing for the organization and for the individual.

CULTIVATION, FLOURISHING, AND THE IMPORTANCE OF LIMINAL SPACES

What if our most productive selves are when we step away from our desks and engage in activity that sparks different synapses in our brains?

Clearly, my walks, my daydreams, and even my naps weren't just procrastination, because they resulted in real, tangible contributions. It was work—just not the kind of work we're used to seeing.

As it turns out, the most important and essential work we do as humans is invisible. I call them the sexy bits of productivity. Now, traditionally, productivity hasn't been particularly sexy. But if we are committed to flourishing, to bringing the entirety of our human potential to our work, it is time to make productivity sexy—to make it alluring, juicy, and fun. Enter the MTR framework.

MTR activity allows your imagination to reign, to spark the synapses that synthesize your best ideas. By redesigning work through the lenses of the uniquely human activities of movement, thought, and rest, we create and strengthen channels of communication between the neurons located throughout the frontal lobes, temporal lobes, and limbic system, the ones that spark generative thinking.

When you are learning a new yoga pose, engaging in meaningful conversation, or taking a break from a tough challenge that has you stumped, the neurotransmitters responsible for generative thinking are still firing. The sexy, juicy bits of work are being done in the moment, for the sheer joy of the process—sometimes with guardrails, but never with benchmarks. There is nothing to achieve, nothing to complete, yet everything to reap. Not simply because MTR activity often yields our most exciting, innovative, get-up-and-start-now ideas but also because MTR activity is the source of work that fulfills us.

While other books have looked for ways to get more productivity out of you through time boxes, stopwatches, and inbox management, this book wants to put productivity to bed. How might we do that? By tapping into what makes us uniquely human—and leaving the unsexy parts to AI and robots. To drive this point home, I offer up the metaphor of cultivation.

When we move from a strictly quantitative productivity mindset to one of cultivation, our focus shifts from what we can make to what we might yield. Think of the produce section in your local supermarket. There, it's clear that the fruits and vegetables are what's made through farmers' labor. But what's yielded is much greater than that: the foundation for healthy individuals and communities, a sense of security, and perhaps even a feeling of abundance.

My provocation to you is to move away from a mindset of "How might I be more productive at work?" toward "How might I cultivate more meaning and value in my role?"

My promise is that in doing so, you, your team, and your organization will make quantum leaps, personally, professionally, and in terms of business outcomes.

The integration of movement, thought, and rest is the key to cultivating meaning and value in your role, and it is much juicier and much more alluring and fun than crossing off items on your to-do list. It will also have a much profounder impact on all the different aspects of your life and your organization's business outcomes. In essence, it leads to flourishing.

In 2021, Adam Grant, noted organizational psychologist and bestselling author, wrote an op-ed in *The New York Times* about the pandemic phenomenon of "languishing." It served as a cri de coeur for a world that felt just . . . blah. Suddenly, everyone was talking about languishing and thriving because we finally had language for what we were feeling and what we wanted. Languishing wasn't quite burnout and it wasn't quite clinical depression, but it was there, omnipresent, a boogeyman to our collective well-being. And everybody wanted to thrive.

Naturally, I found myself as swept up in the emerging discourse as the rest of the lockdown-weary world. At the same time, I sensed something bigger at work. I wanted—I want us all—to flourish.

This nuance, I realized, was what was missing from the conversation.

The word *flourish* comes from the same root as *floral* and *flower*. In the noun version, there's a connotation of ornateness, decoration, and aesthetic beyond mere utility. In contrast, much of the discourse on flourishing simply uses the word as a synonym for *growth* or *thriving*. But that's not entirely accurate.

When we flourish, we're not merely zooming ever upward toward a fixed point. We are acting like a flower—blooming and blossoming in bold, colorful, exciting new directions at times, and retreating into bud form at other times. Flourishing isn't just about mental and emotional health, nor is it just about getting back to a respectable level of productivity. Flourishing includes when we feel fully ourselves and fully engaged in our work. Yes, we're productive when we flourish, but productivity is a mere by-product of a bigger, more expansive state of well-being.

Flourishing can be practiced and accessed through MTR activity. In the world of design thinking, we advise teams to devise design principles, which are essentially guardrails that will be the lighthouses to whatever product, service, or experience they are trying to create. For example, a food and beverage company might develop design principles of *nutrition*, *joy*, and *community*—they would want to ensure that those three principles show up in every iteration of the food product they launch. Similarly, think of MTR activity as a design principle. These are guardrails to help you and your team design great ways to work that incorporate MTR activities and lead to flourishing.

MTR activity may involve discipline and rigor to build into our routines (especially if we're addicted to multitasking and busyness), but it doesn't take any strenuous effort or ironclad willpower. It can be wondrous and improvisational, but it's not so loosey-goosey as to be meaningless. It's creative work that you don't need to be a "creative type" to do. MTR doesn't require us to let go of control entirely. We're not taking our hands off the wheel here; we're just not gripping it so hard. In other words, we're not forsaking the rules; we're just allowing ourselves space and breathing room within constraints. I'll be going into detail about all these dimensions of MTR activity in the book.

It is the integrative nature of MTR activity that helps us and ultimately our organizations to flourish. There are hundreds of books out there focused solely on one of these three dimensions—movement, thought, or rest—with regard to the world of work. Here, I'm promoting an integrative approach that considers all three, while also holistically factoring in the impact on the individual, the team, and the organization. It is not enough to just exercise but neglect your rest. It's also not enough to engage in deep meditation and reflection but neglect your body's need to move. The three dimensions—move, think, and rest—are interdependent. In addition, MTR activity is not sequential; it is situational, relational, and iterative, as you will see. While I have devoted chapters to each dimension, you will inevitably see overlap and cross-references. That's the way MTR works because that's the way humans work.

All three dimensions, when intentionally focused upon, deliver the new operating system we need for work in the twenty-first century.

WHY THIS BOOK, WHY ME, WHY NOW

I've given a lot of thought to creativity. In my last book, I introduced the WonderRigor™ framework. This framework helps us realize that all people (not just artists) are hardwired to be creative. And that our creative capacity increases by toggling between wonder and rigor to solve problems, generate value, and produce meaning.

Flourishing, and the MTR activity that makes it possible, is in many ways a culmination of what I've been doing my whole career. Currently, as CEO of Figure 8 Thinking, I advise leaders on practical ways to catalyze creativity's ROI for inspired business results—by applying wonder, rigor, and foresight. I guide organizations through different ways of becoming more dynamic versions of themselves by designing better experiences, services, and products for their customers. I help them build their creative capacity and improve their productivity to flourish.

But I didn't get there the traditional way.

(I'm not sure I've ever done things the traditional way.)

My background is in anthropology, fashion, and education—yes, all three.

I've worked my way from a solopreneur hat designer to globe-trotting roles at Victoria's Secret and the Limited that took me from Sri Lanka to Portugal and beyond. I went from being an undergrad torn between majoring in English and biology (before eventually settling on anthropology and Africana studies) to a PhD in design management. I was a professor for sixteen years, teaching the business of fashion, and I spent the last six years of my academic career with a diverse group of colleagues building the Strategic Design MBA program at Thomas Jefferson University (TJU).

In all these roles and industries, I've always looked for new lenses, fresh paradigms, and different ways of thinking. Nat's Hats, my first venture into fashion, started as a side hustle to supplement my income as a middle school English teacher in New York City. The Strategic Design MBA we built at TJU was a conscious effort to creatively disrupt traditional graduate business education through a more human-centered approach. In my doctoral studies, I researched how the principles of jazz music provided a perfect heuristic to examine how the Ritz-Carlton hotels designed experiences that delighted their guests.

It was this last remix of paradigms—work as jazz—that led me to where I am now.

After giving a successful talk on this topic at TEDx Philadelphia in 2014, I began receiving invitations from companies to help them actualize those principles: to become more adaptive instead of reactionary, to design more flexible systems, and to create truly innovative workplaces.

What started as a side hustle consultancy swiftly blossomed into Figure 8 Thinking. I began building it full-time in 2017, after retiring from my academic post as an associate professor. Now, as the "creativity whisperer to the C-suite," I bring this diversified approach by delivering keynotes on stages around the globe to major corporate clients like Google, Citrix,

Cooley, Microsoft, and Salesforce; top nonprofit and charitable organizations; and at leadership incubators, start-ups, and all-hands meetings for executive leadership teams.

My broad-ranging professional experience has provided firsthand proof that work is not solely about productivity. At least not the old ways we have thought about productivity.

Meaningful, innovative results happen when our work aligns with our personal passion. And what I'm most passionate about is helping people connect the stuff they assume to be "out there," "woo-woo," or an optional bonus activity *to* the "real" results they're after. Because the truth is that the "extras" and the "work" are inextricably linked. In fact, they're one and the same if we are to flourish.

What I've learned, seen, and taught over my decades of experience is that this "bonus" stuff—what I call *MTR activity*—isn't actually optional. Taking a walk, doodling, and sleeping on it are the wellspring of innovation. Through keynotes, foresight studios, and advisory work, I show team managers, HR executives, and C-suite leaders that real innovation starts with MTR. If you're not leveraging MTR, then you are getting left behind. I've worked with engineers, accountants, lawyers, teachers, app developers, and beyond to help them not just innovate within their industry but also flourish in their daily work.

And I can get you there, too.

To conduct background research for this book, I interviewed over sixty people from a range of industries, professional accomplishments, and ages to understand the real-world application of MTR, which I've included throughout the book. I also incorporated secondary research to understand historical and scientific context about the ideas I have developed and collated. We'll begin by exploring productivity's past. We've got to understand the arc of all the ways we have thought about what makes us fully functioning humans in the world of work to understand the opportunity before us to reframe productivity and work. We will explore the evolution of the boundaries between the workplace and the home, between work and leisure, and how technology is creating the space for us to shift to a cultivation mindset that embraces more leisure *and* more productivity at home and at work. Then we'll move into the MTR framework. I'll break down everything you need to know to incorporate this system into your daily lives. I'm even throwing in a bonus 66-Day MTR Challenge, a series of prompts designed to give you bite-size ways to kick-start your flourishing practice right now, along with a curated MTR Soundscape playlist and a fun MTR BINGO game. At the end of each chapter, I've also included Seeds to Cultivate, a series of reflection questions and exercises for the individual, teams, and organizations, to help you further process everything you learn.

THE ANTIDOTE TO STUCKNESS

As I began research for this book, I was also in the process of developing, scripting, and filming two courses for LinkedIn Learning on creativity, leadership, and collaboration. Specifically, the courses teach individuals how to lead with inquiry, improvisation, and intuition—I call this the *3i Creativity*™ framework. One of the biggest insights I gained from developing those courses as I tweaked and revised my modules is the need to speak to the stuckness that so many people experience at work.

One vice president client at a media firm told me, "Managers are at a loss right now on how to incentivize their teams. We can't bring them this kind of advice fast enough." A similar perspective came from a client of mine at a top-tier law firm, whose team was exploring, "How do we become the law firm of choice for promising young associates, star performers, and excellent lawyers who have a ton of options?"

These might seem like disparate problems, but they are really one and the same. Both burned-out managers and the best of the best are after the exact same thing:

- work that means something;
- a workplace that trusts its employees to think independently; and
- day-to-day work experiences that are filled with thoughtfulness, options, experimentation, and energy.

These are the principles for flourishing. Current technology makes the space for it, and our souls crave it. MTR activity is the means toward the goal of flourishing. MTR activity will change the way you work. And it will do so without demanding that you overhaul your personality, adhere to a rigid protocol, or life-hack the liveliness out of your working hours. When you allow yourself the space and time to pause, to unabashedly pay attention to your human needs, and to allow your intuition to guide you, then you achieve fluency, ease, and even greater productivity.

But more than that, MTR activity will change the way you feel about work and how organizations begin to approach hiring, performance review, incentivization plans, and office design layout. Imagine concluding a workday knowing that you've not only met your key performance indicator (KPI) objectives and crossed off your to-dos but that those same KPIs now include discovery, experimentation, and adding sustainable energy to the work process. For that matter, imagine actually using your imagination and getting something out of it—a new concept for a product that will exponentially shift your market sector, a why-didn't-I-think-of-this-earlier workflow improvement, or an irresistible idea for an article. Now, imagine you've done that without quietly quitting your job.

This book will conclude by showing you how to supercharge MTR activity by spending equal time with your head in the clouds as well as your feet in the trenches. It will help you to design catalysts (rather than deadlines), experiment with modes of working (so that you can always approach a concept from a different angle), and establish a flexible (yet consistent) routine. We will conceive input-based metrics as opposed to strictly output-based metrics that measure the results of MTR activity, so you can know that you're making progress.

MTR activity will help you end your day with work that resonates, satisfies, and is sustainable enough for you to be excited to pick back up the next day.

You deserve to flourish. We all do.

Let's reimagine together.

1

CULTIVATION OVER PRODUCTIVITY

We're so programmed to be transactional that
we don't allow ourselves to be transformational.

—Susan Magsamen, *Your Brain on Art*[1]

I have a question for you.

Why do you work?

Your answers to that question can be varied. It may have to do with very practical reasons—like being able to have money so that you can provide for your family. Perhaps you're part of the lucky few in the world who can attach meaning to their work. That's right, maybe you've been able to climb up Maslow's hierarchy of needs and not only get your basic needs of food, clothing, and shelter met—but your work also gives you a sense of belonging, esteem, and purpose.

I love how Elizabeth Gilbert, *New York Times* bestselling author of *Big Magic* and *Eat, Pray, Love*, outlined categories of work in her now famous 2016 Facebook post "What Are You Doing with Your Life?"[2] In that post, Gilbert delineated the differences between a hobby, a job, a career, and a vocation. By distinguishing work in those four ways, she inadvertently made the case that meaning can be found in each *when* and only when you have clarity about why you are doing one over the other.

She refused to get down on herself about not having a "meaningful" job without first giving clarity to the purpose of each.

Whatever the reasons that prompt you to work, productivity is the undercurrent. You're evaluated by how much you have produced. Companies on Wall Street garner investment dollars (or they don't) based on time markers of productivity: Are they more productive today than they were a month ago? Or one quarter ago? Why or why not? And maybe you ask yourself on a regular basis, *How might I become more productive?*

A concerted effort to systematize productivity emerged during the mid-eighteenth century in Great Britain. This first Industrial Revolution was characterized by the steam engine mechanization and the ability to systematize work and divide it into linear steps. It spread to continental Europe and took off in the United States by the mid-nineteenth century. Productivity became characterized as something that is quantifiable, measurable, speed-based, and centered on volume and outputs. The eighteenth-century Scottish economist Adam Smith's philosophy on political economy influenced the first Industrial Revolution and transcended to the current ways we think of market capitalism. Smith's concept of markets' "invisible hand" pointed out the unintended consequences that our individual human actions can have on society. For example, a small-scale jewelry designer's collection creates demand for suppliers, introduces new products into the marketplace, and could ultimately introduce new trends into society.

In the first Industrial Revolution, work and leisure were siloed in extreme ways. In fact, in a world largely marked by the absence of a middle class, leisure was deemed something that only the wealthy landowning class could do because they could afford it. The peasant class could partake in leisure primarily tied to religious celebrations marked by seasonal cycles (we will dive more into the importance of leisure in Chapter 5, "Rest: Doing Less Better").

The second Industrial Revolution occurred between 1870 and 1914. It was characterized by an increase in electrical power. Inventions that we link to this period include the light bulb, the telephone, the automobile, and assembly line manufacturing. While we were getting great at efficiency and mass production, mass *customization* had not yet been achieved. Thus, Henry Ford famously responded to his customers' customization requests for the cars coming off his assembly line with, "Any color the customer wants, as long as it's black." This period also marked the introduction of Labor Day as an American holiday. It was originally designed to herald the American workforce and the labor movement's efforts to garner fair treatment. It has since evolved to focus on rest and bridges the end of summer with the fall. How timely then that *this* book was published just after Labor Day weekend of 2025!

Engineers like Frederick Winslow Taylor also distinguish the second Industrial Revolution. Taylor's 1911 book, *The Principles of Scientific Management*, introduced an entirely new field called *scientific management*, which paid granular attention to time management and motion studies, standardization, training programs, and pay incentivization. You may recall having learned about *Taylorism* in school at some point. This movement was an attempt to create a science out of managing people. The downside and critique of Taylorism is that it lent itself to equating people with cogs in a wheel, treating individual employees like interchangeable parts and dehumanized labor. On the flip side, Taylorism and its devotees did figure out how to build speed and efficiency into the human touch of work.

I have one degree of separation from Frederick Winslow Taylor. In fact, many of us do. Here's mine.

When I worked in the global apparel sourcing industry at the turn of the twenty-first century (from 1999 to 2001), I briefly lived in Colombo, Sri Lanka. There I worked for a division of a major fashion retailer with a focus on the "intimates" category—that's bras and panties for the rest of us. While a lot of underwear production—especially for brassieres—was increasingly becoming automated, much of the panty production was organized along assembly line production. A lot of apparel production still needs nimble human hands to put together small satin fabric components. It would not be unusual for me to see a factory engineer doing time studies, with a stopwatch, to measure outputs along each step of the production line done by women who were responsible for quickly sewing together pieces of fabric at various stages of the assembly process. Imagine the stress of having an albeit friendly factory engineer looming over you as you ran fabric components through a rapid-fire industrial-strength sewing machine! These sorts of time studies were relics of Taylor's value that faster is better.

Notably, around the same time that Taylor was making his mark, Upton Sinclair wrote his satire *The Jungle* in 1906. The book called out the horrifyingly inhumane treatment of people working in American factories—specifically, poverty-stricken immigrants in Chicago's meat-packing industry. *The Jungle* put a glaring spotlight on the production of goods happening often at the cost of a human limb or, worse, life. The book raised public awareness about the unsafe conditions in which many destitute immigrants worked. Just six months after its publication, *The Jungle* catalyzed the passage of the Pure Food and Drug Act as well as the Meat Inspection Act.

The third Industrial Revolution started in the 1950s. It essentially digitized manufacturing, integrating the internet into more networked production processes, and it made a global supply chain achievable. Mass customization became de rigueur. The third Industrial Revolution added digital electronics to the already existing mechanized and electrical integration of production. Think 3D digital printing, nanotechnology, and biotechnology. That super-dope Nike sneaker that you designed via a selection of options from columns A, B, and C? That's mass customization. So is your ability to customize an iPhone.

A HUMAN REVOLUTION—NOT A TECH REVOLUTION

We are now in the fourth Industrial Revolution, a time when AI, automation, and robotics are rapidly advancing. Often called the *knowledge economy*, this era leverages technology to foster collaboration and continuous learning, enhancing our competitiveness.

But the true opportunity of this revolution lies in rethinking productivity.

Amid this digital boom, there's a pressing need to ensure that humans don't get overshadowed by machines. Some foresee a dystopian future; others, a utopian one. I'm a practical optimist and hold a "heterotopian" (a term I first heard used by futurist Galit Ariel) view, blending a positive outlook with critical insight and questioning. The way I see it, the MTR framework provides an operating system that supports this view by creating a remix of the past, as I'll explain in the next section. It offers us a balanced approach that honors the essence of human creativity and adaptability in this new era.

By focusing on our unique human abilities that AI and automation cannot replicate, we can redefine productivity for the fourth Industrial Revolution and create a future where technology and humanity thrive together. This moment deserves a reframe. Instead of obsessing with "What to do with all of this new technology?!" we should be leaning into what makes us uniquely human. We aren't experiencing a tech revolution—we're experiencing a human revolution. The time that opens up to us because we can arrive at answers more quickly means that we have more time for human interaction, for pausing and spaciousness, and for new opportunities to collaborate. By delegating routine tasks and offloading production-type activity to computers, AI, and technology at large, we can cultivate our uniquely human capabilities to create and flourish. Sustainable growth requires cultivation.

Once upon a time, before the first Industrial Revolution, the majority of societies around the world operated on an agricultural economy. Our sense of time, community, connection to our natural environment, societal structure—and yes, purpose—was connected to what we could yield from the earth. Agrarian societies relied on human and animal labor as well as manual tools. Cultivation (not productivity) gains were a result of better farming techniques, tools, and collaboration methods. Work was linked to the land, and because of that reality, we couldn't force output. It was what it was, based on environmental factors and crop yields.

Back then, boundaries between work and home were blurred because work was often done in proximity to home. It's a relatively recent totem of modernity to assume that work and home should be separated. For as long as societies were based upon agricultural economies, work and home were comparably close together. You woke up in the morning, did your ablutions, ate some breakfast, crossed over the threshold . . . and you were at work. As the last four Industrial Revolutions brought with them innovations in transportation, we increased the boundaries between work and home.

And then COVID.

It's fascinating that the COVID pandemic once again blurred the boundaries between work and home. Commutes to jobs shrunk from hours or minutes to sometimes just seconds, sitting before a screen. For those of us who work from home—either two days out of the week or full-time—the commute and morning rituals are reminiscent of those blurred boundaries of agrarian times—that is to say, we wake up, do our ablutions, drink or eat something . . . and cross over a threshold to a space in our homes that serves as our workplace.

The ways in which we think about productivity today have not really changed since the first Industrial Revolution, where the modus operandi (MO) was measuring time and tangible outputs. But in an agriculturally based economy, the MO is cultivation. As opposed to productivity, cultivation leaves room for things to metamorphose, for ambiguity, uncertainty, and complexity. While we describe today's economic markets as VUCA (volatile, uncertain, complex, and ambiguous) environments, we have to concede that Mother Nature is the OG of VUCA environments. Consider the stressful variability of weather conditions that farmers have to deal with on a daily basis. Now, that's VUCA!

Which makes me wonder: Is there an opportunity to redesign work and reframe our rigid sense of productivity given the more flexible options we have for work, the proliferation of technology that can perform basic tasks, and the fact that burnout is eclipsing well-being at unprecedented rates?

Instead of asking ourselves, our teams, and our companies, "How might we be more productive today / this week / this quarter?" what if we asked a different question?

Try on, "What might we *cultivate* today / this week / this quarter?"

There are big differences in the two questions. The first is mechanical and linear: One plus one equals two. You follow the directions as closely as possible to achieve a desired result. Where this mechanical view of productivity operates under an *either-or* paradigm, cultivation, on the other hand, embraces the *both-and*.

Cultivation values the solo practitioner *and* the collective.

Cultivation values what's happening in the measurable and visible realm *as well as* what's evolving in the dormant invisible realm, in the liminal space of our human creativity.

And cultivation values slow *in tandem with* quick spurts of growth.

Cultivation is what happens when you follow the MTR framework. This is how we redesign work for the future. Cultivation occurs when movement, thought, and rest consistently intersect and holistically integrate—when all three are present and are feeding off one another, it's then that we cultivate the most meaningful and impactful gains. Keep this interplay in mind as you read the subsequent chapters of this book.

Cultivation is happening when we're sitting still and when we allow our bodies to do what they are naturally designed to do—a.k.a., move! So this is a very different paradigm and a new way to think about how you work. Eventually, it will spark new ideas about *why* you work. It's not so much about work segmentation versus work consolidation. It's about more qualitative approaches to the ways we produce. It's about cultivating.

I'm proposing that *all* work is actually about cultivation.

Here's how we do it.

FROM INPUTS TO OUTPUTS TO IMPACT

Traditionally, economists have thought about a country's productivity in terms of output per worker. The gross domestic product (GDP) per hour worked is also a widely used metric for productivity.[3] All those levels of output get neatly wrapped up into GDP, which was dreamed up during World War II by the economist John Maynard Keynes when the British government needed to know how much of its economy could be redirected to the war effort. But the challenge was that they had no idea what the actual size of their economy was. It is widely accepted that these output levels are indicators of economic growth and effectiveness. But GDP is just a snapshot of how large an economy is at a given moment in time. Additionally, it only captures output that is tangible and finite—like cars off an assembly line, construction projects, and semiconductors. For example, economist Daniel Susskind, author of *Growth: A Reckoning*, reminds us that GDP doesn't capture economic activity and output generated by intangibly valuable things such as search engines or email—productivity drivers that we use every day. It doesn't capture the plethora of intangible and infinite output that is possible—for example, the infinite number of combinations of ideas that can produce new innovations to boost an economy. Or things like solar energy, whose costs go down even as its impact and effects increase—unlike fossil fuel energy. So in today's knowledge economy, there are some clear limitations to call into question our strong focus on GDP. We will revisit this limitation even further in Chapter 8, "Cultivating the Imagination Era."

The Organisation for Economic Co-operation and Development (OECD) thinks of productivity as the ratio between the volume of output and the volume of inputs (labor and capital). Nobel Prize–winning economist Paul Krugman wrote in his *The Age of Diminished Expectations* that

> productivity isn't everything, but in the long run it is almost everything. A country's ability to improve its standard of living over time depends almost entirely on its ability to raise its output per worker.[4]

So, we generally tend to think of productivity in terms of how much tangible output we produce—not in terms of impact. Famed motivational speaker Tony Robbins has defined productivity as "getting the results you want with less time and effort."[5] That's interesting because what he's suggesting is another way of focusing on efficiency: reducing time and effort.

I like to think of productivity as the act of creating value. That value could be financial, social, experiential, or cultural. Another definition is "having the ability or power to create." Alternatively, others have introduced the role of impact when factoring in the results we get from being more productive. For example, the Zarvana consulting group has taken the time to explore the multiple dimensions of productivity—not just outputs but also the quality of outcomes. They think of productivity as "the amount of impact you create each hour."[6] Integrating impact into the productivity equation is a welcome addition. That's because impact begins to factor in not just the functional equivalent of the job that's been done (i.e., widgets made, sales generated, or market share accrued) but also the social and emotional effects of the work (e.g., community relationships gained, meaningful employee engagement, emotional well-being achieved, or health outcomes improved).

In modern capitalist societies, because we have historically thought about productivity in terms of volume of output, productivity gets reduced to what is tangible, measurable, linear, and more valuable if done in shorter bits of time resulting in a paycheck at the end of your shift. Therefore, you know you're being productive when you have made a lot of X in a short amount of time. We value thinking about productivity in quantifiable terms. But while sometimes what we yield is tangible (e.g., clothing, vegetables, or cars), at other times, it is intangible (e.g., ideas, services, or peace of mind). The undercarriage of productivity's labor is creativity, but admittedly, not all production processes necessarily feel creative. And interestingly, what we make is not always connected to personal value.

Here lies the rub.

Today, we are at a crossroads and have an opportunity to redesign work. While we have been thinking of productivity as happening on the job once we clock in, cultivation is happening continuously in synchronous ways. Approaching work as cultivation makes more sense in a time where technology like AI and automation can perform basic tasks and amplify what makes us uniquely human in our work.

It's not too much of a leap to shift from the perspective of productivity to one of cultivation. Consider that the word *productivity* stems from the Latin *producere*, denoting what's fertile and abundant. There is a precedent!

LOOK BUSY . . . THE BOSS IS COMING!

Consider the proliferation of productivity apps available on our smartphones: Slack, Asana, Todoist, Trello, Notion, Toggl, and RescueTime—just to name a few. They are all designed to help us manage and track our time, divide tasks into categories, and streamline our workflow. According to research by Gartner, since COVID, the number of large companies using productivity trackers has increased by 60 percent.[7]

This is not a book that will advise you on techniques about how to squeeze more time out of your day. You will not learn how to slice and dice your day into boxes or create a new calendar system.

But one of the big goals of this book is to help you reevaluate your relationship with time. When Western Europe and the United States transitioned from an agricultural economy to an industrial economy, that shift fundamentally changed people's relationship with time. Time became a commodity and a measure of commercial value. But in reality, the way humans experience time is so much more fluid and dynamic.

When it comes to time, there isn't a lot of room for ambiguity in our work lives. Between shared calendars, billable hours, and teams distributed across the globe, we rely on a down-to-the-minute schedule to keep us coordinated. It often feels all but impossible to manage our workflows without some sort of calendaring.

MTR activity thrives in ambiguous spaces. So how do we make time for something that "takes as long as it takes"? And when will cultivating the MTR activity be "done"? To understand this in a bit more depth, consider a range of ways humans have interpreted time.

There are cultural and historical perspectives on time. For example, the ancient Greeks had two perceptions of it: *chronos* time (quantitative, linear) and *kairos* time (qualitative, opportunistic). Chronos is characterized by a sequential, linear, and quantitative approach to the passage of time. It demands constant tracking and control, leading to stress and anxiety about time scarcity. Expressions such as "Time is money" reflect our fear of losing or running out of time, making it restrictive and consuming in the chronos paradigm. Alternatively, kairos time is more qualitative in nature. It's about engaging in the moment when something happens. Ways to engage in kairos time include activities that promote mindfulness and meditation, such as walks, sewing, daydreaming, slow cooking, and listening to your intuition.

Centuries later, the development of Newtonian time is more aligned with the chronos conception of time. When Sir Isaac Newton quantified gravity in 1687, he was capturing a concept of metaphysical absolute time. The world stuck with this concept for another two hundred years until Einstein's theory of relativity came into being. Einstein introduced the idea that "space and time were interwoven into a single continuum known as *space-time*. And events that occur at the same time for one observer could occur at different times for another."[8] The ultimate goal is to integrate the internal reflective time of kairos and the external, sequential time of chronos.

One of the reasons engaging in MTR activity is so important is that it helps you to arrive in a flow state. Psychologist Mihaly Csikszentmihalyi coined the term *flow state* and defined it as a mental state when a person is fully immersed and engrossed in an activity. In a flow state, your sense of time gets distorted. Athletes in Csikszentmihalyi's research described it as time slowing down, even standing still and "as if you're on autopilot"; artists have described it as being "in an ecstatic state."[9] Sometimes people refer to flow as being "in the zone." A flow state is achieved not when you have a loosey-goosey approach but rather when you are intensely focused and concentrating on something. This total immersion often yields a great sense of productivity.

Suspended time is akin to the flow state but isn't quite as all-encompassing. It's a state where we remain aware of time and feel its passing, without having our eyes glued to the clock or our brains distracted by the next item on the day's agenda. Traditional time insists that a session be timed at exactly 12.5 minutes, while suspended time is comfortable knowing it's somewhere between noon and 3:00 p.m. It can help to think of suspended time as the way we experience time on a (phone-free) nature walk, as we notice the sun gradually setting or the tide inching in. We intuitively sense when it's time to head home—without looking at a clock.

If suspended time is what dictates the depth of immersion into work, then *catalysts* determine the breadth and scope of time. In other words, catalysts decide how much time—over the next day, three weeks, or six months—we'd like to spend before we achieve a desired change. Unlike traditional project milestones, the "deliverables" of our catalysts aren't determined by external pressures. Instead, they arise from thoughtful, open-ended questions to ourselves about meaningful progress. Unlike traditional deadlines, catalysts aren't meant to be a stopping point (or a point to keel over and die!) but a moment to recognize change in motion—and then keep going.

For example, in parts of the world where resting during the hottest weather is practiced, it is common to slow down in the afternoon, perhaps for a siesta. It's not a sign of laziness—it's a practiced efficiency to adapt to the environment and be more productive at a different cadence. Similarly, I remember the disapproving cluck-clucking of tongues among my USA apparel-sourcing colleagues in response to our vendor partners in Italy taking off the entire month of August. Some of my American colleagues were aghast. I personally admired the Italians from afar, secretly jealous of an entire nation-state's ability to agree that rest and relaxation are important to the country's overall productivity and economic outlook.

Most Saturdays at 9:00 a.m., I show up for a Tone Zone class at DanceFit—a boutique fitness studio in my community in Philadelphia. Midway through each class, our instructor, Jasmine, starts playing one of the most triggering songs for all of us regulars: Rick Ross's "Hustlin'."

It's a song that really gets you moving. But it also means the beginning of an excruciating series of push-up exercises. My point isn't that by going to exercise class I am being more productive (although exercise does help my productivity—more on that in Chapter 3, "Move: It's How We're Designed"). My point is that we have normalized hustling in our popular culture as if that is the most advantageous way to be productive. And there's even a new term that emerged alluding to this unhealthy drive to push ourselves—*toxic productivity.*

We have come to glorify being busy. We value busyness and achieving more—more money, more growth, more stuff—over rest, pausing, and being content. But busyness is not equivalent to productivity. The result of normalizing busyness means that people are reluctant to take breaks or vacations and that they over-index on output instead of on well-being.[10] In fact, another term has emerged: *productivity theater.*[11] This is when we try to appear preoccupied as if we are accomplishing meaningful work when, in actuality, we are just scanning Amazon reviews for a new home appliance. Research conducted by Visier showed that out of one thousand full-time polled US workers, 83 percent admitted to engaging in "performative work behaviors in the past 12 months."[12] Productivity theater is all sizzle and no meat. It does nothing to move the needle toward achieving significant value, goals, or outcomes.

Activity without purpose isn't the means to the end, and more than likely leads to some form of burnout.

The Anatomy of Work Index published research that 71 percent of knowledge workers experienced burnout at least once in 2020.[13] According to a *PLOS One* Trusted Source study published in 2017, workplace burnout was a predictor of many physical health issues, including coronary heart disease, gastrointestinal issues, and type 2 diabetes.[14] And 2023 research by the American Institute of Stress reported that "job stress costs US industries over $300 billion annually in absenteeism, turnover, diminished productivity, and medical, legal, and insurance costs."[15] In 2019, burnout was classified by the World Health Organization as an "occupational phenomenon."[16] Do you need any more proof?!

Plus, burnout has a business cost. According to Gallup, burnout links to people taking as much as 60 percent more sick days, and it can increase the likelihood of looking for a different job by as much as 2.6 times.[17] That level of recidivism leads to chronic knowledge transfer, and it's a huge business cost.

If burnout is characterized by three dimensions—(1) exhaustion, (2) increased feelings of cynicism related to one's job, and (3) reduced professional efficacy—then our goal should be to feel the opposite in our occupations—that is, we should aim to feel energized, optimistic, and proficient while at work. MTR activity is how we get there.

CULTIVATION 2.0

As I write this in early March in Philadelphia, the natural world all around me is awakening from its dormant winter sleep. Seemingly overnight, I notice new things on my daily walks. Tiny hard buds on cherry trees boldly protrude. Green daffodil shoots and bright purple crocus flowers bravely appear in random patches on my neighbors' front yards. Now that my chin isn't burrowed into my scarf and coat collar on these walks, I observe new activity. I notice the hornets' nest precariously dangling from a chestnut tree and the birds' nest high up on a thick branch of the oak tree in our backyard.

In nature, there is so much cultivation occurring that we cannot see. Generative rebirth and reinvention are happening in integrative and holistic ways. The dormancy of winter—that liminal in-between time where growth is happening under the surface—is as critical as the full-fledged humming, vibrancy, and activity of spring and summer. All of it is cultivation.

What if we brought this sense of cultivation into our work lives?

What if we valued what's occurring during the slow, dormant times as much as the faster, energetic growth spurts?

What if we honored what's happening in the invisible realm as well as the visible realm?

What if we recognized the role of the solitary as well as the communal to get work done?

Both are necessary for a meaningful yield, and I believe this model of cultivation is just what we need.

So, can we give Taylorism a funeral?

In fact, Stuart Crainer, cofounder of Thinkers50, told me in a podcast interview that Frederick Taylor would love that and would be horrified to learn that we still use a two-hundred-year-old model to optimize work.[18] Taylor himself was quite creative.

If productivity can be triggering and sometimes cause us to break out in hives (i.e., are we measuring up to productivity standards?) or experience an inferiority complex because we're not doing enough, we're not grinding and hustling enough—then cultivation might have the opposite, ancillary effect.

This new approach to productivity—cultivation—will tap into what's uniquely human and allow you, your teams, and your organization to flourish.

Cultivation happens in the invisible realm as well as the visible realm— at our desks and while we take a break to move, think, or rest. Cultivation is happening when we are quietly pondering something to ourselves as well as when we are daydreaming or working in concerted effort with teammates. It may not seem as tangible, but it yields far greater results than linear productivity ever can.

A cultivation metaphor for work means that we can amplify what makes us uniquely human in our professional lives. By infusing work with restorative and generative MTR activity, we will add energy and innovation to our days. No more productivity theater. We can integrate leisure into work, rather than treating leisure as a luxury. We can truly allow productivity to be sexy and leave the unsexy parts to AI, robots, and automation.

While this shift might initially feel unsettling, it opens the door for companies to embrace "inside-out" work—work that promotes personal development and encourages professional growth whether in the office or at home.

In our present and future, curiosity, imagination, and creativity are our currency, which means MTR is our way forward.

SEEDS TO CULTIVATE:
PRO TIPS TO MOVE FROM PRODUCTIVITY TO CULTIVATION

The shift from productivity to cultivation requires intentional changes at multiple levels. Here are specific ways to begin implementing these concepts, along with reflection questions to deepen your understanding and application.

Individual Level—Reflections and Exercises
Reflection Questions for You

1. How does your definition of "being productive" limit your potential for deeper, more meaningful work?
2. What would change in your work if you measured impact rather than just output?
3. Where in your work life are you performing "productivity theater" rather than engaging in genuine cultivation so that you can flourish?

Exercises for You

1. Time-Awareness Journal: For one week, track when you feel most energized and creative versus when you feel drained. Notice the natural rhythms of your work patterns without trying to change them. Pay attention to when you naturally enter flow states and what conditions enable them.
2. Cultivation Zones: Schedule ninety-minute "cultivation zones" in your calendar where you work without checking email or messages. During these periods, allow yourself to fully immerse in your work

without measuring immediate outputs. Notice what emerges when you remove the pressure of instant results.

3. Nature-Inspired Workday: Structure one workday using nature's rhythms as inspiration. Include periods of intense focus (like the summer growing season), followed by reflection and integration (like autumn), rest (winter), and renewal (spring). Document how this different approach affects your work quality and energy levels.

Team Level—Reflections and Exercises
Reflection Questions for Your Team

1. How can your team better support both individual deep work and collective creativity?
2. What metrics beyond traditional productivity measures would better capture your team's true impact?
3. How might your team create an environment that values both visible progress and invisible growth?

Exercises for Your Team

1. Cultivation Mapping: As a team, create a visual map of your project cycles (use a whiteboard and markers, or even collage), identifying periods that require intense activity and periods that need incubation and rest. Use this to design more natural work rhythms that honor both active and dormant phases.
2. Silent Cultivation Hours: Implement weekly team "silent hours," where everyone works on individual tasks without meetings or interruptions, allowing natural collaboration to emerge only when needed. Observe how this affects team creativity and output quality.
3. Cross-Pollination Sessions: Schedule monthly sessions where team members share what they're cultivating in their work, including half-baked ideas and works in progress. Create a safe space for sharing uncertainty and ambiguity.

Organizational Level—Reflections and Exercises
Reflection Questions for Your Organization

1. How might your organization's definition of success change if you valued cultivation as much as productivity?
2. What organizational policies or practices currently reinforce traditional productivity mindsets that you need to evolve?
3. How can you better support the natural rhythms of innovation and creativity while meeting business objectives?

Exercises for Your Organization

1. Cultivation Audit: Conduct an organization-wide assessment of current productivity metrics and identify where they might be limiting innovation and sustainable growth. Develop new metrics that measure long-term impact and human development alongside traditional output measures.
2. Seasonal Planning: Align organizational planning cycles with natural seasons, incorporating periods of high activity, reflection, rest, and renewal. This might mean planning for slower periods during summer months or end-of-year reflection periods.
3. Space Design Revolution: Redesign physical and virtual workspaces to support both individual cultivation and collective creativity. Include quiet spaces for deep work, collaborative areas for cross-pollination of ideas, and rest areas for renewal.

LEAVING YOU WITH THIS THOUGHT

Remember that transitioning from a productivity-focused to a cultivation-focused approach is itself a process that requires patience and cultivation. Start small, incorporate all perspectives on your team, observe what works, ask for feedback, and allow new practices to take root naturally. The goal isn't to completely abandon productivity measures but to expand our understanding of what constitutes meaningful work and impact.

As you implement these practices, pay attention to not just what changes in terms of output but how the quality of work, employee well-being, and long-term sustainability of your efforts evolve. Like any good gardener knows, the most bountiful harvests come from patient, attentive cultivation rather than forced growth.

2

WHAT IS MTR?

Most of us think of ourselves as thinking
creatures that feel, but we are actually
feeling creatures that think.

—Jill Bolte Taylor, author of *My Stroke of Insight*[1]

On a beautifully sunny and cold day in March, I visited Le Truc, an internal creativity catalyst at Publicis in Tribeca, New York City, with Dag Folger. Dag is one of the cofounders of A+I ("architecture plus information"), the workplace design firm responsible for designing the unique interiors and layout of this firm, as well as standout spaces like the Peloton Studios in London and New York City's AltSchool. A+I started working on Le Truc's project in March 2020, about one week before the entire world entered a new pandemic reality. They had a very vague design brief because the firm's mission and client base was still evolving. In spite of this ambiguity—or maybe because of it—the A+I team pushed through, in collaboration with their client, and produced an office environment that is unlike any other I've experienced.

At Le Truc, there are a diversity of workspaces—almost a biodiversity of workspaces—that allow a person to sort of choose their work adventure. The rooms range in terms of shape, size, color, lighting, and the type of fabric texture on the walls. That's right, many walls are covered in a vel-veteen fabric, not just paint! Some rooms feel like comforting cocoons for solo work, a few feel like dark caves for subdued conversation, and still oth-ers deliver a bolt of energy with their brighter lighting or natural sunlight streaming through the south-facing windows. The curve—not the straight line—is the architectural motif appearing repeatedly along the ceiling, bor-dering windows, and giving form to the shape of meeting spaces, tables, and even room dividers. Dag told me, "I find that when I work at a more traditional office—say, an open plan with a few breakout rooms—I can probably be found in two or three places during the day. But here, I can easily move between ten spaces because there are just more tools in this box that I can use to do a more nuanced alignment for the kind of work I need to do. You can go from this space to a different space to a different space to a different space quickly so that you can really find the place where you have your best comfort, confidence, and stamina."

Stamina is an interesting word. Its etymology links to the stamen of a flower—the pollen-bearing organ of the flora. Therefore, the stamen is the source of growth for the flower. The Latin *stamina* in the 1600s became associated with the warp threads on a loom. These are the ver-tical threads that literally give the fabric structure, enabling it to be firm and stand upright. So we can associate *stamina* with sources of strength. For Dag, "Stamina means I have more support around me, and I'm able to perform longer and be happier."

Longevity and happiness would be incredible outcomes of productiv-ity, wouldn't they?

Which leads me to wonder: How do I receive my energy to work so that I can grow, be happy, and become strong?

I don't build stamina for my work by pushing through. If I'm honest with myself, pushing through sounds and looks impressive, but it is not sustainable, not for me. Hunkering down at my laptop for hours at a time, barely getting up for a break to use the bathroom or to have a glass of water—all this does is reduce my blood flow and, therefore, oxygen to my brain. As a result, my ideas become stagnant.

The culture of "pushing through" has roots in our learning environments. I recall being a professor in schools of design and business where students pulled all-nighters in preparation for studio crits or final projects. These were badges of honor. Both undergraduate and graduate students passed along tips on how to get by (e.g., Red Bull cocktails and Doritos) as signs of supportive behavior. Some of my colleagues lamented how this culture of learning fostered a problematic disconnect from reality. What passed for impressive on a college campus would surely not be sustainable when balancing a job, familial relationships, and one's physical, mental, and emotional health.

The way to build stamina in our work is to identify sources of renewal and recovery that restore our energy, spur growth, and build strength. And what are the most universal sources of renewal and recovery? Movement, thought, and rest. In other words, MTR is our route to building stamina and, consequently, cultivating a work life that allows us to flourish.

MTR is a framework that helps us redesign *how* we work. It is a provocation to approach productivity in new ways and an opportunity to reframe the ways we think about work. It is a call to reduce our cognitive load (in light of all the technologies that help us to do basic tasks) and use our brains in different and more energizing ways. MTR is especially important in today's world because it is an on-ramp to build our creative capacity.

Creativity is the engine for innovation. If you want to innovate as an individual consistently and sustainably, as a team and as an organization, you must build creative capacity. In my previous book, *The Creativity Leap*, I defined creativity as our ability to toggle between wonder and rigor to solve problems, produce novel value, and deliver meaning. Viewed that way, creativity is not only in the realm of art and design. Every profession—accountants, lawyers, coders, engineers, scientists, artists, and entrepreneurs—are super creative when they are toggling between wonder and rigor to solve problems.

So you might be wondering: Is MTR activity just a bunch of creativity breaks?

For better or worse, the concept of "creative work" has a lot of baggage. I know, from countless keynotes in the corporate world, that this very phrase can make people's hackles go up, especially if they don't consider themselves to be a "creative type." But as I've mentioned, to be human *is* to be hardwired to be creative. If you intentionally make time and space for both wonder and rigor, then chances are that you are engaging in MTR activity.

So now let's consider how to intentionally design wonder and rigor into the workday. *Wonder* is deep curiosity, audacious dreaming, and the ability to pause and sit in awe. *Rigor* is deep focus, discipline, time on task, and skill mastery. In our contemporary work environments, we conflate wonder with woo-woo and rigor with rigidity. Today's work challenges don't need woo-woo or rigidity. They require a curiosity and commitment to flow between wonder and rigor as needed. The MTR framework offers additional skills, pathways, and a road map of habits to intentionally build creative capacity—dare I say MTR activity is the most sustainable, efficient, and enjoyable way to build creative capacity for you as an individual, for your team, and for your organization. In *The Creativity Leap*, I affirmed that creativity has a business ROI. In this book, I am asserting that there is a business cost if we do not make time for MTR activity.

The truth of the matter is that our best work happens if we don't remain confined to the visible realm of work, if we allow ourselves the space and time for restorative and regenerative activities—namely, moving, thinking, and resting.

> **Moving:** Many of us do work that requires us to sit for the majority of the day. Physical movement begins to feel like a luxury instead of an integrated way to optimally function. Movement shakes up the ways that we approach things. It helps us to shift perspective in a literal way because it's impossible to see an object in the same way once you have a new vantage point. Breaking up your workday with movement gets you to new perspectives more quickly.

Thinking: Activities such as responding to emails, paying attention to multiple people's comments and reactions during a Zoom meeting (perhaps while also monitoring the dings of text messages coming through on your phone), and reacting to a client emergency all require skillful thinking on your feet. But that's not the type of thought we lack or that MTR advocates.

The thought dimension of MTR prompts you to explore ways to focus more deeply; dream, daydream, and explore your imagination; actively seek out inspiration; immerse yourself in reflection; engage in metacognition ("Why do I think the way I think?"); and cultivate insight. These are the essential thought activities for twenty-first-century work.

Resting: Rest seems to be the ever-increasingly evasive treasure chest in our twenty-first-century life. We are no longer attuned to the circadian rhythms of our natural environment. That's due to all the technology that can keep us up late—heck, sometimes they may keep us company in positive ways and steer us to our better selves. But at a steep cost.

When we pay attention to the natural world, there is a common theme of contract and release, contract and release, whether that's the way blood pulses through our capillaries, the beating of our hearts, or the function of peristalsis in the esophagus that carries chewed food from the mouth into the stomach. In our external natural environment, we see the theme of contract and release in terms of the change of seasons. The magnificent book *Wintering* by Katherine May does a deep dive into all the possibility, magic, and wonder that is feasible during times of dormancy, solitude, quiet, slowing down, retreating, and cocooning that can happen in winter's shorter days.

While some books have focused only on the value of rest, or have discussed why you should prioritize exercise, or have offered a guide to thinking more deeply, in this book, we explore why all three together are the spark that will ignite your superpowers at work. Moving, thinking, and resting are interdependent and additive to one another. The three activities together help you to systematize a contract-release way of working, to zoom in, then step away, and zoom out. MTR is a tool and framework to help you go all in on the contract phase and ensure that you release—just as nature intended.

I HOPE, I THINK, I KNOW—
VALUING HOLISTIC LIVING TO ENHANCE WORK

One of my favorite T-shirts has this message written on it in bold black capital letters:

I HOPE.

I THINK.

I KNOW.

I am always stopped when I wear this T-shirt. People love the message. And I get it. All great things we now see as companies, products, or experiences started as a dream, an energizing feeling: That's hope. Once that feeling of hope takes root, then that helps to shift our mental model and our worldview. Once our thinking changes, then a deep certainty and knowing becomes our norm.

The body is an integrative and holistic system. Understanding this interconnectedness is crucial for enhancing our cognitive abilities and overall well-being.

The autonomic nervous system (ANS) illustrates the body's integrative nature. Consisting of the sympathetic (preparatory) and parasympathetic (restorative) branches, the ANS plays a critical role in regulating our physical and emotional states. Research by Gary Berntson, John Cacioppo, Karen Quigley, and Vincent Fabro showed that these branches interact in complex ways, co-activating or co-inhibiting based on various stimuli.[2] Emotions are inextricably linked to motor behavior and sensory input from muscles and internal organs, processed by the forebrain, hypothalamus, and brain stem reticular formation. This aligns with William James's assertion that emotion cannot be separated from bodily responses, reinforcing the holistic nature of our physical and emotional systems.[3]

I've gained particular inspiration for my own understanding of the brain's systems design approach through the work of John Medina's *Brain Rules*, Annie Murphy Paul's *The Extended Mind*, and Susan Magsamen and Ivy Ross's *Your Brain on Art*.

I've learned that we must feed our brains meaningful content. That's because our brains absorb stimuli like a sponge in a sudden downpour, soaking up every drop and splash of sensory input, ready to unleash a cascade of creativity and insight at the slightest nudge. For example, engaging in thought activities that stimulate our visual sense, such as doodling, can be particularly beneficial. Doodling taps into our brains' strong visual-processing capabilities, enhancing our ability to think creatively and reflect deeply.

John Medina's research on brain function emphasizes the significance of regular exercise (movement), sleep (rest), and stress management (thinking)—all three![4] No matter how much you may dread going to the gym or committing to regular exercise (whatever that means to you—for me, it's walking, dancing, and swimming), you cannot refute the fact that exercise stimulates the body to renew itself. We are designed to move. When we exercise, there's an increase in blood flow, which circulates vital nutrients and in turn supports brain function. Furthermore, Medina emphasizes the importance of adhering to one's natural sleep cycle.[5] A single night of sleep loss can reduce cognitive skills by 30 percent, and two sleepless nights can result in a 60 percent decline. Chronic stress is another significant impediment to cognitive function, impairing memory and decision-making abilities. By mitigating stress and adhering to healthy sleep and exercise routines, we can significantly enhance our cognitive performance.

Susan Magsamen and Ivy Ross's work on neuroaesthetics, as detailed in their book, *Your Brain on Art*, underscores the profound impact of art on the brain.[6] Neuroscience reveals that only a small fraction of our mental activity—just 5 percent—is conscious, with the majority occurring subconsciously. Artistic activities can lower stress hormone levels, increase neuroplasticity, and improve overall mental health. For instance, a study at Drexel University found that forty-five minutes of art-making can significantly reduce cortisol levels.[7] This principle extends to environments like hospitals, where aesthetics are incorporated into pain-management techniques, enhancing patient well-being through elements such as light, color, sound, and smell. Embracing art and aesthetics leads to healthier, more flourishing minds, countering the rote memorization and standardized testing prevalent in traditional education, which produces staid work habits.

Collective experiences also play a significant role in our emotional well-being. I recall splurging to attend the U2 concert at the phenomenally designed Sphere in Las Vegas. I was already in Vegas for a business trip, and after my work was complete, I went to the Sphere alone. I had no idea what to expect amid the crowd of eighteen thousand people. But I soon felt myself caught up in an energetic wave of pure bliss, fueled by the contagious joy of the strangers around me. Our only connection with one another was our love of U2's music and our shared experience of the Sphere's immersive virtual reality technology. This phenomenon was what the French social scientist Émile Durkheim called *collective effervescence*. It's the synchrony and emotional contagion experienced in group settings, such as concerts, religious services, or team sports. Adam Grant's 2021 op-ed in *The New York Times* highlighted how these sorts of shared experiences foster a sense of unity and exhilaration, enhancing our emotional and social well-being.[8]

Incorporating these insights and experiences into our daily lives and work environments can lead to profound improvements in our cognitive, emotional, and physical health and, consequently, our ability to cultivate great work. By recognizing the body as an integrative system that requires movement, thought, and rest—individually and collectively—we can create a more holistic and meaningful approach to work and life.

MAKING ROOM FOR MEANING

When I present MTR activity to corporate clients or professional organizations, it's at about this point that a particular vibe starts to arise. Now, I can't read minds, but I am pretty good at reading the room. And what I sense in those audiences is something along the lines of, "Okay, this is all well and good so far, but what about my *real work*? I can't realistically dedicate serious time to daydreaming. I'll never get anything done!"

I suspect you might be thinking something similar right now, too.

First, let me reassure you that you will still get things done. But what I really want to emphasize is that MTR activity is not procrastination. Although I won't deny it can look an awful lot like it.

Our grind-heavy work culture thinks of "real work" as "getting things done." Specifically, we see real work as tasks that are provable, measurable, tangible, or otherwise outwardly visible. By contrast, we define procrastination as time that doesn't yield any such proof. Procrastination is literally unproductive—it doesn't produce anything.

MTR activity doesn't always produce something tangible in the short term. That's what makes it so hard to distinguish from procrastination at first glance. The difference between MTR activity and procrastination is that the former is meaningful. It's not hard to understand that thirty minutes spent backyard bird-watching (note the Cordelia Cupp detective character in the hit Netflix series *The Residence*) does not feel the same as thirty minutes spent vegging in front of an episode of *Real Housewives*. But because these activities are, through an outcomes-driven lens, "unproductive," we might struggle to allow ourselves to grab the binoculars. This is why I spent the entire first chapter laying out why rote productivity as the sole metric of worthiness is outdated and no longer useful.

So what would it look like to have a meaning-centric, cultivation mindset?

Let me introduce you to Rhonda and Tom.

Rhonda was a successful mid-career professional whose project management position in the tech sector was running her ragged. Feeling burnout looming, she made the most drastic move possible: She left her job. But not for a competing firm, not even for early retirement.

"I know this will sound very strange," she told me, "but eventually, I think I want to be a funeral director."

In fact, Rhonda took a new job at a church—a religious nonprofit in the suburbs of Philadelphia's Main Line.

Tom, like Rhonda, shifted gears. In his case, literally: He now drives for a car service. We struck up a conversation between the Denver airport and a speaking engagement I had in Colorado Springs. Halfway through the ninety-minute ride, Tom mentioned that he'd previously been a teacher.

"Me, too," I said. "What did you teach?"

"Fourth and fifth grade," Tom said. "At a really nice school in Colorado Springs."

He explained that although he'd loved the kids, he'd grown weary from the demands of the standardized testing, the shoestring budgets, and the sense that he was just a cog in the machine, pushing students along on a conveyor belt. Now, however, he feels like he's doing something useful without being put through the wringer of stress.

"And I get to have so many interesting conversations," he added.

Rhonda, too, has never been happier.

With a conventional mindset, one that values productivity, output, and climbing the corporate ladder above all else, it's hard to understand Rhonda and Tom as two career success stories. They both left more prestigious, conventional lines of work to become . . . a funeral director and a limo driver.

However, Rhonda and Tom have no problem seeing themselves as success stories—because they are. Not only are they both good at their new jobs, working efficiently and (yes) productively, but both Rhonda and Tom are happier at work now. And they're happy because their work has meaning to them beyond sheer output. They're happy because they have a meaning-centric mindset toward their work.

Now, you don't have to quit your job and start a new career to implement this mindset in yourself. You simply have to choose to let meaningfulness have a say in what you prioritize. You have to get comfortable with not always producing something tangible, while still finding that work worthwhile. When you make room for MTR activity, you also make room for meaning. You open yourself up to flourishing.

It's natural to feel a little apprehensive about going all in on the idea of MTR activity, but the blocks in our way can be broken down when we choose a different perspective. To create space for the restorative, invigorating, and, yes, productive practice of movement, thought, and rest, let's defang the guilt that can come with "doing nothing" and quell productivity anxiety by cultivating self-trust.

Backcasting can help you see your career through the lens of meaning and identify new ways to cultivate meaning in your current work, as I'll explain next.

BACKCAST: YOUR INVENTORY OF COURAGE

Being stressed out at work is no fun.

Trust me, I know all about that.

In fact, it was stress and the burnout that I was quickly headed toward that prompted me to leave the safety net of my sixteen-year career in academia. As the founding director of a very new type of MBA program, I was excited for the challenge and impact. However, I was also incredibly stressed out by the recruiting demands and the short staffing that required me to support graduate students and faculty in innumerable ways. All amid extremely limited resources. For example, I recall sharing an administrative assistant with two other faculty members.

Egads.

It took some arduous interior work for me to make the life-changing decision to leave academia and build my own entrepreneurial venture, full-time.

It required that I pause from my jam-packed schedules and engage in some deep thought to rediscover the past activities that yielded energized and triumphant work of which I was proud.

I backcasted.

You are probably familiar with forecasting: sensorially projecting your way into a new and desirable future. Conversely, backcasting is how you make sense of what you have already experienced and the skills you have already acquired. Backcasting builds up what I call our *inventory of courage.*

It's only by taking stock of your failures, lessons learned, and achievements that you have the firm foundation to move forward. And that's because your pains plus your gains equal your assets.

The root of your inventory of courage may be an innocuous and innocent experience. I can trace my inventory of courage to the first grade. During that sixth year of life, I was bullied by a girl who I now know in my adult mind and lens was really suffering: Hurt people hurt other people. And I get it now. While I showed up to school with packed lunches, hair neatly brushed, and smelling like Jergens lotion, she rarely had a homemade lunch, settling instead for the 1970s Philadelphia public school rations of white bread, processed cold cuts, and perhaps a dollop of canned fruit. Of course she hated my guts.

Anyway, one day at the end of recess as we all lined up in the concrete schoolyard to walk into the school building in an orderly fashion, she busted in front of me in line. For whatever reason, on that day, I was not the one. I wasn't going to be pushed around by her anymore.

Being the nice girl with home training that I was raised to be, I tapped her on the shoulder and said, "Excuse me, but you busted in front of me."

She rolled her eyes at me and glaringly said, "So?! What are you gonna do? Kick my butt?!" And then she turned her back on me.

Oooooohh.

Again, that was not the day. I was a bit literal back then. So after staring at the back of her head for about ten seconds, I walked to the back of the line, took a running start, and kicked her in her butt. She toppled forward and looked back at me, shocked. She then left me to my original place in line and walked to the back of the line.

She never bothered me again.

That seemingly innocuous schoolyard moment was the root and foundation of my inventory of courage. It helped me navigate the racially hostile environment of the next school I attended. And because of *that*, I was able to master the steep social and academic learning curve in the prep school I next attended for high school. And because of *that* . . . many years later, I was able to start a hat design business, live abroad by myself in war-torn Sri Lanka, and then earn a PhD in four years while working full-time, et cetera, et cetera, et cetera.

You get the idea.

Your inventory of courage starts with all the little bits that converge to form the greater good of who you are to become.

You can practice backcasting in small increments. Start by considering three positive achievements—no matter how small or how large—on a daily or weekly basis. You don't need more than five to ten minutes to do it.

You can also backcast over longer stretches of time—reflecting over the past month, or quarter, or even years. It really doesn't matter how small the observation of what you have achieved is as long as it can be accounted for on a functional, social, or emotional level.

Something magical happens when we backcast and build up our inventory of courage. It is an energy generator.

PLAY IS THE ORIGINAL MTR ACTIVITY

Another energy generator that we're all familiar with—though maybe we've put it aside in our adult years—is play.

Brendan Boyle, founder of Play Lab and former IDEO partner, defines *play* simply as "engagement." I love that. As he shared with me when I visited his class on play at the Stanford d.school one sunny May afternoon:

Play is a verb. [Play] makes us resilient. We are resilient because we failed so much. . . . For example, my life as a toy inventor. I failed like 99 percent of the time! It's resilience, it's learning to take your lumps. The opposite of play isn't work . . . the opposite of play is boredom. We learn by social play. . . . Most adults think play is frivolous, that it's just for kids. They don't understand that it's lifelong. And then most companies go, "Hey, Brandon, we got play! Look, we got a slide. We got foosball, we got a Ping-Pong table." Play is about engagement. That's the way I couch it with companies and then they have a new KPI.

Drawing from the insights of West, Hoff, and Carlsson, we can also include their definition of play as "an activity that is intrinsically motivated, purposeless, enjoyable, and involves a suspension of self-consciousness."[9] Thought of this way, play can be a three-in-one MTR activity!

So let's talk about play and how it can revolutionize our work lives.

Do you find yourself playing while at work?

It's okay to admit it if you do. In fact, I hope that you and your colleagues do play. The challenge is that play has a PR problem.

Our work would benefit immensely if we took play seriously. And I'm not just talking about the props of play: Ping-Pong tables, a billiards space, or a dart wall. Play of all kind engages your body and mind in ways to help you think critically. Consider that so many of the behavioral attributes required in play are also necessary for critical executive leadership skills: active listening, curiosity, empathy, collaboration, negotiation, the ability to improvise and be experimental, as well as to suspend judgment and then take quick decisive action. Research on rats suggests that "the young mammalian brain is programmed and motivated to engage in playful behaviors, with adverse consequences resulting when opportunities for play are thwarted."[10] We also cannot underestimate that play leads to strategic outcomes. For example, Stanford Graduate School of Business's Jennifer Aaker's research has demonstrated that humor is a secret business weapon.[11] Plus, integrating play at work boosts morale and stimulates greater creativity and teamwork. As a result, work products will be more valuable and collegial interactions will be more meaningful. Annie Dean, a remote work expert and a VP at Atlassian, a software development and collaboration tools company, told me that even in my wider organization of about one hundred people, I think there's something that is always playful about [our work]. You know, it's silly, we joke, we laugh, and I always think of work as fun. There are times when work is *not* fun. . . . Even when it's a very intense, high-stakes, complex problem that needs to be solved, there's always a sense of fun to it.

I'm trying to think about why it feels fun and playful, even in those stressful circumstances. And I guess it's because we are always trying to discover what's true and what's new, and by thinking of these efforts as an adventure where you can kind of uncover a new truth that can benefit your team and can benefit other people—that just feels like a good use of time. That pursuit of coming up with the answer is an energizing and playful experience. . . . So much of what we do is strategy, which is like figuring out a puzzle—and figuring out a puzzle is, by its nature, a playful act.

Imagine incorporating MTR in the form of play into our everyday work environments, especially to something as structured and ubiquitous as meetings. Meetings are artifacts of organizational culture and the host of some very telling rituals in many organizations. Why not redesign them to include elements of play? Research and play go hand in hand because you're allowing people to explore. Consider when Google used to allow their engineers to engage in tinkering with their 20 percent time initiative. Gmail was born from this initiative.

Play helps you to deal with uncertainty. And it doesn't have to be confined to specific activities or designated times. It can be seamlessly integrated throughout the workday. Think of playfulness as a state of being, a mindset that we can bring into our professional lives to foster creativity and productivity. When we adopt this playful mindset, we can transform even the most serious (and uninspiring) business contexts. West, Hoff, and Carlsson assert that play "promote[s] a creative and productive climate in work meetings. These findings are relevant for workplace architects who have long known that contextual cues influence behavior."[12] Their research further offers a theoretical model of team climate for innovation, consisting of four factors: vision, participative safety, task orientation, and support for innovation. Design thinking aligns perfectly with these factors, incorporating play to enhance creative thinking and innovation within teams. Some categories of play include:

- *Physical*—rough and tumble (e.g., on the playground); great for adding movement into the day
- *Role-Play*—get out of the building, into the world, and be an anthropologist for a day
- *Constructive Play*—implementing ideas from prototypes
- *Exploratory Play*—ideation and brainstorming
- *Storytelling Play*—imaginative, narrative play to convey new ideas

Design thinking is a way to integrate play into work. My deep dive into design thinking began while earning a PhD in design management, where I connected with pioneers in human-centered innovation. In the early 2000s, IDEO was the primary consulting firm championing design thinking, and back then, design thinking was viewed as a fringe novelty. Today, major consulting firms like McKinsey, Accenture, and Deloitte have embraced and integrated design thinking into their core methodologies. When we created the Strategic Design MBA (SDMBA) program, design thinking was the through line between every course, from marketing to finance to leadership. In *Strategic Design Thinking*, I defined *design thinking* as a problem-solving process that was 50 percent the application of techniques used in cultural anthropology and qualitative research, and 50 percent the application of design principles, such as prototyping and visualizing concepts.

The design thinking approach dramatically transformed my teaching style. Traditional seminars where I played the role of "sage onstage" were replaced with dynamic, interactive classes. Instead of a single voice dominating the room, there was a constant buzz of conversation, laughter, and collaboration. Classes were noisy. Our graduate students spent only about 30 percent of class time listening to lectures from subject matter experts. The remaining 70 percent was dedicated to peer discussions, laptop research, doodling, prototypes, and using whiteboards that covered the walls—emphasizing the mantra of "show me, don't just tell me."

The energy and joy in the classroom were palpable. When we're at play and joyful, our attention sharpens, and whatever we're working on becomes more memorable and more meaningful. We're inevitably more invested. This playful approach not only sparks dynamic thinking and collaboration; it also aligns with Émile Durkheim's concept of collective effervescence—the synchrony and emotional connection felt in group settings.[13] Such environments are crucial for fostering creativity and deeper thought.

So let's revisit my proposal to reimagine and redesign the standard work meeting. Instead of a rigid agenda, you could introduce playful activities that encourage spontaneity and engagement. Perhaps you start with a quick, lighthearted icebreaker (or fire starter, depending on which metaphor you're in the mood for!) that gets everyone standing and laughing. Then you move into the main discussion but keep the atmosphere light and playful, encouraging participants to think expansively and share unconventional ideas without fear of judgment.

Play becomes a driver to build organizational culture. It doesn't just make meetings more enjoyable; it also taps into the intrinsic motivation and joy that come with play. It fosters a climate where team members feel safe to participate, oriented toward the task at hand, and supported in their innovative efforts. Plus, experts on belonging, like Adam "Smiley" Poswolsky, exhort us to do playful team-building activities.[14] Smiley recommends, for example, "small win parties" to help build belonging. That's important because as of 2024, "only 20% of employees are engaged, the lowest level of employee engagement ever recorded."[15] By infusing play into our daily routines, we create a work environment that is not only more fun but also more conducive to creativity and productivity.

When we are at play, we are priming our best teammate-selves, our best manager-selves, and our best leader-selves. When engaging in role-play, for example, donning the identity of your superhero self helps you to explore other identities, cope with fears, and build curiosity. Play is the number one empathy builder—a mindset and capacity that leaders have proclaimed is a critical skill for twenty-first-century work.[16]

Another great gift of play is failure. I mean that with all sincerity. Growing up on my block in Philly, as my random gaggle of friends clustered around to pick teams for a game of kickball, we fiercely *knew* how high the stakes were: that we could lose! We didn't dodge that reality. We went into our sweaty, awkward, rambling game of missed shots, lucky catches, and trash-talking with the intensity to not only win but to navigate failure.

When we are active throughout our workday and approach it with a spirit of play, we simultaneously raise and lower the stakes. The stakes get raised because of our emotional involvement. The stakes get lowered because we don't take ourselves so seriously. Despite this, we shy away from failure in our work processes. Even if we consider our greatest successes, they are a result of a series of refined failures. One very visible and large-scale way that mistakes have been put on blast is Samuel West's Museum of Failure.[17] It's a traveling exhibit of failed products from food and beverages to technology. It helps you to understand the humor and playfulness of experimentation and mistakes—as well as their necessity.

Another way play can manifest is when we introduce prototyping. An organization that values prototyping is one that has a culture that embraces failure as opportunities for learning. Prototyping at work is play, including props. Prototypes are rough-draft, ugly, cheaply produced mock-ups of an idea. In fact, the messier they are, the likelier you are to receive clarifying questions on your half-baked project. They can be doodles, short video-recorded role-play mock-ups, and, taken to their more polished extreme, pop-up shops. They require active, kinesthetic tinkering to produce new concepts and then collect opinions from others. They are not the result of cerebral exercises. Prototypes build engagement and ensure that your team develops something that others will use. Thus, prototyping also values collaboration because it's about refining through feedback from others. Prototypes also help you to have a low-stakes attitude toward your work and to learn from any mistakes that may happen along the way. And a playful attitude toward your work results in a more exploratory approach, yielding much more interesting and ultimately innovative results and insights. When I interviewed Ivy Ross, chief design officer for consumer devices at Google, she shared the following examples with me:

- She invites each new hire to contribute a favorite book from their childhood to a communal library.
- She organized an off-site trip to a farm, where her team left their job titles back at the corporate office building and got to be, for example, a beekeeper or a flower picker for the day. Time seemed to stand still.
- At the start of COVID, she facilitated an exercise where she asked individuals on her team to create a fairy tale of the future. This helped them suspend judgments on how heavy and burdensome the uncertainty of a pandemic felt and instead to use their imaginations to design an alternative future.

Good play cultivates great leadership. Consider that in a world of increasingly ubiquitous technology, our added value will be the parts of us that are uniquely human. This heightens the emphasis on the value of play and playful interaction. The executive leadership skills that play activates (e.g., collaboration, curiosity, empathy, and negotiation) are soft skills that have become hard-core. Here's a great example from Ivy Ross reflecting on taking a chance on intentionally allowing teams to play *so that* they could more seriously generate great work. When at the toy company Mattel, she realized she needed to design team formation differently. She converted the first two weeks of a twelve-week product development cycle as follows:

I wondered what would happen if I changed it up. In the first two weeks, the team really got to know each other. Who are we? What are our gifts and talents? We got to learn new things at the same time, because everyone comes in with different life experiences. And then when we worked together for ten weeks . . . would the results be better at the end?

So I played with this idea for the first two weeks, we didn't quote-unquote produce anything; there wasn't an outcome. There was playful exploration.

Then sure enough, after the next ten weeks, we got down to work, and now there was a common language, there was a bond; we learned new things together. And then we had what was called *the desk of twelve brains*, where we would start to throw out ideas. We ended up winning the Chairman's Award for sustainability of the company, because of this methodology, because [of] the toys and the ideas that were coming out of those sessions.

Ross's experience at Mattel demonstrates how intentionally creating space for play and human connection can lead to breakthrough innovation and sustainable business outcomes. This insight became even more relevant as the world faced unprecedented challenges in the years that followed 2020. The COVID pandemic not only revealed systemic inequities, it revealed ways of working that didn't necessarily make sense anymore. As a loneliness epidemic became an outcome of COVID, people began questioning why well-being wasn't a greater part of how they worked. As Adam Piore stated in his 2023 *Newsweek* article, "Americans have been prioritizing work over play, leading to increased loneliness and isolation."[18] Research shows great benefits to adults engaging in play. It fosters connection, creativity, bonding, stress reduction, job satisfaction, workplace performance, overall well-being, and flow. In fact, post-pandemic play has seen an uptick in the likes of adults putting together more jigsaw puzzles, buying more video games, and attending adult summer camps. Toy sales in the "kidults" category (ages twelve and older) reached $9 billion in 2022.[19]

The risks of not playing are pretty high—namely, isolation, apathy, and languishing. More cities have invested in public policy that sparks play-based learning landscapes.

What could happen if we begin to prioritize play? I'll take it a step further: What if our workplaces transformed into communities of play?

COMMUNITIES OF PLAY TRANSFORM THE WAY WE WORK

Communities of play are not only essential for flourishing; they are the perfect setup to make MTR activity more resonant, more satisfying, and more sustainable. But play is about more than just out-and-out enjoyment: whether it's Candy Land or kickball, when we play, we play by rules. And those rules—and the potential to win or lose—not only keeps us accountable and honest participants but also heightens the reward of success. In other words, it's the rigor of group play that enables its wonder.

Ann Thorsted's insights into the concept of "communities of play" suggest that such environments are essential for flourishing because they result in meaningful, transformational, and resilient experiences.[20] Hans-Georg Gadamer, a German philosopher known for his work in hermeneutics and phenomenology (a fancy way of saying he specialized in being a text detective and explaining how we experience the ordinary), beautifully encapsulated the essence of play. He believed that the purpose of play is simply to . . . play! According to Gadamer, play mediates personal and trust-based relationships, unfolding us as individuals and as a collective, thereby enhancing meaningful and personal human encounters.[21] One of the most profound aspects of play is that it shifts our focus away from "What's the answer?" to "What's the process?" This aligns with the concept of liminal space, an important theme in shifting to a cultivation model of work, where play acts as a vehicle for sense-making, social negotiations, and conversations between people. It builds trust and fosters deeper connections.

A cool example of this comes from a study with LEGO executives in Denmark.[22] During this study, participants engaged in a variety of playful activities: They collaborated on drawing exercises, helping one another create individual portraits. They used LEGO bricks to visualize their dream team, they engaged in heroic role-play, they shared stories to create a shared understanding of their existing team, and they even cooked dinner together. Additionally, they brought their favorite toys to introduce themselves to the group, a practice reminiscent of the Strategic Design MBA orientation program where, on the first day of orientation, we invited new graduate students to bring an object to introduce themselves. These playful activities helped the LEGO executives enter a space of freedom and safety. They became more natural and honest with one another, establishing a genuine community of play. As a result, the managers' commitment shifted from purely professional relationships to more trusting and honest ones.

Thorsted's research highlights that communities of play can transform the ways we work.[23] By fostering environments where play is integral, we create spaces where people can connect on a deeper level, build trust, and ultimately enhance their professional and personal lives. Feeling good while we work is not just a throwaway emotion. Companies like Google, Pixar, Remedy Health Media, and MKG all encourage play and movement in the workplace. From Google's colorful beach bikes that employees ride from one end of the campus to the other, to Pixar's secret speakeasies, these environments show that the fear that participating in play will result in demerit is reduced. Such environments realize that inspiration comes because of the resulting serendipity of interpersonal interaction.

Imagine a city where play isn't confined to playgrounds and schoolyards but is woven into the very fabric of daily life. Adam Piore, in his article "Do You Play Enough? Science Says It's Critical to Your Health and Well-Being," delved into how public policy can spark and catalyze more play in urban environments, transforming them into vibrant, interactive spaces for all ages.[24] Walking through the vibrant streets of my hometown of Philadelphia, I have seen this vision coming to life and get a glimpse of how these playful public policies can bring people together. Whether it's a game of hopscotch painted on the sidewalk or interactive sculptures at bus stops, these playful elements invite spontaneous interactions and shared moments of joy. They remind us that play is not just for children;

it's a vital part of being human, a source of creativity, and a catalyst for community.

Toward the end of COVID, Philadelphia's Parks & Recreation department created a large-scale play area at the end of the Benjamin Franklin Parkway, just across the way of the iconic Philadelphia Museum of Art. It's a lively space where families gather, children run freely, and the joy of play fills the air.

This local initiative echoed broader movements seen across the globe in cities like Duncan Village, Buffalo City Municipality, South Africa; Tulsa, Oklahoma; Chicago, Illinois; and Brooklyn, New York. They create environments where play is not just an activity but a fundamental part of the urban experience, promoting creativity, connection, and well-being. For example, Houston has published an "Outdoor Bill of Rights," emphasizing the importance of outdoor play, while other cities are striving to become "child-friendly cities." And a 2023 report from the Center for Universal Education at the Brookings Institution highlights the success of Playful Learning Landscapes (PLL) projects.[25] These projects incorporate playful elements into everyday public spaces, making play an integral part of city life. Installations include games painted on sidewalks, signage placed in grocery stores, and large physical designs integrated into bus stops. These designs aim to foster actively engaged, meaningful, socially interactive, iterative, and joyful experiences for children and families.

These initiatives show that cities can take a proactive role in promoting play in our work environments. Piore even states, "Work that embodies elements of play, where individuals operate at the edge of their abilities, can lead to feelings of creativity, productivity, and energy."[26] By embedding play into the public realm, cities can support sustainable MTR activities that extend beyond work into everyday life. This not only enriches the lives of children but also fosters a sense of community and joy among residents of all ages. Note that Piore's reference to play "leading us to the edge of our abilities" points out again the value of liminal space.

Dr. Stuart Brown, a psychiatrist and founder of the National Institute for Play, a nonprofit designed to advance the appreciation and application of play, goes so far as to say that we have a "play deficiency" and that it is a public health problem. "No one has measured the effect on neurotransmitters if you don't play; . . . But there is a reasonable biological parallelism between sleep deficiency and play deficiency, which is why I think play is a public health necessity. Play deficiency, from my standpoint, is a very real phenomenon."[27]

So, let's redefine how we approach our work. Let's embrace the power of play, as considered by West, Carlsson, and Boyle, and integrate it into our professional lives. Whether it's through redesigning meetings or adopting a playful mindset throughout the day, we can enhance our creativity, foster a supportive team climate, and ultimately make our work more fulfilling and what we cultivate more meaningful.

At the end of the day, organizations are organisms. And that's because they are made up of humans. Why do we insist on overlaying a model of productivity from two centuries ago, one that assumed humans could replicate the machine? Why would we even want humans to replicate machines with their lack of imagination, insight, and capacity for innovation?

Now that we have technology that takes over basic tasks, we have a great opportunity to redesign work in a way that leverages the best of what we can cultivate as humans. And we can do so by making space for movement, thought, and rest.

SEEDS TO CULTIVATE:
PRO TIPS FOR IMPLEMENTING MTR
AND PLAY IN LIFE AND WORK

Individual Level—Reflections and Exercises
Reflection Questions for You

1. How does your energy level fluctuate throughout the day, and what patterns do you notice?

2. What childhood activities brought you joy, and how might their essence be incorporated into your work?

3. When do you feel most creative and engaged in your work? What conditions enable this state?

Exercises for You

1. Personal Play Audit
   - Track your daily activities for a week, noting moments when you feel most energized and engaged.
   - Identify activities that bring you into a state of flow.
   - Document when you naturally incorporate movement, thought, and rest into your day.
2. MTR Scheduling
   - Block fifteen-minute periods throughout your day for intentional movement.
   - Create personalized "Spark Moments" in your calendar where you step away from your desk to daydream, read a poem, or answer a riddle.
   - Schedule micro-rest periods between intense work sessions—try starting with increments of five minutes to fifteen minutes.
3. Playful Problem-Solving Practice
   - Try the Superhero Method: Choose a superhero (e.g., Wonder Woman for confidence, Spider-Man for agility) and tackle your challenge from their perspective. Use the free Random Word Generator tool (randomwordgenerator.com) to force creative connections between your challenge and unrelated concepts.
4. Visualizing Complex Problems
   - Try the free Excalidraw.com sketching tool for creating playful diagrams and mind maps.
   - Use the Sketchnote technique: Combine simple drawings with text to create visual notes (download the free Sketchnote Handbook starter guide).

5. Role-Play for Better Decision-Making
   - Use Edward de Bono's Six Thinking Hats method (available as a free PDF template online).
   - Try the Disney Creative Strategy: Approach your problem from three perspectives—the Dreamer, the Realist, and the Critic.

Team Level—Reflections and Exercises
Reflection Questions for Your Team

1. How does your team currently make space for play and experimentation?
2. What barriers prevent you from incorporating more MTR activities?
3. How can you better support one another's need for movement, thought, and rest?

Exercises for Your Team

1. Playful Meeting Redesign
   a) Start meetings with a physical warm-up activity.
      - Use the free Energizer deck from SessionLab.com, which offers more than fifty quick team warm-ups.
      - Try Kahoot! (kahoot.com) for interactive quiz warm-ups that get people moving and laughing.
      - Use Random Team Generator (teammateapp.com) for quick pair-ups and breakouts.
   b) Incorporate creative brainstorming techniques using visual tools.
      - Use Miro's free tier (miro.com) for collaborative virtual whiteboards.
      - Try FigJam's free templates (figma.com/figjam) for visual brainstorming.
      - Use Google Jamboard for quick, accessible visual collaboration.
   c) End meetings with a collaborative game or challenge.

- Try Gartic Phone (garticphone.com) for remote team drawing games.
- Use Random Acts of Kindness Resources (randomactsofkindness.org) for team challenges.
- Implement Mentimeter (mentimeter.com) for interactive word clouds and quick polls.

2. Team MTR Challenges

   a) Create a monthly movement challenge.
      - Use Stridekick (stridekick.com) for team step challenges.
      - Try Move Minutes on Google Fit for tracking active time together.
      - Use Microsoft Teams' Virtual Commute feature for structured movement breaks.

   b) Establish quiet zones for deep thinking work.
      - Use the Focus@Will app (focusatwill.com) for productivity music.
      - Implement Clockify (clockify.me) for team time-blocking.
      - Use Forest App (forestapp.cc) for group focus sessions.

   c) Develop team rituals for celebrating rest and recovery.
      - Use the Calm for Business platform for team meditation sessions (health.calm.com).
      - Try Todoist (todoist.com) for tracking and celebrating completed tasks.
      - Implement Bonusly (bonus.ly) for peer recognition of rest champions.

3. Cross-Functional Play Sessions

   a) Organize skill-sharing workshops.
      - Use Skillshare (skillshare.com) for structured learning sessions.
      - Try the Pecha Kucha presentation format (pechakucha.com) for quick knowledge shares.
      - Use LinkedIn Learning paths for guided team development (linkedin.com/learning/).

   b) Create collaborative art projects.
      - Use Canva for Teams (canva.com) for group design projects.
      - Try Figma (figma.com) for collaborative digital art.

- Implement MURAL (mural.co) for visual collaboration.
c) Design team-building activities.
  - Use TeamBuilding.com for virtual team activity ideas.
  - Try Gather (gather.town) for virtual team spaces.
  - Implement Gatheround (gatheround.com), FLOWN (flown .com), or Workfrom (workfrom.com) for spontaneous virtual meetups.

Organizational Level—Reflections and Exercises
Reflection Questions for Your Organization

1. How does your organizational culture currently support or hinder MTR activities?
2. What systemic changes would make your workplace more conducive to play and creativity?
3. How can you measure the impact of MTR and play initiatives on your organizational success?

Exercises for Your Organization

1. Workplace Environment Transformation
   a) Design spaces that encourage movement and different working styles.
     - Use the Steelcase Office Planner tool (steelcase.com/resources) for layout optimization.
     - Implement Room Booking by Robin (robinpowered.com) to manage flexible spaces.
     - Try OfficeSpace Software (officespacesoftware.com) for visualizing and testing different workplace configurations.
   b) Create dedicated areas for rest and reflection.
     - Use Acoustic Design Tool by Armstrong (armstrongceilings.com and armstrongceilings.com/drop-ceiling-calculator/en-us/) for sound management.

- Implement Lutron lighting systems (lutron.com) for circadian-friendly environments.
- Explore meditation pods by OpenSeed (openseed.co)—they've collaborated with companies such as Deloitte and Morgan Stanley, as well as the US Department of Veterans Affairs.

c) Install interactive elements that promote playful engagement.
- Use GestureTek (gesturetek.com) interactive floor and wall displays.
- Implement Bloomberg Connects (bloombergconnects.org) digital engagement platforms.
- Use Eptura (eptura.com) for meeting room and space analytics.

2. Cultural Initiative Development

a) Implement company-wide policies that support MTR activities.
- Use Culture Amp (cultureamp.com) for measuring MTR initiative impact.
- Try 15Five (15five.com) for tracking well-being metrics.
- Implement Officevibe (workleap.com/officevibe) for regular pulse checks on engagement.

b) Create recognition programs that celebrate playful innovation.
- Use Kudos (kudos.com) for peer recognition of creative solutions.
- Try Assembly (joinassembly.com) for gamified recognition.
- Implement Bonusly (bonus.ly) with custom categories for MTR achievements.

c) Develop training programs that incorporate movement and play.
- Use Trainual (trainual.com) for interactive onboarding.
- Try Bridge LMS (getbridge.com) for creating movement-based learning modules.
- Implement WorkRamp (workramp.com) for gamified skill development.

3. Community Play Integration

a) Partner with local organizations.
- Connect via Catchafire (catchafire.org) for nonprofit partnerships.

- Use VolunteerMatch (volunteermatch.org) to find local community projects.
- Try HandsOn Connect (handsonconnect.com) or Hivebrite (hivebrite.io) for coordinating community initiatives.

b) Organize company-wide events.
- Try Confetti (withconfetti.com) for structured team activities.
- Implement TeamBuilding.com for large-scale virtual events.

c) Build organizational connections.
- Join Culture First Community (cultureamp.com/community) by Culture Amp.
- Participate in Great Place to Work (greatplacetowork.com) networks.
- Connect through LinkedIn's Workplace Innovation Groups.

Here are some implementation tips:

1. Start with a pilot program in one department or location.
2. Use Monday.com or Asana to track initiative progress.
3. Create a cross-functional play committee using Microsoft Teams or Slack for coordination.
4. Use SurveyMonkey or Typeform for regular feedback collection.
5. Document success stories through Loom videos or Notion pages.

A few examples of measurement tools that you could use include:

1. Track engagement using Gallup Q12 (gallup.com/q12) metrics.
2. Measure space utilization with VergeSense (vergesense.com) sensors.
3. Monitor well-being with the Personify Health platform (personify health.com).
4. Analyze collaboration patterns using Microsoft Workplace Analytics.

LEAVING YOU WITH THIS THOUGHT

Remember that successful implementation of these activities requires the following:

- Gradual integration rather than sudden change
- Regular assessment and adjustment based on feedback
- Clear communication about the purpose and benefits
- Leadership support and active participation
- Flexibility to adapt activities to different work styles and preferences

The key to sustainable change is starting small and building momentum. Choose one activity from each level that resonates most with your current situation and begin there. As these become natural parts of your routine, gradually incorporate additional elements.

The goal isn't to force play or mandate specific MTR activities but rather to create conditions where these elements can naturally flourish and enhance both individual and collective work experiences.

3

MOVE: IT'S HOW WE'RE DESIGNED

It is solved by walking.

—Saint Augustine

In 2023, I pushed myself out of my comfort zone.

I embarked on an open-water swimming holiday in Crete, Greece, organized by a British company called SwimTrek.[1] Swimming is a natural extension of my lifelong affinity for the water. It calms and energizes me, offering both physical rejuvenation and emotional contentment. I learned to swim at the Germantown YWCA as a bubbly toddler in Philly, honed my skills at the Jersey Shore as an awkward teenager, and perfected my technique studying abroad in Salvador da Bahia, Brazil, at age twenty. At the ripe age of thirty-eight, I taught myself how to do flip turns by watching YouTube videos.

Water is my sanctuary. It calms and mesmerizes me. Sitting in the shallow parts of the Indian Ocean by an atoll in the Maldives or gazing at the jagged boulders on the seaside of Marin County, California, has felt like church to me.

But despite my love for water, I had never tried open-water swimming seriously. The sea is a powerful force, and the absence of a swimming pool's clear black lanes felt risky.

Every year, I commit to one personal development experience, so at age fifty-three, I decided to jump in—literally. Nervous but determined, I reminded myself of my MO: wade into new and possibly uncomfortable situations.

Arriving in Chania, Crete, after a delayed flight, my friend Tori and I took a ninety-minute drive down to the southernmost coastline of the island, through mountainous olive groves to the Port of Sfakia, culminating with a ten-minute water taxi to Loutro. This tiny village, accessible only by boat, is a hidden gem with its hilly paths, pebble beaches, whitewashed homes, and turquoise waters. It was like stepping into a postcard. That first evening, our British guides asked us to don our "swimming costumes" for a test swim, which comprised of three loops around buoys in Loutro Bay. Our group of thirteen averaged sixty-three years old, and our guides included accomplished swimmers, one of whom had swum across the English Channel. We plunged into the clear, refreshing water and began swimming.

Then I panicked.

Comparing myself to others, I lost my breathing cadence. I had to float on my back several times to catch my breath. I finally came ashore after only having completed *two* loops around the buoys. Dripping and deflated, I felt devastated, thinking, *I should never have come. . . . I'll slow everyone down. . . . I'm gonna drown!*

But then I noticed a heart-shaped pebble by my foot. I took it as a positive sign. I picked it up, clutching it tightly as I walked back to my hotel room. That night, a pep talk from my husband, John—despite his dry-land advantage—boosted my spirits. By morning, I had reconciled myself to being in the "slow group," deciding to enjoy the swims for the joy they brought me.

As I swam in the vibrant blue waters, I toggled between total sensory immersion and focusing on my technique. Gradually, I relaxed into my body, finding my rhythm with long, slow, extended strokes. That evening, our guides, having observed us, moved me to the "fast group." I was shocked to learn that long, slow, extended strokes—the way I love to move through water—are ideal for open-water swimming. My anxious energy and ruminating mind had been holding me back, not my technique.

For the rest of the week, I listened to my body and stopped comparing myself to others. Immersed in the water, with only the steady sound of my breathing and deep awareness of my body, I became attuned to when my negative self-talk would start to emerge, swatted it away, and shifted to gratitude. Swimming in flow with the sea in such a beautiful place was a gift.

OUT OF MY HEAD AND INTO MY BODY

That swim adventure taught me the profound value of movement and being in tune with my body—specifically by thinking *less*. It was a poignant reminder for me to get out of my head and into my body. As Dr. Bessel van der Kolk emphasized in *The Body Keeps the Score*, the body has its own intelligence.

Profoundly, the chapters that follow this one—focused on *thought* and then on *rest*—are actually dependent on movement. Throughout my interviews, people shared repeatedly how their best thinking seemed to come after a brisk walk. Others shared how exercise recalibrated and calmed them to have deeper sleep. I'm reminded of my conversation with Samantha Skey, the CEO of SHE Media who grew up as an athlete and still regularly plays tennis, surfs, and walks some mornings with friends. Sam told me,

> I think productive thinking is really different from what I feel as constant rumination. So productive thought is where you figure things out and ideas generate and then, you know, execution on an idea clicks. That to me is often associated with physical movement. . . . I mean, in tennis, everything feels like a metaphor for business, for life . . . really I apply them to our business. Like I write things down after a game of tennis because I see so many things that are applicable.

Humans were built for endurance, responsiveness, and play—not stagnation or rote repetition. After all, the spinal cord is an extension of the brain, connected by the medulla oblongata. When we are hunkered over a laptop all day, we constrict and restrict blood flow and therefore reduce the flow of oxygen to the brain. This makes us tired, cranky, and uninspired. Alternatively, when we are in motion, it's like putting various tissue systems in the body through the washing machine. They get a good cleanse as they are tugged and pulled, invigorating our overall system and making it healthier.

Studies show that movement helps cognition, sleep, vigor, and task focus—categories that some researchers call *resource caravans*.[2] This is because exercise reduces stress hormones like cortisol while increasing endorphins.[3] Endorphins are known as your body's natural mood boosters. One research study showed that as little time as ten minutes of walking before a test improved high school students' performance in memory and detecting details on a math test.[4] For adults, research has shown that physical activity can improve focus when there is a match between the intensity of the exercise and how motivated the person is to do the exercising.[5]

Mood, focus, and overall health outcomes improve when diverse physical activity is integrated throughout the workday.

That's the good news.

But the disappointing news is that globally, we are operating at a movement deficit. Just about all the research agrees that the majority of working adults spend way too much time being inactive. For example, American adults spend, on average, 7.7 hours a day sitting, leading to preventable health risks and diseases such as diabetes and cardiovascular disease.[6] This has a negative cascading effect on not only physical health but mental health, social health, and healthy aging.

A 2018 report from the World Health Organization stated, "Worldwide, 1 in 4 adults, and 3 in 4 adolescents (aged 11–17 years), do not currently meet the global recommendations for physical activity set by WHO. As countries develop economically, levels of inactivity increase.

In some countries, levels of inactivity can be as high as 70%, due to changing patterns of transportation, increased use of technology and urbanization."[7]

That same report targeted the year 2030 to reach a "15% relative reduction in the global prevalence of physical inactivity in adults and in adolescents."[8]

Now, some of this infrequent movement makes sense from an evolutionary standpoint. We don't need to hunt for our food, because our greatest threats have shifted away from being physical ones (a hungry lion) to existential ones (climate change). Daniel Lieberman, author of *Exercised: The Science of Physical Activity, Rest and Health*, believes that our physical strength has regressed while our brains have advanced. That's because, he writes, we tend to think about problems and solve them creatively rather than trying to run away or fight our way out of them.[9]

My research, based on over sixty interviews with a range of working adults, shows that movement is consistently a catalyst for better thinking and resting.

MOVE YOUR BODY, EXPAND YOUR MIND

There's something about moving my body that makes me feel truly alive with possibility.

One day while swimming laps, I had a revelation. In the midst of raising my right arm, extending my left arm in front, rotating my head to take a breath, and then exhaling heartily through my nose as I submerged my face back into the water, I thought, *Wow! I'm so happy right now!* This same feeling of being alive and vibrant hits me when I'm dancing. Being in motion, whether through swimming, dancing, or learning in an interactive setting, brings me profound joy and fulfillment.

Any kind of movement activity can spark joy and benefit the mind.

Movement activities get your body in motion and out of a sedentary position. When we move, different synapses ignite and connect in the brain, beyond the prefrontal neocortex, parietal cortex, and basal ganglia that integrate neural networks for rational cognition. Movement allows the brain to unburden cognitive load and activate different and equally important regions.

Getting more ambulatory and using your arms is a subtle reminder that our brains are not disembodied entities separated from the rest of the body. In fact, the brain needs the body in motion to be optimally stimulated. In *The Extended Mind*, Annie Murphy Paul wonderfully challenged the metaphors that we have accepted of "brain as computer" or "brain as machine" and instead used an analogy from nature.[10] She compared the ways our brains work best to the ways the magpie constantly flits around and resourcefully gathers what it needs to build a nest from its immediate environment. Similarly, the brain is at its prime and is most ripe with great thinking when we can integrate movement and spark a feedback loop. As Samantha Skey told me, "Moving organizes my thoughts better. So those [movement and thinking] are often hand in hand. If I can get into the flow zone, then I can quiet my thoughts, which is useful."

Some of the types of movement that you already may be doing throughout your workday include walking, stretching, using a standing desk, alternating between standing and sitting, taking dance breaks, intentionally taking the stairs instead of an elevator, holding walking meetings, or even eliminating chairs and hosting standing meetings. Taking a dance break in the middle of the day is one of my tried-and-true methods for incorporating movement and shifting my state of mind. I'll select a favorite hip-hop or R&B song from my self-curated "My Happy Place" playlist, crank up the volume, and dance for five minutes. During these moments, I feel free, joyful, and reenergized. It's a type of role-play—I become a sultry Donna Summer, a sassy Megan Thee Stallion, or a bold Bono from U2. The possibilities of who I can be and what I can do expand.

If you're looking for a boost in confidence, a challenge, or a way to strengthen your brain and improve skills like leading or following, maybe dance can bring out the best in you, too.

Some folks feel intimidated by dance, thinking that if they can't perform high kicks or complicated moves, they have no business dancing. But to the extent that you can move, you can dance. Dance is a universal language, one of the most expressive forms of communication and one that engages our entire being. Dr. Peter Lovatt, noted expert on the psychology of dance, emphasizes in his work that dance benefits "four aspects of human behavior—social connection, thinking and problem-solving, emotions and our physical and mental wellbeing." In a viral Instagram clip, Dr. Lovatt shares how movement through dance changes the way we think, solve problems, and connect with others because of the hormones (e.g., endorphins, dopamine, and serotonin) that are released while moving.[11]

Dance as a MTR practice carries so many benefits that have flowed into my work life. Here are just three examples, which I refer to as *the ABCs of dance movement*—Attention, Bravery, and Cheer:

- *Attention:* I'm naturally a big-picture person, not great with minutiae. Studying dance, however, requires attention to detail—arm placement, executing a pivot versus a turn, head positioning. This attention to detail has transferred to other areas of my life, like improving my focus on the financial aspects of my business.
- *Bravery:* When we're young, we embrace "bravery before mastery," but this diminishes with age as we grow older and society begins to reward certainty over inquiry. Dance has revived this spirit in me, encouraging me to try new things, to play, even though I'm still an awkward, clumsy student. I've discussed the power of play as a MTR practice in Chapter 2. Bravery is not the absence of fear; it's trying something despite the fear. Being brave before you're an expert is the only way to advance, and in the process, you learn a lot about yourself.
- *Cheer:* Laughter makes you fully present. It's a catalyst for the body to release serotonin, the feel-good hormone that benefits

the entire body. According to the Cleveland Clinic, laughter aids in learning, digestion, and mood regulation.[12] Dance cheers me up and keeps me laughing—mostly at myself, but it works! These qualities have made me a better collaborator and leader.

The complement to dance is stretching. By its nature, stretching expands the mind because you're incrementally working on reconditioning and lengthening your body in ways that are imperceptible in the moment. Only retrospectively do you realize that your mental intentions have a physical result. One of my favorite apps for stretching is STRETCHIT, which I have used two or three times a week. It offers a variety of customized stretching exercises that target different parts of the body. They even gamify the process for friendly competition. One of the instructors, Alicia Archer, an integrative movement coach, guides us through the routines in a way that makes it feel like a community, and achieving goals earns you fun labels like Boss or Chief.

When I interviewed Alicia, she explained,

I emphasize that [exercising] doesn't have to look like everyone else's routine. Social media presents this picture that you have to do "the most," and when people feel they're not doing the most, then they must not be doing it correctly. There's no such thing as "correct," because it's on a continuum based on your lifestyle and what you can afford to do with your time. And that might mean if you have an office job that's at home, you might have to just walk around your house a few times between meetings. You might have to do counter push-ups. Or if you have a baby, you do squats with the baby. It's not going to be glamorous, but there are always opportunities to exercise. But when we hear *exercise*, we think Peloton, we think marathon, we think of Pilates or going to a yoga class. . . . With the body-positivity movement, people use the word *movement* because the word *exercise* is too triggering for them. At the end of the day, we need exercise.

Exercise propels you to make those harder decisions easier. . . When I think about my 155-pound front squats, it's scary! But when I'm there, and I'm looking at the bar—I'm saying to myself, "This is gonna be hard. It is a little scary." But you come out on the other side. That process just makes it easier, and it conditions your anti-fragility.

Alicia's wisdom reminds us that movement, in whatever form it takes, is about progress, not perfection. Whether it's through stretching, dance, or simply taking small steps, we can all find ways to strengthen both our bodies and our minds—transforming life's challenges into opportunities for growth.

LET YOUR PEOPLE MOVE

When I was a professor of fashion management, I taught a required course on global apparel sourcing. While many aspects of my syllabus changed over the years, I consistently required that my students read *Let My People Go Surfing*, the memoir of Yvon Chouinard, founder of outdoor clothing and gear brand Patagonia. The book happens to be a brilliantly simple outline of the apparel sourcing process—from fiber development to logistics and delivery to distribution centers. But that's not why I mention it here in this chapter. Consider its title. Chouinard was committed to a flexible, *macro*management way of leading. His perspective was that an employee who wants to surf in the middle of the day should be able to do just that. Chouinard's assumption was that she would build in the time required to get the work done before and after surfing, even if it meant coming back to the office and working a bit into the evening.

When I first came across *Let My People Go Surfing* more than fifteen years ago, I was struck by how radical a leadership style it seemed: "What? Just allow your people to exercise in the middle of the day and trust that they'll get their work done? Wow!"

Management styles like Chouinard's are fundamentally based on the principle of trust. It assumes that if you hire the right people and give them the space and time to do their job, they will be intrinsically moti-vated to do their best work. It also assumes people cannot be expected to come up with their best ideas and to give you their best work product within the confines of rigid thirty-minute time blocks. Annie Dean, the VP of Team Anywhere at Atlassian and an expert on remote work strat-egies, emphasized that

> meetings are such an overused and broken tool. Coming together to be creative is really important and it shouldn't be forced into a thirty-minute meeting. You can do very little in thirty minutes. You cannot have an original conversation or idea in thirty minutes. So, you know, it's about breaking people's frames and thinking about "What does it mean to work together?"

You and your team must be able to move about and be *in* the world to deliver their most valuable work. After all, no matter the company or organization, the purpose of doing the work is not control—the purpose of the work is to deliver the best product, services, and experiences for the people who are your customers. Isn't it?

When we integrate opportunities for movement into the workday, we enable a work process that will ensure that result.

Other companies have embraced creative ways to incorporate move-ment into the workday: At Airbnb's headquarters in San Francisco, the environment itself invites movement. With open staircases, walking paths, and flexible workspaces, employees are encouraged to get up and move around. The company also provides standing desks, ergonomic furniture, and on-site fitness classes, making it clear that employee well-being and health are top priorities.

REI, known for its outdoor gear, takes a similar approach by integrat-ing movement into its company culture. Employees at REI can take paid time off to enjoy outdoor activities like hiking, camping, or skiing. This not only promotes physical health but also aligns with the company's mis-sion to enable life outdoors. By encouraging employees to step outside and explore, REI fosters and inspires a work environment that values balance and active living. Nike's headquarters in Beaverton, Oregon, is another great example. The campus includes on-site sports facilities, such as basketball courts, running tracks, and gyms. The office layout is designed to promote movement with open spaces, natural light, and walking paths that encourage employees to stay active. Additionally, Nike offers fitness classes, wellness programs, and incentives for employees to participate in sports and recreational activities. This focus on physical activity helps to create a dynamic and energetic workplace where innovation thrives.

But companies don't need to invest in resplendent gym equipment to get their employees moving. One simple solution is to bring back recess and encourage outdoor activity. Ideamix Coaching advocates for recess, stating in a 2023 blog, "Companies can avoid the steep costs associated with fitness facilities by allowing employees time for a 20-minute walk outside, just as they allow time for lunch breaks."[13] Brendan Boyle, toy inventor and founder of Play Lab, also advocates for recess in our work environments:

> Once a week for an hour and a half, you go out and just wander around and bump into people for meetings. And I can find the VP out there because the VP is right there [with me]. . . . That's the way recess works, right? You just sort of go out and everyone's there. There might be some ground rules like "No conversations more than three minutes long!" But you're moving, you're bumping around [and it] doesn't feel formal. That's great. The conference room should be redesigned, every table should be a circle, or just have standing room meetings!

In some workplace environments, standing meetings and walking meetings are commonplace. For example, the US Navy has instituted standing meetings for years, finding it a much more effective way to efficiently collaborate. These types of meetings not only promote physical activity but also foster more dynamic and engaging discussions. Gamifying movement opportunities through friendly competitions is another effective strategy. For example, a tech company could implement a Step Challenge Month, where employees form teams of four or five people. Each team chooses a fun name (like the Walking Devs or Quality Assurance Questers), and members track their daily steps using fitness trackers. The company could create a digital leaderboard in the break room showing team rankings and individual achievements. To make it more engaging, they could add different categories for winning beyond just total steps—such as Most Improved Team or Lunch Walk Champions. Teams that hit certain milestones could unlock small rewards, like a healthy team lunch or the ability to choose the office playlist for a day. The competitive element motivates people to take the stairs instead of the elevator and walk to nearby meetings rather than booking conference calls. This example shows how turning movement into a team-based game with varied achievement categories can make physical activity more appealing, motivating, and sustainable, encouraging employees to incorporate more movement into other areas of their daily routines.

Another innovative approach to promoting movement at work is the concept of an *unconference*. Unlike traditional conferences, an unconference is built from the ground up, with the agenda created by the participants themselves at the start of the convening. This format allows for a more democratic process that is fluid and fosters dynamic interaction. Attendees can freely move from session to session based on their interests. This constant movement not only keeps participants physically active but also sparks more innovative thought and collaboration. The very first unconference I ever attended was held in an outdoorsy arts center, just south of Pittsburgh. It felt a bit like a nerdy day camp for adults.

The attendees were folks who worked for big tech firms in Silicon Valley, as well as entrepreneurs in human-centered innovation. Admittedly, this was a group that was a bit more open to such an experimental way of meeting. In the morning, we crowdsourced potential topics by volunteering brief descriptions of ideas that were written on Post-its and taped to a crude grid made from blue painter's tape on a cabin wall. We

voted for our favorite topics after reading the descriptions and applying dot stickers. Within an hour, we had crowdsourced an orderly and
interesting agenda. Ultimately that day, I floated between sessions on
fractals, project management, and the value of doodling. I had never
before been so energized at a conference. I was sold! I went on to host
unconferences over the subsequent years. The informal, flexible structure of an unconference breaks down barriers and encourages spontaneous, creative exchanges of ideas.

Further still, there are additional ways on a macroscale that you can
use to encourage movement in the workplace. And that's through travel.
Take, for example, Visit Philadelphia. When I interviewed Angela Val,
the CEO of Visit Philadelphia (the official tourism and marketing organization for Philadelphia), she shared some of the dynamic ways that they
incentivize movement and getting out of the office so that her team can
do their job more effectively and gain new perspectives. Angela's view
on productivity is to measure results—not time. Staffers are required to
be in the office three days (everyone is in the office on Tuesdays), and are
allowed to be remote the other two days:

> We try to be flexible and look at people's lives and to make accommoda-
> tions. . . . For example, we have a Love & Lift group here, who takes the
> pulse of the organization, to say, "Hey, this is working, or not working.
> Can we do more of this and less of that?" Those ideas have to evolve with
> the staff. . . .
>
> We let the staff person and the team figure out what the other days are
> that you are remote or in the office. We do ask for that to stay consistent
> for at least a quarter at a time. Not that you can't make adjustments. But
> we also know that there's a seasonality to life.

In addition to six weeks of paid leave (with a goal of getting to twelve
weeks of paid leave), Visit Philly gives ten bereavement days and allots
a $500 travel stipend where staffers visit other cities and report back on
competitors, based on a list of questions they are required to answer.

You may be thinking, *Well, sure, visiting other cities works for a tourism-focused organization. But I work in education / tech / finance / fill in the blank!* Then consider how you can incorporate microdoses of movement throughout the day. And wouldn't your business benefit from a dose of fresh perspective that comes from zooming out, visiting a competitor, or checking out a new environment in which your product or service could launch?

Incorporating movement into the workplace isn't just about physical health; it's about creating an environment that supports holistic well-being and fosters innovation. It's about signaling our awareness of basic biology: Our best work doesn't come from a disembodied brain but from holistic integration within our bodies and with other people.

PUTTING IT INTO PRACTICE

Movement is important for our personal and professional success. We've talked about some progressive companies that promote movement in their work environments. But what if you don't work at a company that is willing to invest in fitness and movement or change company policy to add in recess? Here are some ways you can start incorporating movement into your day.

1. STAND AND DELIVER

When I was a middle school English teacher and then years later a professor, the ability to move while I worked was one of my favorite parts of those jobs. I could teach while standing, in motion either in the classroom or walking across campus to get to the next class or meeting. I loved that my job required me to be in motion, indoors and outdoors, to be on my feet, and to interact dynamically with my students rather than be confined to a desk all day.

Simply standing up throughout the day is an amazing way to get some movement in without even leaving your office. Many offices are now installing adjustable workstations to transition from sitting to standing seamlessly throughout the day. If you don't have an adjustable desk, you could look into purchasing a modular add-on that simply sits on your desk, allowing you to take standing breaks while you work.

If that's not in your budget, simply try standing up throughout the day. Roll or shake out your wrists, give your neck a stretch, relax your shoulders, and then sit down when you're ready.

With the evidence strongly supporting the advantage of a sit-to-stand work culture, you could even try putting in a request with your manager. For example, you could present the research that Steelcase reported. They conducted a "stand to work" study, adding to the growing evidence that workplace design can significantly impact employees' physical, cognitive, and emotional well-being. According to their research, 65 percent of participants with height-adjustable desks reported increased productivity after one year. They also noted better concentration abilities and felt more active, refreshed, awake, limber, and energetic.[14]

2. WALK IN ORDER TO WORK

Walk away from your work to propel your work.

In my experience, you do not need to walk for hours at a time to reap the benefits. I pepper my days with very short walks that are part of my breaks. I have pre-mapped walks: one that takes five minutes, one that's twelve minutes, another that's fifteen minutes, and, for when I'm feeling really luxurious, one that is thirty minutes. Regardless of the length, I always return to the work at hand refreshed and renewed.

And walking doesn't need to happen outside to reap the benefits. Simply getting up from your desk or station and walking the halls a little to stretch your legs will work.

3. GO OUTSIDE

Historically, cigarette breaks provided people with a sanctioned opportunity to stand up, move, and get outside, albeit in an unhealthy manner. These breaks were an attempt at recovery from fatigue.

How might we re-create the positive benefits of a cigarette break without inhaling cancer-causing chemicals?

The easiest thing to do is just walk out your office's door and step outside. It can even be for two minutes. The act of just exiting your building and exposing yourself to natural light may be all you need to feel recharged.

Ideally, immerse yourself as much as possible in nature when you step outside. If you have this luxury, you could try a few minutes of forest bathing, or *shinrin-yoku*, a nature immersion practice that originated in Japan in the 1980s as a response to the rise in stress-related chronic diseases, such as heart disease, hypertension, diabetes, depression, and suicide.[15] Japanese leaders established certified trails for people to "bathe" in nature during the workday. The purpose is to immerse yourself in the sounds, sights, and smells of nature. Allowing yourself to hear the birds or the rain, for example. An experiment with twenty-three burned-out physicians showed remarkable results. One hundred percent of participants rated the experience as very or extremely valuable, 96 percent were interested in more frequent forest therapy sessions, and 100 percent would recommend this practice to others. Additionally, 94 percent reported that forest therapy could help them cope with stressful events and setbacks.[16]

Now, forest bathing might not be easy or enjoyable if you're working in a busy city and the most you can hear are sirens blaring. But what else might you be able to observe in a similar way? Perhaps you can notice the sun or clouds in the sky or notice the trees if there are a few lining the streets. Taking just five minutes to do this throughout the day can make a major difference.

If getting outside isn't feasible, biophilic design offers an alternative by incorporating natural elements into the workplace. Biophilia, a philosophy introduced by Edward Wilson in the 1980s, emphasizes the connection between the workplace and nature. Biophilia improves productivity, reduces stress, and enhances creativity. Ivy Ross exemplified this in her redesign of Google's office space for the design team, using wood tones, glass walls, and access to natural light. Companies like Apple, Amazon,

Microsoft, and Google have all embraced biophilic design, seeing positive results in employee well-being and performance.

You can try bringing a succulent to your desk, or hanging a few photos of nature in your cubicle to stop and look at throughout the day.

WHO GETS TO MOVE?

Even as I write this chapter on movement, I'm astutely aware that the ability to get up and move throughout the day is a privilege. It's a privilege from an ability perspective as well as from a socioeconomic perspective. Bear in mind that one in four US adults aged eighteen to sixty-four lives with a disability.[17] These individuals often face significant challenges, whether it's difficulty walking or climbing stairs, hearing, seeing, or even concentrating and making decisions. Adults living with disabilities report fewer neighborhood environmental supports (such as sidewalks, public transit, and walkable shops) and more barriers (such as traffic and crime) for walking than people not living with disabilities.[18]

Aerobic physical activity, such as brisk walking or wheeling oneself in a wheelchair, can significantly reduce the impact of chronic diseases associated with disabilities. Yet nearly half of all adults living with disabilities get no leisure time or aerobic physical activity.[19] This lack of movement not only affects physical health but also mental well-being. Adults with disabilities report experiencing frequent mental distress almost five times more often than those without disabilities, according to the CDC's report on the mental health of people with physical disabilities.[20]

Mary Hale, a certified personal trainer with UNC Wellness Centers, has shed light on the mental barriers and anxiety that people living with mobility issues might face when considering exercise. Hale emphasizes that finding movements that work best for one's body at the present moment is key. It's important to recognize that with the right guidance and support, these challenges can be reduced.[21]

Imagine the transformative impact if more adults who live with disabilities could integrate more physical activity into their lives. Not only would it improve their physical health, but it would also offer significant mental health benefits. It's a powerful reminder that movement is a vital part of human well-being and should be made accessible to everyone with support and encouragement.

But sometimes it is the people with limitations in their physical abilities who prioritize movement the most. Take Tyler Turner, an award-winning Canadian para-snowboarder and athlete. A catastrophic skydiving accident left Tyler as an incomplete paraplegic and a double below-the-knee amputee. Living with a disability has made him much more mindful about his body than so many of us who have full use of our limbs. When I talked with Tyler, he was just coming off an incredible week of winning the Crystal Globe in snowboarding-cross for the World Cup's 2023/24 season. He's already won four World Cups. Pre-accident, Tyler took his physicality for granted. Now he intentionally moves, thinks, and rests with consistency:

> I'm always thinking before moving. For me, *execute* means *move*. So, I like to really have a good solid plan that limits variables. . . I want to be James Bond, not Evel Knievel. . . . I like to think, then move, and I like the idea of rethinking.
>
> I've become a master of rest. . . . I used to skip rest, and now that's all forced upon me—if I don't rest, then my prosthetics are gonna force the rest upon me. . . . I will have a cyst, I will have, you know, skin breakdown, whatever it is. So rest is now essential in my life. I have "legs-off days."

What if we *all* had legs-off days? Weeks when we were so purposely moving that we also intentionally incorporated rest, a.k.a. legs-off days?

It's not only people living with physical disabilities who must be creative in integrating more movement throughout their day. Consider people who have restricted movement because they live in high-crime areas. For aerobic activity, the CDC recommendation is at least 150 minutes of moderate-intensity physical activity per week.[22] But not everyone has a job where they are able to go surfing whenever they want; and similarly, not everyone lives in a neighborhood where they feel safe moving about freely. If you live in an urban area with a high crime rate, with minimal to no green space (let alone highly functioning recreation centers), going for a leisurely walk or a jog is not practical.

That's why the pioneering work of Dr. Toni Yancey, cofounder and former codirector of the UCLA Kaiser Permanente Center for Health Equity, is so invaluable. Yancey was particularly concerned with the socioeconomic disparities around movement. Before her tragic death to lung cancer at age fifty-five, she designed and planned movement activations. Instant Recess was an award-winning program dedicated to "making America healthier 10 minutes at a time" that was embraced by former First Lady Michelle Obama's Let's Move! initiative.[23] It promoted short exercise breaks at offices, schools, and places of worship. Instant Recess introduced a new paradigm for fitness that didn't require lots of space, expensive gym memberships with fancy equipment, or access to open parks. It proposed regular ten-minute exercise breaks that are easily incorporated into school, work, and community life utilizing music and dance. Activations of Instant Recess happened at the UCLA and UC Berkeley campuses among faculty, students and staff, and the benefits were phenomenal:

> It wasn't so much the physical benefits as it was the behavioral impact: The ten-minute activity served as a wake-up call for adults who had been sedentary for years, motivating many of them to do more.[24]

To get very practical about movement when considering both physical limitations and safety concerns, here are some inclusive movement opportunities:

- Ten-minute dance breaks at home or in the office, inspired by Dr. Yancey's program. These can be done in small spaces and don't require special equipment—just put on your favorite music and move to the rhythm in whatever way feels comfortable and accessible.

- Chair-based exercises during work or leisure time, such as seated arm circles, leg lifts, ankle rotations, and gentle torso twists. These can be done in short bursts throughout the day, making them ideal for people with mobility challenges or those who need to stay in one location.

- Indoor walking or wheelchair rolling circuits—creating a safe route within one's home or workplace, perhaps doing a few laps around the living room during TV commercial breaks or circling the office floor during phone calls.

- Strength-building exercises using household items as weights (like soup cans or water bottles) while seated or standing, which can be done safely indoors regardless of neighborhood conditions.

- Gentle stretching routines that can be done in bed or upon waking, taking inspiration from Tyler Turner's mindful approach to movement. This could include simple joint mobility exercises or gentle reaching movements.

- Social movement groups within apartment buildings or community centers, where people can exercise together in a secure indoor environment. This addresses safety concerns and also creates accountability.

- Short exercise breaks during religious services or community gatherings, following Dr. Yancey's model of integrating movement into existing community structures where people already feel safe and comfortable.

- Adaptive video game workouts using consoles with motion controls, where people can participate from a seated position and adjust the intensity and range of motion to their abilities. Similar to Tyler Turner's strategic approach to movement, people can plan their gaming sessions thoughtfully and incorporate rest periods as needed.

- Water-based movement in a supportive pool environment (where available through medical facilities or rehabilitation centers), as water can reduce the impact on joints and provide natural resistance while supporting body weight. Aquatic exercise can be highly customizable to individual abilities and comfort levels.

These suggestions emphasize accessibility, safety, and the ability to break movement into small, manageable segments throughout the day, similar to the Instant Recess concept.

THERE'S AN APP FOR THAT

Perhaps you're one of the millions of people who use a tech-based app to help them move and exercise regularly. I've already referenced my appreciation for the STRETCHIT app. According to the National Institutes of Health (NIH), almost one-third of Americans use fitness trackers to help prompt movement; additionally, the Pew Research Center has found that 21 percent of US adults wear a fitness tracker or a smartwatch.[25] Globally, the World Economic Forum estimates that 8 percent of the world population uses a fitness tracker,[26] and 2024 research from Statista estimates that the projected global market value for fitness trackers will be $56.82 billion by 2029, with an annual growth rate of 5.62 percent.[27] It makes sense that wearables are a popular accessory: Technology is increasingly not just an add-on to our lives but is integrated into how we are motivated, perceive, and connect to others.

When we can't rely on being intrinsically motivated, it's our technology that can get us up and moving. Take the Apple Watch, for instance. It's not only a timekeeper; it's a movement motivator. Periodically, it gently nudges us with a reminder to stand up, stretch, or take a short walk. These simple prompts can break the cycle of prolonged sitting, encouraging us to incorporate more movement into our daily routines. But the influence of fitness trackers extends beyond Apple. Devices like Fitbit, Garmin, Samsung Galaxy Watch, and the Oura Ring have revolutionized how we improve with our physical health. Sam Skey, CEO of SHE Media, told me that "the Oura Ring or [other] wearables are very effective for people with my general approach, because they are goal oriented."

A study published in *The BMJ* by Danish researchers found that physical activity monitors led people to take an extra 1,235 steps per day and engage in forty-nine additional minutes of moderate-to-vigorous physical activity each week. Although participants only stood for an extra ten minutes per day, the overall increase in activity was significant.[28] As with Dr. Yancey's Instant Recess activations, the longer-term benefit was in the behavioral impact.

The magic behind fitness trackers lies in several psychological factors. They create a sense of achievement, foster self-competition, and provide an honest feedback loop that keeps users motivated. There's something deeply satisfying about completing a task, even if it's just hitting a daily step goal. Fitness trackers tap into this intrinsic motivation—the sheer satisfaction of accomplishment. They give immediate feedback, prompting engagement and self-satisfaction. But we need to hold all of this in perspective. Dr. Pamela Rutledge, a professor of media psychology at Fielding Graduate University, emphasizes the importance of not becoming overly reliant on numerical metrics provided by these devices. While the quantitative data can be motivating, it's crucial not to lose sight of qualitative health and wellness goals. Balancing the numbers with a mindful awareness of our bodies' needs is key.[29]

Building movement into the ways we work doesn't have to be an arduous chore. It doesn't require fancy and expensive gym equipment in every single workplace. It doesn't even require the HR department to offer discounts for gym memberships at partnering companies. Fitness trackers demonstrate that incorporating movement into your day doesn't require grand gestures. It can be as simple as standing up when your Apple Watch tells you to or competing with yourself to reach a new step goal on your Fitbit. And if you don't have a tracker, you can simply schedule these same reminders on your work calendar or on your phone. What matters most is creating a rhythm that keeps you connected to your body—because even the smallest act of movement can spark a ripple of energy, clarity, and creativity throughout your day.

SEEDS TO CULTIVATE:
PRO TIPS TO MOVE BY DESIGN

The following questions encourage reflection and practical steps for incorporating movement into daily routines for better mental, physical, and creative outcomes.

Individual Level—Reflections and Exercises
Reflection Questions for You

1. How do you currently incorporate movement into your workday? What barriers prevent you from moving more?
2. When do you feel most energized and creative during your day? How might movement play a role in those peak moments?
3. What small changes could you make to your workspace and daily routine to encourage more natural movement?
4. What's your favorite way to get out of your head and into your body? Can you commit to doing that activity for five minutes daily?
5. How can you incorporate regular moments of movement into your day that also encourage creativity and reflection? Could you use timer reminders to stand up from your desk once an hour? Think about walking meetings, standing breaks, or stretching routines that allow your mind to wander and process ideas.
6. How do you currently engage with your physical body during work, and how might more intentional movement improve your productivity and well-being? Reflect on whether you feel disconnected from your body during the workday and identify simple actions like stretching or walking that could help.

Exercises for You

1. Movement Mapping: Create a "movement map" of your workplace identifying opportunities for natural movement (stairs, walking paths, standing areas). Set goals to use these spaces intentionally throughout your day.
2. Movement Breaks: Schedule three five-minute movement breaks into your calendar each day. Use these for stretching, walking, or simple exercises. Start with times when you typically experience energy dips.
3. Movement Journaling: Keep a two-week log tracking when you move and how it affects your energy, focus, and creativity. Note patterns to optimize your movement schedule.

Team Level—Reflections and Exercises
Reflection Questions for Your Team

1. How does your team's current work structure support or inhibit movement?
2. What meeting formats could you redesign to incorporate more movement?
3. How might movement-based activities strengthen team relationships and creativity?
4. What playful rituals or activities can you introduce to your team or workplace to encourage collective movement and creative thinking? Could you set up at least one meeting a week as a walking meeting outside? Consider activities like brainstorming walks, team yoga, or even spontaneous dance breaks to energize the group.
5. How could your team redesign your work environment to promote both movement and rest, creating a balance between physical activity and mental rejuvenation? Look at your workspace—can you incorporate standing desks, open spaces for walking, or quiet zones for thought and relaxation?

Exercises for Your Team

1. Walking Meetings: Convert one weekly team meeting to a walking format. Start with shorter, two-person meetings and gradually expand to small-group discussions.
2. Movement Champions: Gamify this initiative by designating rotating "movement champions" who lead brief movement breaks during long meetings and encourage active participation.
3. Team Movement Challenge: Create a monthly team challenge incorporating movement goals. Focus on collaboration over competition, celebrating collective achievement.

Organizational Level—Reflections and Exercises
Reflection Questions for Your Organization

1. How does your workplace design and culture impact movement opportunities?
2. What policies could you implement to normalize movement during the workday?
3. How might investing in movement-friendly spaces affect productivity and innovation?
4. What opportunities does your organization have to use movement as a tool for both professional growth and personal well-being, and how can these opportunities be integrated into work routines? Think about how movement like walking or exercising might help teams solve problems, de-stress, or come up with innovative ideas, and plan to make it part of the organization's culture.

Exercises for Your Organization

1. Space Audit: Conduct an organizational audit of movement opportunities and barriers. Include employee feedback about desired changes and concerns.

2. Policy Innovation: Develop clear policies supporting movement during work hours. Examples: "Walking meetings welcome," flexible break schedules, standing desk options.

3. Movement Infrastructure: Create dedicated spaces for movement—quiet walking paths, standing meeting areas, stretch zones. Start small with pilot areas to test effectiveness.

LEAVING YOU WITH THIS THOUGHT

Movement hygiene isn't just about exercising; it's about integrating motion into our daily lives in ways that connect the mind and body. In the fast-paced, screen-dominated world we live in, it's crucial to intentionally break away from the desk to fuel more generative thinking and creative breakthroughs. When we move—whether it's through walking, stretching, dancing, or simply standing up and taking a break—our thoughts become more fluid, our ideas more expansive, and our bodies more attuned to the world around us.

No matter what our mobility access and ability is, the journey to incorporating more movement begins with small steps. Start by choosing one action item from each level—individual, team, and organization—to implement over the next month. Begin with what feels most achievable and track the impact on your personal energy and focus, team collaboration and creativity, and organizational culture. Remember that sustainable change happens gradually; the goal is to make movement a natural part of how work gets done, not an additional obligation.

Movement interacts with both thought and rest to support the process of cultivation—much like tending to a garden, where each element works in harmony to produce growth. To nurture this garden, establish regular check-ins: weekly self-reflection on movement patterns, monthly team discussions of movement initiatives, and quarterly organizational reviews of movement-related policies and spaces. This rhythm of reflection helps maintain momentum while allowing for necessary adjustments.

The value of movement extends far beyond physical activity—movement's value is in how it connects us to our physical selves, engages our minds, and invites us to cultivate a more thoughtful, rested, and creative way of working. Success looks different for every person and organization. Focus on progress over perfection, celebrating small wins and adjusting approaches based on what works for your specific situation. Let the benefits of increased movement—enhanced creativity, better focus, stronger relationships—guide your continued evolution. Through this intentional integration of movement, we create spaces for deeper insight and innovation, fostering both individual and collective flourishing.

4

THINK: THE INSIDE-OUT WORK OF CULTIVATION

We do not learn from experience. We learn from reflecting on experience.

—John Dewey, American philosopher
and education reformer[1]

Where do you do your best thinking?

I do my most *expansive* thinking when I am in steady motion.

Whether I'm taking a leisurely walk, dancing, or swimming laps, movement ignites my thoughts. It's no surprise that I'm also at my happiest when I'm in motion. As a kinesthetic learner, I thrive on moving and tinkering to create and figure things out. Even when I'm doodling and sketching out ideas with rough-hewn circles, squares, arrows, and lines, my hands' movement helps me process and explore concepts.

There is something to be said for stepping away to think more creatively. Even for a portion of writing *this* chapter for *this* book, I had a walking meeting with Nick Begley, founder of Illume and the former head of research at Headspace. Begley brings a unique scientific and experiential perspective to understanding how movement, meditation, and cognitive processes interact to influence productivity and well-being.

His insights particularly emphasize the importance of understanding different types of thinking modes and how physical movement and meditation can be used strategically to enhance different cognitive processes. He told me, "I find it easier to structure my thoughts when I'm moving. And I do find it easier to do creative thinking while moving." In fact, he wrote a lot of his doctoral thesis dictating into a recording device while walking along the River Thames.

For truly *deep focus*, I need a clear and organized space. In college, I used to think I was procrastinating when I tidied up my dorm room and desk before diving into reading or writing assignments. Often, I'd light some incense. I now realize that these rituals are essential prep; they set the stage for my best deep thinking. A clear space and sensorial cues like the scent of incense help me find my way into a focused mindset. When the space around me is uncluttered, it signals the clarity I seek for my mind. This habit has carried over into my adult home office, where my design aesthetic is clean and minimalist, with occasional pops of color. This environment not only supports my need for physical and mental space but also creates a harmonious backdrop for creativity and reflection.

During college, I also tackled difficult material by heading to a quiet sanctuary away from my dorm room. My refuge was the basement of the beautiful Thompson Library at Vassar College, a secluded area known as "the stacks." There, enveloped in a cocoon of silence, all I could hear were the gentle hum of the radiator and the occasional clanking of the heating pipes. The stacks were sparse and cozy, a perfect retreat where I never felt spooked despite the isolation. The stacks offered an environment that made me feel cloaked and comforted by the quiet. I wonder how many students today seek out such secluded, quiet spaces in libraries or their equivalents. For me, it was the ideal setting for deep focus and study, and I highly recommend it.

Years later, while writing my previous book, *The Creativity Leap*, I found myself yearning for a similar cocoon to finalize my manuscript. Driven by this need, I returned to my intellectual roots at Vassar College, spending a week immersed in the familiar ambiance of that beautiful library. Just being in the space triggered a visceral, almost cellular memory. The atmosphere of the library (the smell of old books, light filtering through stained glass windows, shadows in the nooks of Gothic archways), reminiscent of my college days, put me in the perfect mindset to deeply immerse myself in the writing and editing process.

The experience reaffirmed the importance of finding a personal sanctuary—a place that feels like a second home, where one feels free to get lost in thought.

When I reference *thought* in the MTR framework, I am referring to the range of mental activity that helps us with both deep thinking *and* sparking new ideas. We can backcast through reflection, metacognition, and memory; we can forecast through imagination, curiosity, inspiration, dreaming, and daydreaming. All these activities help us develop our capacity for creative thinking. And this matters now more than ever. The World Economic Forum's *Future of Jobs Report 2023* predicted that by 2027, creativity would rank number two as the most in-demand leadership skill.[2] Just look at some of the statistics from a November 2023 Linearity blog post[3] and 2024 research from ThriveMyWay[4]:

- 80 percent of people believe unlocking creativity is critical to economic growth;
- 75 percent of respondents are pressured to be productive rather than creative at work;
- 60 percent of polled CEOs say that creativity is an important leadership skill, but 46 percent of workers say they are only given a few times a year to be creative at their places of work;
- 75 percent of respondents don't believe they are living up to their creative potential, yet seven out of ten people believed that creativity was an important driver in the economy; and
- creative problem-solving sessions with groups trained in creativity tools and principles generated 350 percent as many ideas, which were 415 percent more original than those from untrained groups.

Given these numbers, don't you want to carve out more time for thought activities?

DEEP FOCUS AND MENTAL FREEDOM

Culturally in the United States, we often equate busyness with productivity. This mindset is especially prevalent in fast-paced environments where the pressure to perform and deliver can lead us to juggle multiple tasks. However, this approach can lead to burnout and decreased overall effectiveness. In contrast, many cultures emphasize the importance of focus and single tasking. For instance, the Japanese concept of *ichigyo-zammai* encourages concentrating on one act with full attention, which can lead to more meaningful and high-quality outcomes.

We may fool ourselves into thinking that doing multiple things at once will make us more efficient. However, multitasking is incredibly inefficient and counterproductive. True productivity and meaningful completion of tasks require us to cultivate focus and intentionality. By attempting to multitask, we defeat the very purpose of being productive. Reflecting on my own attempts to multitask, I've concluded that multitasking is essentially a form of intentional distraction. It's taxing on the brain, requiring constant cognitive switching. This consumes a lot of mental energy and dilutes the impact of my thinking.

More companies are trying to make deep, intentional, and thoughtful work part of their organization's culture. For example, 3M has a "15 percent culture" that encourages employees to set aside a portion of their work time to "proactively cultivate and pursue innovative ideas that excite them."[5] And software company Zapier, which has a global and remote workforce, implemented a no-meeting week in 2022. After this Get Stuff Done (GSD) week (I love the title!), here's what they found:[6]

- 80 percent of respondents would want to do another GSD week in the future;
- 80 percent of respondents achieved their goal(s) for the week; and

- 89 percent of respondents found communication to be about as effective during GSD week as during a typical week.

See what happens when we leave one another alone a bit and just trust that our colleagues will get the work done?

As Nir Eyal wrote in a blog post featuring ideas from Ian Bogost, a video game developer and professor at Washington University in St. Louis,

> Finding novelty is only possible when we give ourselves the time to focus intently on a task and look hard for the variability. The great thinkers and tinkerers of history made their discoveries because they were obsessed with the intoxicating draw of discovery, the mystery that pulls us in because we want to know more.[7]

Focusing is immensely important—it helps us sift and sort through the noise of life. But finding time to focus is increasingly challenging these days with all sorts of distractions vying for our attention: work demands, family commitments, and the constant dinging of our phones. Johann Hari, in his book *Stolen Focus*, notes that while our cognitive capacity hasn't changed in the last forty thousand years, the amount of information we process has skyrocketed.[8] Productivity expert Cal Newport offers these four strategies to minimize distractions and commit to the practice of what he calls *deep work*:

1. A monastic approach—where you go off somewhere by yourself with no distractions
2. A bimodal approach—which involves setting a clearly defined, long period of seclusion for work
3. A rhythmic approach—for example, working in seventy-five-minute increments
4. A journalistic strategy—where you grab any unexpected free time that comes along

What all of Newport's strategies have in common is that they make depth our default, while also scheduling in focus breaks—times when we allow ourselves to "give in completely to distractions," as he put it. Most of us do a combination of these strategies; I know that I do. For example, to write this book, I tried a bimodal approach for the first time. I took a two-week writing sabbatical, inspired by Bill Gates's Think Weeks. I rented a beachside condo in Miami from my friend Ivy and immersed myself in research, writing, and reflection. This period of deep focus and play (swimming every afternoon and taking Cuban salsa lessons two nights each week) while also engaging in relaxing conversations (sometimes with strangers and often with old friends) rejuvenated my mind. The experience was so valuable that I have since committed to annually investing in similar sabbaticals in whatever ways are affordable and time-feasible.

Such modes of working are examples of the contract-release, converge-diverge processes so prevalent in our natural environments: For everything, there is a season; for every dormant winter, there's a jubilant spring. Our attentional system consists of different networks in the brain that coordinate skills such as sustaining awareness, prioritizing tasks, using working memory, and practicing self-regulation—all of which require lots of cognitive energy! And as a result, the best way to remain focused is actually to take regular breaks—which most people do *not* do.

Finding balance between focused work and mental relaxation is essential. We flourish in that liminal in-between space where we forgo doing to simply be. Practices like the Japanese *shinrin-yoku* (forest bathing) emphasize the importance of nature in rejuvenating the mind and body. Similarly, the Italian's *dolce far niente*, or the Trinidadian's laid-back "liming" (the art of doing nothing while sharing food, drink, conversation, and laughter, typically in a public space) celebrates the sweetness of hanging out and whiling away the day, highlighting the value of taking time to simply be. And intermittent work can result in greater productivity. As Hari shared, "[When] a Toyota factory in Gothenburg cut its workday by two hours, workers actually produced at 114 percent of their previous capacity, and the factory reported 25 percent more profit."

But taking breaks is different from task-switching or multitasking, as it's commonly known.

Consider those moments when you try to answer emails during a meeting, jot down notes, *and* plan your grocery list for dinner—all at once. You end up missing important insights from the meeting, sending poorly thought-out emails, and possibly even messing up your dinner plans. The brain is not wired to efficiently handle multiple complex tasks simultaneously. Multitasking spreads our attention thinly, leaving us less effective and more stressed. Embracing a focused approach can transform our productivity, allowing us to complete tasks with greater quality and satisfaction.

Gloria Mark, a researcher on distraction, has shared that on average, people in the workplace spend about three minutes on a task before switching to another. And while on the computer, they switch attention—from one website to another, for instance—every two and a half minutes. Now that was 2004 data—by 2021, they'd started switching their attention every forty-seven seconds.[9] That's very different from taking a break. The more we are interrupted externally, the more we begin to interrupt ourselves. While these interruptions may seem to provide brief mental breaks, they actually drain our cognitive resources and prompt cortisol hormone release, which adds to stress and leads to endless scrolling spirals from which we walk away beating ourselves up for having wasted time.

Reflecting on my own experiences, I find deep thought challenging to do sometimes, but I recognize that it is absolutely necessary. Mark's insights remind me that creating the conditions for deep thought is essential. And this need for focus isn't exclusive to sedentary office workers.

It's not every day that you meet a residential electrician who's also a Jungian dream aficionado. Tyler Blaetz, our family's electrician, is one such unicorn. Tyler relies on focused, deep concentration to solve complex problems safely. I became interested in interviewing Tyler after overhearing him talking to himself while working through an electrical wiring challenge in our attic. He explained to me,

> Sometimes I have to step into a space and imagine the history, you know, imagine the way that it used to look, and so it starts in the very room the project has to take place. And when we're up in your space, I have questions—I have questions for the house, and maybe I'll ask them to myself. I don't know why, but I guess it's helpful to think out loud. Yeah, I wonder, "What would Natalie think if the cable just dove into the wall in this pocket? Would it be worth it to make that portion disappear? Or would that be too much work? Probably. Is there a big gap back there? Oh, yeah, I'm sure there is. Oh, no. There's not a big gap back here. Well, what do we do now?" . . .
>
> The questions I ask for problem-solving can be as simple as where to place a light in relation to another fixture. What shadow is it going to cast? What might the effect of this be if this fixture or fan started to move? How's the person going to use this outlet? Why? Why should this outlet go in here? And what's it going to be for? Should it go like this? Does it make sense? . . . And then, you know, obviously, it scales all the way up to identifying, you know, what does this person really want? What do they really need? My favorite question is, "What if this was *your* house?" So, I'll ask that of myself. I'll ask that of my apprentice. . . . And I'll tell somebody that if this were my house, you know, here's what I would do. And I think it just takes you right to the most satisfactory solution and it asks, "What is really worthwhile?"

Tyler applies a jazz improvisational approach to his problem-solving and to the ways he works with his apprentices and fellow electricians. I was pleasantly surprised to learn that as a devotee of Jungian dream philosophy, he applies that same affinity for deep reflection to figuring out residential rewiring challenges. He pointed out to me that Elias Howe, inventor of the sewing machine, and Thomas Edison both used dream inspiration and sleep to arrive at insights.

The hope that I subscribe to is that the dream has some information that we don't consciously know already. . . . Maybe there could be some information in there; things that our attention needs to be drawn to or things that might need to bubble to the surface. You're tasked to ascribe the symbols in your dream to associations that you personally have with those symbols and then retell the dream.

It's really very fascinating stuff. . . . Sometimes you have to wait for the fruit to ripen, so to speak. And sometimes it comes from dreams. That's one of the channels I explore.

As with Tyler, sometimes your best thinking can come from paying attention to your dreams, and sometimes it can be possible to find your zone for deep thought among a group of people—not holed up somewhere alone. Well, kind of. Recently, I experimented with joining a cool online community called FLOWN—a platform that provides what I call *asynchronous synchronicity* as a way of working. Founder Alicia Navarro's impetus to start FLOWN was this question: "What if I could bring the same vitality and energy that Peloton or SoulCycle instructors bring into an exercise class . . . while people were working?" Sign me up! So I did. I committed to regularly immersing myself in a variety of FLOWN sessions while editing a book chapter, replying to emails for a block of time, or mapping out a slide deck for an upcoming keynote.

At first, I was skeptical: Would this feel like Big Brother was watching me? What if creepos interrupted my workflow? And then I tried it. And I've grown to enjoy it and look forward to it.

Here's how FLOWN works. You sign up, then decide if you want to drop in to an open session or join a more facilitated session. The first time, I had my camera on, ready to do some writing for this very book. It felt in many ways like entering a hushed library. The Zoom screen was full of *Brady Bunch* boxes of people writing, reading, some at walking-standing desks—all with their audio off, and all working. It had a quieting effect on me. I hunkered down to do my own work. There was a bit of peer pressure at play, I must admit—but in a good way. They were all working, and I didn't want to stick out. I could see how this online community could transform people's ability to focus. I could even add background sounds (for example, rain, or the ocean waves) or music. Facilitators regularly shared their favorite Spotify playlists to facilitate deep, focused work. And of course, there were timers so that I could choose my increments of work: ten, twenty-five, or fifty minutes—and at the end of each session, I was prompted to take a break.

The breaks were well curated with scenes of nature and fun facts about a lot of things I am writing about in this book. For example, the importance of taking breaks and pausing; playing; immersing yourself in nature and daydreaming to get your default mode network (DMN) going. Through FLOWN, I found a balance between deep focus and mental relaxation, focused productivity and creative exploration. FLOWN isn't just about getting work done; it's about how we work. It's about creating new habits that ground us in the present, while offering a sense of accountability and community that can be elusive when we're working solo.

By embracing both deep focus and moments of mental freedom, we can create a more balanced and meaningful approach to work and life. Joining communities like FLOWN and integrating practices from different cultures can help us navigate the challenges of modern distractions and cultivate the conditions needed for deep and creative thinking.

MEDITATION STRENGTHENS OUR ATTENTION MUSCLES

Meditation isn't just something that happens on a cushion with your eyes closed—it can take many forms, including those sparked by movement. The academic literature tends to break down meditation into focused attention meditation (e.g., focusing on a particular object) and open monitoring meditation (e.g., awareness of your sensory experience without judgment). There's a hybrid between these two types of meditation that can occur when we are in motion.

For example, I fall more easily into meditation when I am doing consistent physical movement, such as swimming laps. Luke Bloom, director of integrated well-being at Miraval Resort in the Berkshires, helped me to reframe meditation in this way:

> For me, personally, [meditation] always seemed like an unachievable thing. . . . I always had this notion of somebody sitting next to a waterfall and "ohming" in a very peaceful manner. . . . I have something known as a "monkey mind," right? It just jumps all over the place. So, it seemed like the doorway was very narrow, and it was one that I wouldn't fit through.

But Luke now realizes that he can meditate through a different doorway, when he is physically active. It is called *kinetic meditation.*

Deep thought without distraction is like a muscle that can be strengthened with practice. Mark's research shows that most people focus best around 11:00 a.m. and 3:00 p.m., with the biggest dips in focus occurring after 1:00 p.m.[10] Structuring your day to align with your own natural peaks and troughs can enhance productivity. Meditation can also be a powerful tool to cultivate deep thought because it provides a structured way to clear the mind and enhance focus. (But it's not the only way. As a counterpoint to meditation, I will be discussing daydreaming later on in this chapter. It also plays a significant role in fostering creativity and deep thinking.)

The effects of meditation, when done in moderation, are downright amazing. Meditation promotes neuroplasticity, which is to say that the brain is not a rigid structure but one capable of continuous growth and change. It can be rewired—or, stated another way, human attention is a trainable resource.

Meditation offers numerous benefits that are increasingly recognized in the workplace. David Gelles outlines in *Mindful Work* the ways that meditation can significantly calm the area of the brain responsible for self-referential thoughts, enhancing overall mental clarity.[11] This insight presents an opportunity for workplace or technology interventions to harness these benefits. The most popular form of meditation training today is mindfulness-based stress reduction (MBSR), which focuses on the physical sensations in the body. Mindfulness, the practice of directing and redirecting attention by observing thoughts, helps bring oneself back into focus.

The key benefits of mindfulness include the following:

1. Enhanced focus: Meditation helps improve concentration and the ability to stay on task.[12]
2. Improved emotional recovery: Mindful leaders can be more focused on their goals, while also effectively responding to challenges, be more self-aware of their own emotions, and listen more attentively.[13] This awareness positions them to make decisions based on honesty and compassion, aligning with emotional recovery (more on that in Chapter 5, "Rest: Doing Less Better").
3. Healthier immune profile: According to an article by Black and Slavich, preliminary findings suggest that mindfulness meditation can lead to a healthier immune profile by reducing inflammation and enhancing cellular defense mechanisms.[14]

These insights underscore the potential of meditation to not only improve individual well-being but also enhance cognition and leadership qualities and boost immune health, making it a valuable practice in both personal and professional contexts.

For me, doodling is akin to a variation of focused attention meditation. It's an incredibly relaxing and enjoyable low-stakes thinking activity with no judgment. In fact, the cruder and more imperfect the doodles, the more they invite engagement and interesting questions. Doodling is a powerful form of thinking that transcends the need for artistic talent. It is a form of play that taps into visual thinking, allowing us to delve deeply into our thoughts, visualizing our ideas and working through complex problems in an intuitive and enjoyable way. Embracing this practice can enrich our thinking processes and lead to unexpected insights and solutions.

Warren Berger, the author of *A More Beautiful Question*, has aptly said that asking questions is a way of thinking.[15] Well, so is doodling.

Think of doodling as your gateway tool to deeper reflection and creativity. The beauty of doodles lies in their simplicity and lack of intimidation. Your ability to doodle has nothing to do with your drawing skills or whether you've taken advanced art classes. Instead, it taps into your capacity for abstract and complex thinking. They're just lines, stick figures, and circles, yet they invite really good questions and spark curiosity.

Doodling also allows you to explore liminal spaces—the in-between areas where creativity thrives.

IT'S OKAY TO DAYDREAM—REALLY

I know I just extolled the benefits of meditation, but truthfully, I've never been a big meditator.

I actually find it quite challenging, even though intellectually I understand that meditation is good for me.

But daydreaming? I'm a natural.

I regularly take daydream breaks. They leave me feeling revived and energized every time I return to the work at hand. Sometimes, all I can manage is a ninety-second daydream. At other times, I indulge in five minutes, and on particularly luxurious days, I might even enjoy a fifteen-minute daydream.

Being in nature is a wonderful place for me to let my mind wander. The biodiversity creates pattern interruptions—like watching the ocean waves, with their constant yet varied motion, or observing the asymmetry in a grove of trees. Even just standing by a window and observing a cloud drift by can be incredibly refreshing. Gazing at a piece of visual art is another great cue for daydreaming. The same goes for listening to soft music—whether it's jazz, classical, or some chill electronica. These activities create an in-between space where my mind can relax, my brain's DMN takes over, and creativity can flourish.

To me, daydreaming is the perfect counterpoint to meditation. It shouldn't be dismissed as useless or equated with distraction because it's far from that. Daydreaming and mind wandering might seem like idle pastimes, but they play a significant role in problem-solving and creativity. Nick Begley explained to me that

> mind wandering, it's actually all about the self, and it's projecting you in different places, it's projecting you in different times, the past, the future. . . . The default mode network is just helping project the self into lots of different situations.

This sort of projection can be a very useful way to engage in scenario planning, as a way to work through challenges and strategize. While you daydream, you're freeing up the cognitive load in your neocortex and activating the other synapses in your brain's DMN. Susan Magsamen, an expert on neuroaesthetics, director of the International Arts + Mind Lab at Johns Hopkins University, and the coauthor of *Your Brain on Art*, broke down the DMN for me in the following way:

> So the default mode network is in the frontal, parietal, and temporal cortices of the brain. That's where it's primarily activated. And the default mode network goes to work when you are not bringing the world in, right? . . . It goes to work when you're not engaged [with the world]—so when you're taking a walk in nature, or if you're passively listening to music, or taking a shower—where you have these aha moments.
>
> This is a part of the brain that is really the meaning-making part of the brain. It's where your brain connects the dots. It finds patterns, it makes sense of the world. It also is this place that can recognize what you think is beautiful, or things that you like and don't like. And so it goes to work when you're in between the notes, when you're quiet, when you're allowing your system not to be overflooded with different things.
>
> So that's why I think it's really important to pause—it's where you daydream, it's where your mind wanders. It happens through this default mode network.

In other words, the DMN is kind of like the washing machine for our ideas! Interestingly, it is located above our brains' saliency network (regulating "What do I need to survive?"), which is above the limbic system, the most ancient part of the brain, responsible for autonomic and parasympathetic systems to keep us alive (e.g., raw feeling to detect danger). As Susan explained to me, "So the default mode network is actually taking the most salient, the most deeply felt information and making sense of it! That's extraordinary, right?" The DMN thrives in liminal space and gets to work when we allow ourselves to tap out and tap into MTR activity.

I view daydreams as inside-out work. As Diane Barth wrote in her 1997 book, *Daydreaming: Unlock the Creative Power of Your Mind*, every daydream is an attempt by the psyche to redirect attention from external tasks to internal processes.[16] There's so much invisible labor, activity, and synthesis happening beyond the conscious level. So to make us more aware, our bodies give us cues—such as a daydream—and permission to indulge.

Markus Baer and his colleagues, in their study "Zoning Out or Breaking Through?," highlight that daydreams, particularly problem-oriented ones, can be a valuable source of creative inspiration under the right circumstances.[17] For professionals facing cognitively demanding problems, daydreaming may lead to breakthroughs that structured thinking cannot achieve. Baer outlines a typology of daydreams that includes both problem-solving daydreams and bizarre daydreams. When individuals deeply engage with their challenges, their daydreams can become a potent tool for creative problem-solving.

I was thrilled to see Danah Henriksen and her colleagues' findings highlight the benefits of daydreaming and mind-wandering in their research on mindfulness and creativity.[18] While mindfulness involves focused attention, mind-wandering—especially deliberate mind-wandering—can enhance creativity. Combining mindfulness with mind-wandering fosters fertile ground for creative thinking.

Jill Suttie, in her article "What Daydreaming Does to Your Mind," discusses the neurological basis of this phenomenon.[19] She notes that daydreaming increases alpha waves in the brain's frontal cortex, a pattern linked to enhanced divergent thinking and creativity. Furthermore, she wrote,

> Practicing mindfulness and increasing awareness of our thought patterns during mind-wandering could serve as an intervention to control and redirect thoughts. This awareness might not only boost creativity and happiness but also productivity, especially when mind-wandering is applied during less critical tasks and not at the expense of tasks requiring sustained attention.[20]

So, practicing mindfulness and daydreaming simultaneously can help control and redirect thoughts, boosting creativity and happiness as well as productivity when applied during less critical tasks. That's pretty cool! Claire Zedelius and Jonathan W. Schooler's 2015 study supports this finding, also showing that mind-wandering aids in aha moments of problem-solving.[21] However, in full disclosure, another study, "Dimensions of Experience: Exploring the Heterogeneity of the Wandering Mind," found that daydreaming can lead to creative problem-solving but also unhappiness, highlighting its diverse cognitive impacts.[22]

Steve Bradt's article "Wandering Mind Not a Happy Mind" cites research indicating that we spend about 47 percent of our waking hours thinking about what isn't happening.[23] This type of mind-wandering, according to the Killingsworth study conducted at Harvard, occurs during nearly every activity and is often linked to unhappiness. In other words, we do seem to be obsessed with what is *not* in front of us in the present. However, this mental drifting might also be a survival mechanism. Think about how incredibly beneficial it has been over eons, to generate possibilities so that we are prepared for various scenarios.

The type of mind-wandering thought activity I'm discussing here, though, isn't about escaping reality; it's about giving the mind a chance to rejuvenate, freeing up the cognitive load in the cerebral cortex, and allowing synapses in other brain regions—such as the limbic and saliency networks—to activate. Embracing these moments of mental freedom leads to unexpected insights and, consistently, a renewed sense of energy and focus.

BOREDOM IS AN INVITATION TO INSPIRATION

Just as daydreaming catalyzes creativity and greater productivity, so does boredom.

Boredom is an invitation.

There's a reason every single human has the capacity to feel bored. It's not a behavior to reprimand ourselves for but rather a cue and an invitation to find new sources of stimulation. Perhaps my take on this stems from my mother. When my sister and I were young and dared to tell her, "Mommy, I'm bored," she would look at us directly and very matter-of-factly state, "Only boring people get bored." Not one to shy away from a challenge, and quickly perceiving that this was some sort of ninja mind trick, we would scramble to find activities to occupy our minds. This usually meant diving into play, using our imaginations, asking each other questions, and finding *something* to do. We knew that if we didn't, the next option would be to help our mom with chores around the house.

Reflecting on those moments, I now understand boredom to be a cue and an opportunity—it's an invitation to activate the mind, to start noticing and to ask questions. When we are bored, just as when we daydream, the DMN in the brain gets activated. As explained earlier, the default mode network, or DMN, comprises neural regions of the brain that are activated when you are not laser focused on a task external to yourself. It turns out that it's really important for the DMN to be active for synthesis as well as for emergent thought. Ivy Ross, chief design officer for consumer devices at Google and coauthor with Susan Magsamen of *Your Brain on Art*, told me,

We don't realize, especially in these times when we think it's all about information and stimuli [that] none of that will have any impact without you being in the default mode network, without you being able to have the time to make those connections. And that's why I get my best ideas when I'm walking in the woods, or flying up in an airplane—when I'm forced not to be doing.

Time often seems to slow down when we allow ourselves to go inward and for the DMN to become activated. As adults, boredom creates space and time for noticing and for reflection on both our cognitive and emotional states. In that way, boredom is a trigger for curiosity and sparks a feedback loop. Curiosity requires the opposite of self-centeredness—we must step outside of ourselves. It requires humility and engagement with others. When we're curious, we're acknowledging that we don't have all the answers and that our best insights can come from other people, other cultural contexts, other fresh, new, and different sources of experiences. Thus, curiosity is really key to sparking the imagination.

Boredom is a signal that we need to engage in something new, to tap into our curiosity, and to connect with our surroundings and one another. Instead of viewing boredom as a negative state, we can see it as a catalyst for exploration, imagination, and stimulating our inner world.

Which leads me to inspiration.

Inspiration comes from two sources: the past and the present. The past, with its rich tapestry of memories, gets stimulated by our interactions and experiences in the present. This realization underscores the importance of engaging in MTR activities and stepping away from our screens. Sitting sedentary at a computer doesn't necessarily spark the most poignant memories. Those come alive through interaction and immersion. Touchpoints with people, places, smells, sounds, and visual cues are what truly ignite our memories and help us notice what's presently in front of us to gain inspiration.

This is why it's so crucial to step away and engage with the world around us. Whether it's taking a walk, having a conversation, or experiencing new environments, these activities are essential for sparking creativity and inspiration. Our minds thrive on the stimuli of our environments, making every interaction and experience a potential source of inspiration.

INTENTIONAL NAVEL-GAZING: MEMORY, RECALL, METACOGNITION, AND SRL

One of the first things I learned to do as a student of cultural anthropology was to question my own objectivity. Because anthropology uses research methods such as interviews, deep observation, and contextual inquiry, it's really important to probe how objective one's insights are. This requires intense navel-gazing; well, the more professional term is *self-reflexivity*. Such introspection has its place as long as you don't go too far down the tunnel. There has to be a moment when you stop, you zoom out, and you make some decisions. But it's valuable training to go inward and challenge your own assumptions.

The ability to be self-critical is an important progression in learning. If we are trying to become learning organizations and have cultures of learning, then we need to extend these forms of metacognition. Carla Silver, cofounder of Leadership+Design, goes so far as to say, "We don't have learning organizations. We have *knowing* organizations." And the latter is a dangerous place to be. Because when you err more on the side of certainty than curiosity, you notice less about yourself and about those around you. You miss a lot. What if our organizations developed true learning environments and cultures of learning? What if we had environments and practices that sparked metacognition to be aware of how we learn and to create conditions where we will learn better?

Memory and recall are fascinating processes that shape how we learn and interact with the world. According to the Derek Bok Center at Harvard University, memory operates through two main systems: recall and application.[24] These systems function across three stages: encoding, storage, and retrieval. Encoding is how we initially learn information, storage is about retaining that information in either short-term or long-term memory, and retrieval is accessing the stored information when needed.[25]

Understanding our own cognitive abilities and strategies for learning is crucial. David Perkins categorized learners into four levels of metacognition: tacit, aware, strategic, and reflective.[26] Metacognition goes beyond "thinking about thinking"; it involves actively monitoring and adjusting one's learning strategies based on self-assessment. This is particularly important in self-regulated learning (SRL), where students engage with academic tasks by setting goals, selecting strategies, and monitoring their progress, making adjustments as needed to overcome obstacles and stay motivated. Feedback plays a key role in SRL. It's described as a "dynamic, recursive information flow" that helps learners adjust their strategies and improve their understanding. Regular feedback helps learners stay on track and refine their approaches.[27]

Carla Silver offers all sorts of creative approaches to fostering reflection and memory. She described to me the following example. She gave each of her team members a blank journal and an instant Kodak camera, encouraging them to print one photo per week that captures a learning, a wondering, or an inspiration. They then pasted the photo in the journal and wrote a short reflection. By the end of the year, each team member accumulated fifty-two photos and reflections, which they shared monthly during team meetings. This practice not only enhanced memory and recall but also fostered a culture of continuous learning and reflection.

These insights highlight the importance of understanding how memory works and applying strategies to enhance it. By actively engaging in metacognitive practices and SRL, we can improve our ability to learn, recall, and apply information effectively. Whether through traditional methods or innovative activities like Silver's photo journals, the goal is to create a rich, reflective learning experience that supports ongoing personal and professional growth.

COLLECTIVE WISDOM: BRAINSTORMING IS ALL THAT IT'S CRACKED UP TO BE

Sometimes we dread brainstorming activities. You know, people don't necessarily look forward to what can feel like forced optimism ("There are no bad ideas!") or contrived team-building activities. Or to that moment when the bossy-pants extroverts in the room inevitably take over.

But when done correctly, brainstorming is truly all it's cracked up to be.

Brainstorming is a powerful form of collective intelligence and wisdom. We genuinely are better when we come together, even if that sounds clichéd. I can take an idea only so far on my own, but when I'm surrounded by others with diverse perspectives—stemming from their unique expertise, lived experiences, or even their mood that day—the potential for innovation grows exponentially.

For brainstorming to be effective, it must allow everyone to be heard and incorporate the diverge-converge method I referenced earlier. Cultivating our best ideas often happens in a brainstorm when we structure them to include both divergent and convergent thinking.

A practical approach is using the think-pair-share method. Imagine that the brainstorming prompt is "How might we develop a better marketing strategy for Q2?" or "What are ways we could design more rest into our working weeks?" (Wink, wink.) Instead of the boss standing at the front of the room asking for *your* best ideas—which can be a little intimidating—how about she writes the prompt on the whiteboard for all to see?

Then this is what comes next:

Think: Participants have a brief period, say, anywhere from ninety seconds to five minutes, to quietly think through their own ideas and jot them down on a piece of paper.

Pair: Participants are paired up (or put into small groups, depending on the size of the brainstorm) to share their ideas, answer questions, and receive feedback.

Next comes another quiet period for individuals to refine their ideas based on what they've heard.

Then the small groups do a mash-up, discussing which ideas they find most interesting, practical, or innovative, whatever parameter is most important to the business.

Share: Finally, the groups share their synthesized ideas with the larger group. This is where the magic happens.

The first time I used this approach, I noticed a significant shift in myself. In traditional brainstorming, if "my" idea didn't make it to the final list, I was disheartened. But with this method, the ownership of ideas morph. It was no longer about "my" idea versus "your" idea, because you lose track of where your idea ends and a colleague's begins. It becomes a collective vision. This integrative approach fosters higher engagement and buy-in, as everyone feels their input contributes to the final outcome.

Moreover, this method curtails the dominance of extroverted participants. By giving everyone time to think, quieter individuals, such as introverts or those who are neurodivergent, feel more included and valued in the process. This balance creates a richer, more inclusive brainstorming environment, with space for a wider diversity of thought to merge into innovative solutions.

Brainstorming is a powerful tool for helping us understand the dynamic role of human interaction in problem-solving. Research from Ethan Bernstein sheds light on the benefits and costs of this process.[28] The benefits include higher average solution quality, as participants build on existing ideas through social learning—ideally in a playful and open environment. However, the cost is often a lower maximum solution quality, because individuals might not explore novel answers as thoroughly.

This insight underscores the importance of moderation and aligns with the principle I emphasized at the start of this book: to approach work and learning with a diverge-converge mindset. Brainstorming is inherently divergent, encouraging a wide array of ideas. Solo thinking after brainstorming, on the other hand, can be convergent, refining and focusing those ideas. Both methods are essential for enhancing creative outcomes.

Bernstein advocates for a strategy he calls "intermittent social-influence treatment," which involves alternating periods of interaction with periods of separation. This approach ensures that the benefits of social learning are balanced with opportunities for individual exploration.[29] It echoes the wisdom of allowing ideas to incubate, to sleep on it, and develop both collectively and independently. Part of Bernstein's recommendation includes turning off technology during high-touch, collective, and communal situations. This practice enhances the quality of interactions, ensuring that the focus remains on the people and the ideas being shared, rather than being distracted by screens.

Blending Bernstein's research insights with the think-pair-share method can further enhance the effectiveness of brainstorming sessions. Imagine starting with individual reflection, then moving to small-group discussions, and finally converging on a collective mash-up of ideas— all with no outside distractions. This structure allows for the dynamic interplay of divergent and convergent thinking, fostering an environment where creativity will thrive. And by intentionally stepping away from technology during these sessions, we can ensure that our interactions are genuine and our focus remains sharp.

It's all about finding that sweet spot where the energy of collective thought is tempered with the depth of individual insights, leading to richer, more innovative outcomes. This integrated approach not only improves the quality of our ideas but also makes the process more inclusive and engaging for everyone involved.

INTUITION: WORKING FROM THE GUT UP— THE REAL HUMAN RESOURCES

When I worked in the global fashion sourcing industry, I was rarely confined to a desk all day. We were in the business of creating three-dimensional physical objects—clothes—for people's four-dimensional daily experiences. Although a great deal of strategizing and knowledge work shaped our day-to-day, the fact remains that fashion doesn't happen in a cubicle. So we made time to "shop the market." We visited stores. We saw the garments in person and touched the fabric. We observed how salespeople and customers interacted with one another and with the clothing on display.

Similarly, when I worked at factories in Sri Lanka and Portugal, manufacturing bras and panties, I noticed that the best engineers were the ones who left their desks and walked the factory floor. I followed suit. I walked the floor. I moved my body, and I observed others in motion at their workstations. In observing, I realized that the best garment factories—the ones with happier people, higher efficiency, and greater productivity—didn't get there through some stroke-of-genius management technique from the C-suite. Those companies designed their workstations to work *with* the human body, not in spite of it.

Unfortunately, most of us in the knowledge work sector have grown significantly disconnected from our bodies while we work. We've come to assume intense focus—working from the neck up—is what brings insight and breakthroughs and flashes of genius. And occasionally, we include working from the heart up. But that's not how breakthrough work manifests. The truth is that cultivating your best creative work demands that you engage both your brain *and* your body. In other words, we do our best work when we work from the *gut* up.

You might not see the point in reconnecting with your physical self to cultivate your best work. You may even find the idea a little woo-woo or New Agey for your taste. But hear me out. Gut-up work where you have astute awareness of your body is an inherently human way to navigate the world. This is because we are sentient beings. We are constantly sense-making—making meaning of the signals in our environments through our senses. Newborn infants rely on their tongues, noses, ears, and *then* their eyes, in that order, to inform the development of their brains.[30] Salespeople have long known that plying customers with pleasant bodily sensations—like flattering lighting, tempting smells, or comfortable chairs—can motivate us to linger longer and buy more. Even "shower moments" are the result of our repeated physical actions (like soaping up and scrubbing) occupying *just* enough of our brains' conscious thinking so that our subconscious DMN has the spare cognitive power to let loose, synthesize all the varied input from the day, and think big.[31]

We would like to assume that we simply read, watch, and listen to information, then process it in our brains to generate ideas. However, we're also wired to use everything *below* the neck, too. Ivy Ross shared the following with me:

I remember when early in my career here, when we were trying to convince the product managers of a certain color, I think it was blue at the time, they said, "Well, where's the data for blue?" And I said, "The data is in my subconscious. Do you know that 95 percent of what we take in goes into our subconscious and only 5 percent into our cognitive mind?" That stopped them in their tracks. And so when I get a strong hit, that's coming from actually more data than my cognitive mind [it's because], you know, we all walk around with antennas.

Gut-up work is ultimately what makes MTR activity the powerful practice that it is. That's because MTR activity helps you to be in tune with your intuition and to literally think on your feet.

Scientists have names for processing these sensations within ourselves: *interoception* and *proprioception*. Interoception is the awareness of internal bodily sensations and cues, such as, "I am hungry," "I am tired," "I feel safe," or "I feel cold." Proprioception is our awareness of where our body is in space without having to actually touch our body limbs. Dancers, for example, are really good at proprioception. When it comes to gut-up work, interoception is what's at work. Interoceptive signals originate from receptors in organ tissue, and then particular areas of the brain process those signals. For example, the insular cortex in the brain helps to make sense of bodily sensations and helps with emotional response and self-awareness. Interoception is linked to our ability to make better strategic decisions and employs the vagus nerve as its highway to convey interoceptive information.

The vagus nerve is the longest cranial nerve, extending from the brain, through the heart, and into the gut. So when we say things like, "My gut is telling me to do X instead of Y," it literally is! Intuition is powered by interoception and integrated in our physiology. It conveys bodily signals and provides the brain with updates about our internal organs, which is really important for homeostasis. It helps to regulate our heart rates, internal digestion, and breathing, which has an effect on our sense of calm. It can help us process our emotional states. And very importantly, there is a two-way feedback loop between the vagus nerve and the brain, allowing the brain to adjust bodily functions in response to external situations, which in turn affects our stress levels.

I like the way Arpana Gupta, PhD, codirector of the Goodman-Luskin Microbiome Center at UCLA, and Dr. Kelly Bender, ND, have described it in a *Katie Couric Media* interview, respectively, as, "a two-way superhighway that connects the brain to other parts of the body like the gut. The vagus nerve will 'sense' what's going on in the gut and report back to the brain," and it is "one of a few nerves that's bidirectional—most nerves only [communicate in] one direction, but the vagus nerve does both."[32] Research in 2009 by Natalie Werner and others pointed out the connection between the vagus nerve, interoception, and stronger strategic decision-making. Their experiment required people to tap out the rhythm of their heartbeat—on their laps, without touching the pulse in their wrist!

Some people could easily do this ("interoceptive awareness"), and others could not. Their study concluded that "enhanced cardiac perception is associated with benefits in decision making."[33] In other words, there is a direct correlation between your inner awareness—that nudge—and your ability to make strategic decisions. So intuition is not New Agey woo-woo. This all adds up to the gut-feeling sensation we have all experienced at one time or another. The vagus nerve communicates sensory information from the internal organs to the brain, playing a crucial role in our intuitive sense-making and interoception.

Intuition is a form of knowing—a type of pattern recognition. While in many cultures, intuition is deeply valued as a source of wisdom, in North American society, we are biased to act mainly on what's visible and rationally defensible. Thus, sitting with the ambiguity of intuition is a challenging supposition for a lot of us raised in Western cultures. Learning to navigate and accept the intuitive process takes practice and self-acceptance. It's a journey through liminal space, the threshold between the known and the unknown.

Jeff Rosenblum is very attuned to interoceptive awareness. Jeff used to be an executive with FS Investments and has a thirty-plus-year career in health care and disease management. After contracting a stomach bacterium (the campylobacter infection called Guillain-Barré syndrome) that left him physically compromised, he began a journey of astute emotional and mental acuity.

> My immune system went nuclear. And instead of attacking the bacteria, it took out the myelin on my arms and legs, my whole neuromuscular system. So, I was in a wheelchair for a number of months. I was on a walker basically for a year. I wasn't ambulatory, and my nerves had to regenerate. You lose all your muscular connectivity; so, if and when you get it back, you then have to reprogram the whole system. You've got to rewire it, and then your brain has to get out of the way and your parasympathetic system has to kick in.

He learned to work through and embrace what's uncomfortable and rewired what he calls his "internal integrative operating system." Slowly but surely, he was able to walk again, and has even taught himself how to swim in a nontraditional way. From Jeff's perspective, "I'm actually having the chance to fix all the movement-pattern flaws I had previously. . . . I don't think most people realize how often they are in fight-or-flight mode and how often their cortisol is firing. And how uncreative they are when those times happen."

MTR activity is work that only humans can integrate. Not because AI hasn't advanced that far or because algorithms aren't sophisticated enough yet. It's work only humans can do because our bodies, with their manifold physical inputs and sensations, have the unique equipment required to activate MTR activity.

Maybe this still feels a little touchy-feely to you—and it is, literally. But you owe it to yourself and your work to harness all the human resources you've got and to tap into the power of working from the gut up.

Very excitingly, research shows that enhanced interoceptive awareness and interoceptive accuracy are linked to greater emotional regulation and better decision-making abilities. In 1994, Antoine Bechara, Antonio

Damasio, Hanna Damasio, and Steven Anderson concluded a ground-breaking study that connected the dots between our emotions and rational decision-making. It was called the Iowa gambling task and was originally done with patients who had damage in the prefrontal cortex region of their brain.[34] As the Iowa gambling task test has played out in years since, participants choose cards from different decks, each with a different reward, punishment, and overall balance. Some decks are advantageous over time, while others are disadvantageous. Those who do well seem more attuned to the emotional signals (often referred to as "gut feelings") that warn against bad choices or reinforce good ones. Later, a 2006 study by Barnaby Dunn and others showed a correlation between heartbeat perception (interoceptive awareness and accuracy) and performance on the Iowa gambling task, concluding that people with higher interoceptive awareness were better at making decisions in risky contexts.[35]

I've become comfortable sitting with the discomfort of intuition's ambiguity.

I first started observing the role of intuition in strategic decision-making when I began interacting with more entrepreneurial start-up leaders from various sectors. I noticed that in their origin stories, they frequently credited their intuition when making pivotal decisions. I would regularly hear them say things like, "Something told me not to do the deal," or "My gut told me that I should go this way and not the other." These leaders paid close attention to their gut feelings, which guided them in making strategic decisions. Researchers have categorized intuition in a range of ways. One that I like for its simplicity is from research by Giulia Calabretta and others, which divides intuition into two categories: intuition that is quick and automatic, and intuition that's emergent and deliberate.[36]

Admittedly, there is a tension between intuition and rationality. Intuition can feel like a mysterious instinct that defies logic. But intuition and rationality are not mutually exclusive. They coexist and complement each other, requiring what Calabretta calls *paradoxical thinking*. Joel Pearson has taken grappling with the coexistence of intuition and rationality a step further through the research he's done at his Future Minds

Lab at the University of New South Wales. They've developed a scientific method to measure intuition. Pearson's study involved exposing participants to subliminal emotional images while they performed conscious tasks, similar to the subconscious influence depicted in the movie *Inception*.[37] This groundbreaking research provides evidence of intuition's existence and offers a way to objectively assess it. It's being applied in military training, too—a space where even with all the technical preparation and planning in the world, levels of uncertainty are extreme, so practicing how and when to follow that nudge is tantamount to survival.

Isn't this nimble and adaptive way of thinking what we were aiming for in the early 2000s when the concept of learning organizations dominated discussions on LinkedIn and at conferences? The goal was to become an organization that fosters continuous learning. Key characteristics of learning organizations include systems thinking and addressing interrelationships within an organization; personal mastery; mental models that promote reflection; shared vision stemming from a common sense of purpose; and team learning. And as discussed in Chapter 2, embracing design thinking is a way to deploy MTR activity, fostering playful and interactive learning environments that prioritize deep thought and reflection. These principles to create an environment where deep learning and metacognition are valued also extend to helping teams reflect on strategic initiatives. Learning organizations not only enhance strategic thinking but also attract and retain better talent. Integrating these insights into our work environments can significantly enhance productivity and innovation. MTR activity has the potential to drive us closer to becoming true learning organizations by powering up our intuitive sense-making capabilities.

AI AS A THINKING PARTNER

It's interesting to consider what it means to think in a world of ubiquitous technology.

If so many answers are at the tips of our fingers . . . then, what more is there left for the brain to do?

Well, plenty!

Increasingly, a world full of clicks and algorithms that can get us answers at the blink of an eye will mean that the most valuable thinking will happen in the spaciousness created at the end of a ten-second ChatGPT reply to a prompt. Invaluable, uniquely human thinking will be in the form of the questions we ask, as well as our ability to reflect and discern meaning. The technology is only part of the means to the problem-solving; it's not the end. Large language model (LLM) technologies like Claude and NotebookLM are our thinking partners, our cocreators, even our coconspirators.

In this moment, we can reimagine Carol Dweck's growth mindset work. A growth mindset is a belief system that your abilities and intelligence will improve by reconceiving challenges and criticism as opportunities to learn and grow. The opposite of a growth mindset is what Dweck calls a *fixed mindset*, one characterized by avoiding challenges and feedback, and not acknowledging critique as a source of growth and learning.[38] If we adopt a fear- and scarcity-based mindset, then AI is a doomsday bell ringing loudly in our ears. But if we try on a growth mindset, then AI offers tools and opportunities—such as increased efficiency and new job creation—about which we can be positive, open-minded, and excited. As David Bentley, former CEO of Porter Novelli, told me, "AI can be the prompt to help us jump across a chasm of fear." There are of course challenges that we must keep top of mind as AI creeps into creative territory. For example, how do we leverage existing people's work while giving the people who originated the idea their due credit? How do we ensure ethics and accountability? And is our imagination under threat with this injection of generative AI?

With regard to the last question, I think *not*. And here's why.

While functions such as ChatGPT seem on the surface to take away the work of humans, let's not go so fast. Generative AI is neither a dystopian quagmire nor a utopian panacea. Brilliant and rambunctious imagination is required now more than ever. Whatever algorithms spit out are only the starting place. And the algorithms still need humans who know how to frame better questions. Remember that the coders who design the algorithms must possess deep thinking skills to ask better and different questions. At the root of every great algorithm was a really amazingly framed question. And the better we get at asking questions (a catalyst for building our creative capacity), the more effective ChatGPT, Claude, or whatever your technology of choice will be.

Even with AI, critical thinking and integrity remain supreme. As I write, ChatGPT's training data is only through 2021, and the world is changing rapidly. We still have to be diligent about doing our background research. Big data and mechanisms such as ChatGPT can reveal patterns—but they don't necessarily discern the *meaning* of the patterns. That is in part because of the way ChatGPT functions. It is scrubbing the internet—which is only representative of the people who use it. Its inputs are limited. As Seth Godin wrote in his January 6, 2023, blog post, "GPT and other AI tools don't actually *know* anything. They're pattern matchers and pattern extenders. And those patterns are called culture."[39]

Josh de Leeuw, a cognitive science professor at Vassar College, is exploring the possibilities of how this technology can enhance learning. He teaches students to explore LLMs by getting them to think about thinking and to probe intelligence.[40] After all, if the word *intelligence* is in *AI*, it's a good idea to start by pondering, "What exactly is intelligence?" And that's what Josh makes his students do on the first day of class. His own version of a ChatGPT learning buddy is PAT (which stands for "philosophical artificial thinker"). Rather than being a one-directional technology, he coded and designed PAT for dialogue. Not only can the students ask the technology questions, but the tech asks questions back to the students, requiring them to think more deeply about their answers and work. It creates a dialogue with students, enhancing their critical thinking and question framing.

AI technology can help train us to become better critical thinkers. And it can also support our deep thinking, just as the FLOWN online working community did for me. In fact, I asked ChatGPT for ways that technology can enhance our thought and thinking process. Here's what it responded (with some editing, background research, and due diligence on my part, of course).

Distraction-blocking apps: Certain apps available can help minimize distractions by blocking access to social media sites, news websites, or other distractions for a set period of time. This can help you stay focused on your thoughts without being tempted to check your phone or browse the internet. *A few examples:* Freedom, Forest, and the Stay Focused apps.

Focus-enhancing tools: Tools like ambient noise generators, meditation apps, or even simple tools like Pomodoro timers can help create a focused environment for deep thought by providing a steady background noise or structuring your work into focused intervals with regular breaks.

Digital notebooks and mind-mapping tools: Using digital tools for note-taking and mind mapping can help you organize your thoughts more effectively and explore ideas in a structured way. This can support deep thinking by allowing you to visually map out connections between different concepts. A few examples of digital notebooks include One-Note, Evernote, and Google Keep. And two examples of mind-mapping tools are MindMeister and Coggle.

Research and reference tools: Having quick access to research materials, articles, and references through online databases, search engines, or academic platforms can help support deep thought by providing a wealth of information at your fingertips.

Collaboration tools: Technology can also support deep thought by facilitating collaboration (such as Miro or Mural) and discussion with others who share your interests or expertise. Tools like online forums, collaborative documents, or videoconferencing platforms can help you bounce ideas off others and gain new perspectives on your thoughts.

Digital decluttering tools: Keeping your digital workspace organized and clutter-free can help minimize distractions and create a more conducive environment for deep thought. Tools that help you declutter your email inbox, clean up your desktop, or organize your files can support a clear and focused mind. Three examples are Unroll.Me (a tool that unsubscribes you from emails and sends a single digest/roll-up of emails at the end of the day), Dropbox, and Evernote (helps to organize files, notes, and ideas).

We need not only big data (the bird's-eye view) but also what I would call *deep data* (the worm's-eye view)—the data that comes from exploratory observations, interpersonal interactions, and story.

So, take heart. The *I* in *AI* stands for *intelligence*—but you're still in charge of your own intellect, intuition, and imagination to uniquely create.

WONDERING WILL DO YOU ALL THE GOOD

Imagine standing at the edge of a lake on a cool summer morning. The view is breathtaking, with bits of mist hovering on the surface, reeds of tall grass swaying in a gentle breeze, and the early-morning sun casting sparkles over the lake's surface. Birdsong surrounds you, with an occasional heron flying just overhead and then perching on an inlet. The combined smell of lake water, moist soil, and grass, along with the mild temperature, prompt you to inhale deeply. You feel a profound sense of wonder and awe as you gaze out at the vast expanse of nature before you. This feeling, as described in multiple ways by psychologist Dacher Keltner in his book *Awe: The New Science of Everyday Wonder and How It Can Transform Your Life*, does more than just inspire—it transforms us. Awe has the power to reduce stress by lowering cortisol levels, and it broadens our perspective, enabling us to see the bigger picture and understand our place in the world:

> [A]we, activated by the vagus nerve, is not just an emotional experience; it's a catalyst for prospection—the act of looking forward into the future, the opposite of retrospection.[41]

As Keltner said in a 2023 interview,

Awe is an emotion; a brief experience we have in response to vast and mysterious things we don't understand. And as I've studied it over the years, I've come to believe—like Jane Goodall and Albert Einstein—that awe is in many ways our most human emotion. We encounter these vast mysteries: What is life? How do I make sense of the solar system? Why are mountains so large? How can you make music? And the mind has this emotion that kicks things like wonder, curiosity, and exploration into gear.

According to Adam Bulley and Muireann Irish in their exploration of prospection, this forward-looking imagination supports goal-directed behavior and flexible decision-making.[42] Goals are inherently prospective, guiding us toward future achievements. Furthermore, the physical benefits of awe are profound. Keltner's research highlights how awe activates the vagus nerve, enhancing heart health and reducing inflammation in the immune system. It alleviates depression and anxiety, making us feel more connected and less lonely. Even listening to a piece of music alone can reduce feelings of isolation.

Emotions play a critical role in this process. It turns out that emotion precedes and catalyzes rational thought. Dr. Lisa Feldman Barrett has made the significant point that emotions are not pre-wired in the brain but rather are constructed by our experiences—our emotions are predictors of (versus reactors to) rational thought. In her book *How Emotions Are Made: The Secret Life of the Brain*, Barrett wrote,

Emotions are not reactions to the world. You are not a passive receiver of sensory input but an active constructor of your emotions. From sensory input and past experiences, your brain constructs meaning and prescribes action. If you did not have concepts that represent your past experiences, all your sensory inputs would be just noise. You would not know what the sensations are, what caused them, nor how to deal with them. With concepts, your brain makes meaning of sensations, and sometimes that meaning is an emotion.[43]

This means that awe, like other emotions, is not something we pas-sively feel—it is something we actively create through the interplay of our perceptions and memories. When we consciously seek out experi-ences that evoke awe—whether through nature, music, or even quiet reflection—we are not just enriching our lives but reshaping our emo-tional and cognitive landscapes. This underscores the idea that awe is a skill we can cultivate, a practice that not only enhances our emotional well-being but also fuels our creativity, empathy, and resilience. And as Keltner points out, emotions are brief mental states that in addition to motivating action and guide cognition also help us navigate our social lives. This power of awe—bridging emotion, cognition, and connection—reminds us that wonder is not a luxury but a necessity. It compels us to pause, breathe, and engage with both the mysteries of the world and the opportunities ahead. When we embrace awe and wonder as part of our daily lives, we don't just dream bigger; we gain the courage and creativity to act on those dreams. So the next time you stand at the edge of a lake, or hear a stirring piece of music, or marvel at the grandeur of a star-filled sky, know that you are not just witnessing beauty—you are equipping yourself for growth, healing, and transformation.

Thus, we truly do feel before we think and know. This sequence is essential for effective decision-making. What a different paradigm to embrace, prioritizing emotion over rational thought. I also noticed the value of paying attention to emotion from a business perspective when, in the early 2000s, I attended a fascinating conference hosted by the Design and Emotion Society. The name alone intrigued me. At the time, I was an assistant professor of fashion management, and I was eager to explore this unique intersection between design and emotion. The con-ference was held in Chicago, and I was absolutely captivated by the diver-sity of participants (engineers, artists, marketing experts, anthropologists, psychologists—just to name a few) and the wide range of topics. The idea that we should design around and for emotional responses and that we need to pay attention to the intersection of design and emotion is a miss-ing link in many business initiatives.

The opportunity before us in the fourth Industrial Revolution is to harness these human thought activities—deep focus and reflection, daydreaming, metacognition and memory, brainstorming, intuition, awe, and prospection—and integrate them into our daily lives to cultivate better work. By doing so, we can amplify what makes us uniquely human, leveraging technology as a copilot rather than a replacement. This new approach to productivity emphasizes holistic well-being and the profound impact of our emotional and imaginative capacities.

SEEDS TO CULTIVATE:
PRO TIPS TO THINK DEEPLY AND BROADLY

To foster deeper thinking, three key criteria must be met. First, people must model this behavior—leaders can show their teams the value of taking reflective pauses. Second, process matters—organizations can incentivize deep thought by embedding reflection into their culture and performance goals. Finally, place plays a critical role. Consider where you do your best thinking and how space at home or in the office can be designed for this purpose. Even if your workday or organization is nowhere near meeting these three criteria currently, the following questions encourage reflection and practical steps to begin inching toward incorporating deep and inspired thought into daily routines for more generative and innovative outcomes.

Individual Level—Reflections and Exercises
Reflection Questions for You

1. When and where do you do your best thinking? What conditions enable this?
2. How often do you allow yourself to daydream? What insights emerge?
3. What practices help you achieve deep focus?

Exercises for You

1. Create a "think diary" tracking when/where breakthrough ideas occur.
2. Schedule fifteen-minute daydreaming blocks and/or doodling sessions with no devices.
3. Design your ideal focus space based on environmental cues.

Team Level—Reflections and Exercises
Reflection Questions for Your Team

1. How does your team balance individual reflection with collective brainstorming?
2. What barriers prevent deep thinking in your workplace?
3. How might you incorporate more metacognition into team processes?

Exercises for Your Team

1. Implement the think-pair-share brainstorming method described in this chapter.
2. Establish regular no-meeting blocks for focused work.
3. Create team reflection zones with minimal tech distractions.

Organizational Level—Reflections and Exercises
Reflection Questions for Your Organization

1. How does your culture support or hinder deep thinking?
2. What systems could you implement to protect focused work time?
3. How might you measure the value of reflection and ideation?

Exercises for Your Organization

1. Adopt a 15 percent culture like 3M for innovation time.

2. Design physical spaces that support both focused and collaborative thinking.
3. Implement organization-wide Get Stuff Done weeks, modeling Zapier's example, with minimal meetings.

~~~~~~

LEAVING YOU WITH THIS THOUGHT

In our fast-paced world, making time for deep thought, reflection, and daydreaming is more crucial than ever. The practice of inside-out work emphasizes the necessity to carve out intentional time to step away from the constant stimulation of screens and embrace moments of solitude and internal reflection. Whether it's taking a midday shower—as is a common cultural practice in Brazil during hot-weather months to refresh the body and mind—or finding quiet time for deep thinking, it's essential to move inward before stepping outward into collaboration and action. People need to diverge and converge, balancing solo reflection with collective work in ways that aid a deeper connection to their thoughts.

Thoughtful workspace design that encourages moments of quiet introspection, whether through designated reflection zones or environments that prioritize calm and focus, will support the cultivation of ideas. By integrating these practices, we create spaces where thought can flourish and cultivate more meaningful work outcomes and personal fulfillment.

5

REST: DOING LESS BETTER

The average person doesn't
overtrain; they under-recover.

—Alicia Archer, movement specialist and wellness mentor

I was raised in the Jewish faith.

And, yes, I am African American.

As a kid, I grew tired of hearing white people tell me, "You can't be Jewish—you're Black!" and Black people tell me, "You can't be Jewish—you're Black!" I learned very early in life to never discuss my family's faith practice. (Perhaps that's a chapter of my life that I will write about in a future memoir.)

While my religious beliefs became a private matter in my childhood, it definitely laid the foundation for a lifelong value of resting. You see, my father was one of the hardest-working men I've known. At one point, in addition to holding his full-time job in pharmaceutical sales, which kept him traveling a ton, he built an entrepreneurial firewood business where he fit in deliveries on early mornings, some evenings, and Sundays. And he attempted, unsuccessfully, to own income-generating real estate—all to put my sister and me through six years each of private school. I saw him leave very early in the mornings as we were groggily getting dressed for school and come home, tired, needing to write out sales reports after dinner. And then he'd go off to bed to do it all over again the next morning. I also saw him fastidiously observe the Sabbath. Saturdays in our home were devoted to rest and religious observance. If we weren't at our tabernacle, then we would sit quietly at home. My father cherished Saturdays. He called it the time when he could "get my rest." He never strayed from that.

My dad was also devoted to ensuring that we took vacations. Now mind you, we were what I would call *middle-class aspirational*, living in a solidly upper-blue-collar neighborhood in Philadelphia. People on my block were cops, nurses, secretaries, and homemakers. The fact that in the 1970s my dad piled us into our 1976 Plymouth Volare station wagon and drove our family eleven hours down interstate 95 South from Philadelphia, Pennsylvania, to Hilton Head, South Carolina, was a novelty and an oddity—to both our neighbors and to the majority of white vacationers at 1970s Hilton Head Island. He was committed to exposing us to spans of long-term rest in luxurious environments.

My dad seeded in me an incredible work ethic, and he's also my reference point for knowing that rest is not a luxury. He understood that rest, as Tricia Hersey, founder of the Nap Ministry says, "is a human right" because it helps us to do what Hersey calls "dream work."[1]

There are other touchpoints in my life that have been reminders of that foundational value of activity without purpose. I haven't always been great about practicing it, but the foundation is there.

For example, I went to a Quaker high school, where we were required to attend a weekly meeting for worship. Sitting still for forty minutes as a teenager felt impossibly boring (see Chapter 4's section "Boredom Is an Invitation to Inspiration") and a good excuse to either take a nap or mentally review for an upcoming test. But slowly and surely, the recentering of a Quaker meeting for worship became ingrained. Many alums of Quaker schools, whether or not they are practicing Quakers, nostalgically relish the time to be physically still and allow the mind to quiet.

Years later in college, I studied abroad in Salvador da Bahia in Brazil. My host family would sometimes take off to the country homes of friends and family, outside of the sweltering heat of Salvador in March. It felt indulgent, sitting around on a Sunday, eating delicious feijoada, and passing the time just talking and listening to music. Those times reminded me of my own growing up, making the rounds with my parents to visit with our family members, specifically, my great-aunt Mildred and great-uncle Leon. My sister and I would sit patiently on her plastic-covered sofa while the adults talked about whatever pressing current-event issue of the day. The point there, as it was on those Sundays in Bahia, was to slow down, connect with others, and just . . . be.

I earned a master's of science degree that brought me to Reutlingen University in southern Germany for a portion of my studies. I arrived in Bavaria with some stereotypical images of Germans in mind. For example, that they are strict timekeepers and really hard workers. (Spoiler alert: Not all German trains run on time—the Swiss ran their trains much more impressively!) But what I didn't count on was the German commitment to rest and relaxation, especially on weekends. They worked hard and they played hard: A day's work tempered by a nice cold pilsner on a warm afternoon hits the spot. I observed weekends full of family time, hiking and being outdoors, and visiting with friends. From my American perspective, this really stood out to me as admirable. Sure, we in the United States have prided ourselves on working hard vis-à-vis "the American work ethic," but we don't take the time to carve out the counterpoints to hard work: rest and play.

Then, years later still, in my early thirties, I lived and worked abroad in Colombo, Sri Lanka. I so appreciated the time my colleagues in the Sri Lanka office took to ensure we had a nice and relaxing lunch break. They'd bring out tins of delicious Sinhalese food, prepared at home, that we'd eat with our hands, just chatting and laughing with no references to work. Some of those same colleagues became friends, and while I didn't speak Sinhalese, there was something very familiar about the family dinners they would invite me to: Crowded around tables, the hubbub felt familiar, the bowls and plates of food clattering, the invitation to connect, relax, and just . . . be.

LIMINAL SPACE: THE MAGICAL IN-BETWEEN

I used to hate the winter until I read *Wintering* by Katherine May.

Her book helped me to understand and embrace the value and beauty of cold, dark, still days where the sun coats the cloud-covered sky in a specifically beautiful, muted pale indigo. Her book helped me to understand that it is only through the dormancy, cocooning, and slowing down, which winter requires, that we can truly be restored. The evidence is all around us in nature. May's book spelled it out for me. She uses winter as a metaphor for reflecting on her *seemingly* barren seasons, which she learned to embrace. As she put it,

> Wintering brings about some of the most profound and insightful moments of our human experience, and wisdom resides in those who have wintered.[2]

Dormancy is not inactivity; it's just a different type of activity. The brain powers up alternate synapses when we are at rest. Think of it as the difference between a subtle simmer versus a high boil when the flame is turned up.

Another writer I love, Bonnie Tsui, articulated the value of fallow time in her 2019 *New York Times* op-ed, "You Are Doing Something Important When You Aren't Doing Anything." She described fallow time as

> a period of rest and rejuvenation that is crucial for creativity and productivity. Fallow time is not merely about being idle; it involves engaging in activities like reading, visiting museums, or simply being still, which are often not recognized as work but are essential to the creative process.[3]

We need fallow time to restore our dynamic thinking.

Hundreds of years earlier—in fourteenth-century Japan, to be precise—there lived a monk and poet named Kenkō. His collection, *Essays in Idleness*, was his reflection on, among other things, the beauty of the time in between flowering and fullness. Here's an example of his perspective:

> Are we to look at cherry blossoms only in full bloom, the moon only when it is cloudless? To long for the moon while looking on the rain, to lower the blinds and be unaware of the passing of the spring—these are even more deeply moving. Branches about to blossom or gardens strewn with faded flowers are worthier of our admiration.[4]

May, Tsui, and Kenkō were all meditating on liminal space: the value of pausing and the magic of undefined, impermanent, transitional in-between time. Rest is liminal space.

The word *liminal* comes from the Latin *limen* and refers to the transitional phase between two states or phases—in betwixt space and time, the edge where things are temporal and transitory. Liminal space can be physical (like a tunnel or a bridge), emotional (like a graduation or a divorce), or metaphorical (like Kenkō's cherry blossoms). Due to its ambiguity, liminal space can wreak havoc on your emotional state and spark anxiety. But it can also be wonderfully restorative and a rich breeding ground for our best, most innovative work.

I think of ambiguity in two ways: anxiety-provoking ambiguity and restorative ambiguity. The anxiety-provoking type is the sort you experience when you've been sitting in an airplane for seventy-five minutes, on the tarmac, and you have no detailed information about how much longer you will be stuck there as you deduce the unlikelihood of catching your connecting flight at the next destination city. Anxiety-provoking ambiguity is also experienced by people whose homes have been decimated by natural disasters or whose lives have been uprooted by war. The restorative ambiguity is the kind where you feel expectant and at peace in the not knowing. For example, when you are falling in love with someone and the discovery process of getting to know them fills your days with wonder. Or when you decide to go on a stroll in a new city and wander about aimlessly. Both require work on your levels of self-awareness. According to Kimberly

Dawn Neumann in her *Forbes* article "Liminal Space: What Is It and How Does it Affect Your Mental Health?," techniques to move through emotional liminal space include writing things down, learning to meditate, and focusing on what you can control.[5] Asking the 5 Whys is one way to do this. The 5 Whys were originally developed by Sakichi Toyoda, the founder of Toyota Industries, to help drill down to the root cause of a problem. It is a question-asking process used in problem-definition processes like design thinking where you ask "Why?" five times to surface a root cause and offer actionable solutions. The 5 Whys can also be applied for personal challenges. For example, "I feel constantly exhausted."

1. *Why?*
   - Because I'm not getting enough sleep at night.

2. *Why?*
   - Because I stay up late scrolling on my phone.

3. *Why?*
   - Because I feel like it's the only time I have to myself after a long day.

4. *Why?*
   - Because my day is packed with work and responsibilities, leaving no room for personal downtime.

5. *Why?*
   - Because I haven't set boundaries to protect my time and prioritize self-care.

In this way, reflection through self-inquiry can identify that a root cause of exhaustion stems from a lack of boundaries to protect personal time during the day, leading to late-night scrolling as an escape. You might resolve to address this insight by scheduling thirty minutes of "me time" earlier in the day and implementing a nighttime routine that limits screen use before bed.

Times and spaces of dormancy, fallow times, and cocooning are all examples of liminal spaces. Waiting for a pot of water to boil is a great opportunity to experience restorative liminal space. Another example of restorative liminal space is waiting in line at a coffee shop: Instead of reaching for your phone, you can take a moment to breathe deeply, observe your surroundings, or daydream about a project or idea. And still another example is sitting in your car at a red light: You can use this brief pause to notice your posture, unclench your jaw, or take a few calming breaths while letting your mind wander freely. These moments, much like waiting for water to boil, offer pockets of stillness where the mind can reset and recharge.

Rest is also a version of liminal space. Liminal states when we are neither fully awake nor fully asleep have an underappreciated value. And it's actually during these transition points to sleep—the hypnagogic state as we drift off to sleep and the hypnopompic state as we awaken—that are critical for creativity, problem-solving, mental rejuvenation, and regenerative thinking.

The hypnagogic state (the transitional period between wakefulness and sleep) is a fertile ground for creativity, problem-solving, and intuition. Psychotherapist Edward Traversa, in a 2022 LinkedIn discussion, described the hypnagogic state as involving the simultaneous presence of alpha waves (associated with relaxation) and theta waves (linked to deep meditation and creativity).[6] This combination makes the hypnagogic state conducive to producing unexpected changes and creative insights. In this state, there's no ego, and in the liminality between the conscious and unconscious mind, your intuitive and innovative thoughts can surface. Thomas Edison famously used this state to enhance his own creativity: "The inventor is said to have napped while holding a ball in each hand, presuming that, as he fell asleep, the orbs would fall to the floor and wake him. This way he could remember the sorts of thoughts that come to us as we are nodding off, which we often do not recall."[7] Inspired by Edison's predilection for slumber, researchers at the Paris Brain Institute and Pitié-Salpêtrière Hospital conducted a study that showed that hypnagogic rest can significantly enhance problem-solving abilities. In a 2021 experiment, participants who engaged in hypnagogic rest while holding an object in their hand were more successful in solving a hidden-rule challenge compared to those who stayed awake or fell into deeper sleep.[8] This suggests that the hypnagogic state fosters novel ideas and creative thinking.

The hypnopompic state, as coined by Frederic Myers in 1904, is the dreamlike state between deep sleep and full wakefulness. It is in this period that logical thinking often recedes, allowing for a free flow of ideas and insights that can be remarkably creative and innovative. In a 2016 article for *Inc.*, Susan Steinbrecher highlighted the potential of this mental state for fostering creative thinking and problem-solving.[9] During this time, the brain's rigid logical structures are relaxed, enabling it to form connections between seemingly unrelated concepts. This process can lead to innovative solutions and novel ideas that might not emerge during fully awake and rational states.

Research supports the idea that the early-morning hours, including the hypnopompic state, are also optimal for creative endeavors. A recent study from MIT in 2023 on targeted dream incubation underscores the benefits of utilizing this state intentionally. The study found that participants who napped with specific task prompts during their sleep produced more creative stories and performed better on divergent thinking tasks compared to those who napped without prompts or stayed awake.[10] These findings suggest that the brain, during the hypnopompic state, can make broader and more innovative connections between different ideas, thereby boosting creativity. When we dream, especially during the transition from sleep to wakefulness, our minds can link disparate ideas effortlessly. This capacity for enhanced creativity during the hypnopompic state can be harnessed by setting intentions for the day upon waking slowly and being receptive to the ideas and messages that surface naturally.

Both the hypnopompic and hypnagogic states offer valuable liminal spaces where creativity and problem-solving abilities can be significantly enhanced. While we are resting, we can tap into a reservoir of innovative potential that lies dormant during our fully conscious hours. And there are broader implications from these findings. For example, the World

Economic Forum emphasizes that creativity and innovation are crucial for addressing economic, social, and sustainable development challenges. Cultural and creative industries play a significant role in generating revenue and supporting jobs globally. Thus, embracing the potential of restful liminal spaces like the hypnopompic and hypnagogic states is not just beneficial for personal creativity and problem-solving but also for broader economic and societal development.

OVERCOMING OUR BUSYNESS ADDICTION

Have you ever noticed that so many world religions, in addition to Judaism, emphasize rest? Many a minister has jokingly reminded parishioners that "even God needed a day off!" So why do we push and run ourselves into the ground with work at an unsustainable pace?

You may have read Robert Fulghum's 1986 longstanding bestselling book *All I Really Need to Know I Learned in Kindergarten.*[11] Interestingly, of the sixteen points he makes, there are three that are particularly relevant to our discussion on the value of rest:

- Live a balanced life.
- Take a nap every afternoon.
- Be aware of wonder.

Embedded in Fulghum's three pieces of advice is the reminder that we cannot work nonstop. The puritanical work ethic of the early-American ethos has a shelf life, and it has expired. It is neither sustainable nor healthy. Even the gents of *Mad Men* took three-hour martini lunches! Taking cues from nature and understanding the ebbs and flows of life are important to living our best lives and doing our best work. They give easily accessible lessons about the importance of balance and cycles, about honoring the push, the pull, and the nebulous time in between.

Naps aren't just for babies and for the elderly. I recall first reading about *nappuccinos* in Daniel Pink's *When: The Scientific Secrets of Perfect*

Timing and getting so excited about the prospect of normalizing a midday twenty-minute snooze. Studies show that there is a synergy created during coffee naps between the caffeine from the coffee imbibed just prior to the nap and the body's production of adenosine, a chemical found in our cells that plays a role in slowing down our heart rate: "Caffeine works by blocking adenosine, and since adenosine levels are at their lowest right after a nap, this might account for the extra increase in alertness."[12]

And finally, my favorite of Fulghum's encouragements: to be aware of wonder! Wonder is about awe, deep curiosity, dreaming, and daydreaming. As I wrote in Chapter 4, "Think: The Inside-Out Work of Cultivation," wonder is a catalyst for prospection—the act of looking forward into the future, of inspirational thinking. But we cannot wonder when we're going eighty miles an hour. It's impossible. To wonder requires us to slow down and to pause.

Now, more than ever, we need to reengage with rest.

A 2021 survey by TORK (a global leader in workplace hygiene products) found that a high majority of employees (91 percent) and bosses (93 percent) agreed that taking breaks was essential for maintaining mental focus.[13] And here's a stat that should make the C-suite's ears perk up: nine out of ten employees stated that they were more likely to stay at a company where breaks were encouraged by management.[14] I cannot underestimate how important it is for leaders to model this behavior. And all of this in light of research that shows "reducing hours to manageable levels can enhance productivity."[15]

So how and why did we stray so far from this good advice about rest?

The same survey found that we're still not even taking lunch breaks—even though 94 percent of employees felt happier when they took a lunch break during the day and agreed that it gives them the opportunity to step back and gain perspective on their work.[16]

I think it's because we have a busyness addiction. And like with all addictions, the satiation is only temporary and the consequences are negative. They include a loss of control and self-neglect, as well as, ironically, missing the details in our lives and work, and not paying attention—to anything—with deep, intentional focus. Northwestern University's Adam Waytz, a management professor, has written that "once upon a time, leisure was a sign of prestige. Today that idea has been turned on its head, and busyness is the new status symbol."[17]

I couldn't agree more.

London-based social scientist Katie Jgln pointed out in one of her essays on Medium that people in the world's wealthiest countries don't believe they have time to rest. She muses that taking almost a month off from work is normal in Europe, but Americans refuse to take time off: 58 percent of people say because of money, but also because it compromises their perceived work ethic.[18] With an addiction to being busy—and appearing busy—life takes on a surface, survival-only quality. This can ultimately be catastrophic. Neuroscientist and Stanford University professor Robert Sapolsky makes this point by comparing the body to a house: "Suppose the owner only focuses on and prepares it for external events that are—or seem to be unavoidable—like hurricanes or heavy rainfall. In that case, he will likely neglect the necessary maintenance. And eventually, the house will become a ruin."[19]

A 2023 article in *Money* magazine by Pete Grieve cited that Americans work almost four hundred more hours per year than their German professional counterparts.[20] And a 2021 World Health Organization report pointed to higher risks of stroke, heart disease, and ultimately death due to overworking.[21]

We have gotten ourselves wound up in what Michelle Braden calls "a cycle of dissatisfaction," where we tie self-worth to accomplishments.[22] But what if we suspended judgment and attempted the following thought experiment? Instead of tying our self-worth to what we accomplished, what if we tied it to what we were *cultivating*? This would direct us toward a dynamic focus on process instead of a static emphasis on results. Such a mental model would require greater individual and organizational self-awareness and the inside-out work I mentioned in Chapter 4.

It would require us to push back on hustle-and-grind culture and all the mantras to which we've become accustomed:

Just do it.

Push through.

Grind now, shine later.

Every day I'm hustlin', hustlin', hustlin' . . .

These mantras keep us in survival mode. But if you're just surviving, that's a mindset based on competition, fear, and there never being enough.

You see, I don't believe there is any such thing as competition—as much as scrolling through social media and Instagram would have you and me think otherwise. In those moments of malleable self-judgment, the sage words of Theodore Roosevelt—"Comparison is the thief of joy"—ring true. The reason I don't believe in competition has to do with an interview I read decades ago from a Grammy Award–winning musician. She said that she didn't believe in competition because (to paraphrase) "everyone has access to the same eight notes in an octave; I have my technical training and you have yours; I have my God-given talent and you have yours. I can't do what you would do with that—and you cannot do what I would do."

Wow. I was floored by that insight and have never forgotten it. What if we all thought like that? What if we shifted away from a single-focus, competitive survival mode to a multidimensional, creative flourishing mode? One of the results would be to ease up on a furious race to the end and instead refocus on more self-compassion and the MTR activities that relax and renew our bodies and minds on our own time frame and under our own conditions. Getting more intentional about rest, engaging in activity without purpose, and embracing the ambiguity and blurred boundaries of liminal spaces—both as individuals and within our organizations—would help us to do that.

RECOVERY IS NECESSARY ON MULTIPLE LEVELS

Flo at the Fitler Club makes the best oat milk matcha lattes in Philly. Her commitment to rest is likely a large part of why she's so good at her job. Instead of letting her vacation days pile up, she has begun to do intermittent resting. She incorporates a vacation day on a Monday or Friday (or both) to give herself longer weekends throughout the year, using the time just to be at home, enjoy her garden, trim her shrubs, take a walk, and get in a nap. This thoughtful approach to her recovery has helped her achieve more without burning out.

We are entering a new era, the Imagination Era (more on that in Chapter 8), where the value of rest and intentional pausing is essential for productivity, creativity, and well-being. This shift requires a fundamental change in how we approach leadership—moving from micromanagement to macromanagement. In this new model, employees are trusted to manage their own time and energy, with the autonomy to take breaks and rest as needed. As Erin Shrimpton, an organizational psychologist, noted in a 2022 LinkedIn post, "One of the biggest buffers to workplace stress is autonomy. The sense that you—along with your colleagues—have agency when it comes to the things that affect you most."[23] Companies like Shopify have led this charge by implementing policies such as No Meeting Wednesdays and their forward-thinking "calendar purge," which eliminates unnecessary meetings and empowers employees to prioritize their focus. Cal Thompson, VP of design at Headspace, shared about a similar practice at Headspace:

> We have a four-day workweek twice a month; and then the other Fridays are No Meeting Fridays, and those are truly honored as No Meeting Fridays. It is deeply unusual to have a meeting on a No Meeting Friday. . . . And we used to have "MINDAYS"—days for Headspace employees to care for their minds. I used to go to art museums, to galleries, or work on a painting project, or go to a doctor's appointment. You know, it's these things where you [realize], "Oh, I have a free day. What do I want to do with it?"

These experiments give people the agency to shape their own workday, emphasizing the importance of rest and reflection.

This cultural shift is not only about fostering individual well-being but also about creating a sense of belonging within organizations. Employees feel more connected and engaged when they are trusted to balance their work and personal lives. Reflecting on my time in global apparel sourcing, I saw firsthand how women thrived in modular production settings (where each woman was cross-trained on multiple operations instead of only being responsible for a singular operation in a linear production line), where they had the autonomy to manage their work processes. They showed up more fully, bringing their knowledge and agency to the table, which ultimately led to better outcomes. This is a perfect example of how macromanagement fosters an environment of experimentation and trust, a concept echoed by Scott Peltin, cofounder of TIGNUM, who emphasizes the importance of emotional recovery for leaders and employees alike. My own perspective on the value of recovery evolved after my conversation with Scott. He helped me to broaden my understanding of recovery to include cognitive and, crucially, emotional dimensions, especially within work environments.

Scott is an expert in performance development for executive leaders. He told me that for leaders, the ability to manage and recover from emotional labor is just as critical as maintaining cognitive function. Leaders today face immense emotional fatigue, exacerbated by events like the COVID pandemic, necessitating a more comprehensive approach to recovery. Emotional recovery is not just about alleviating immediate stress but about managing the ongoing emotional load that can significantly impact decision-making and leadership effectiveness.

Effective leadership, therefore, involves recognizing and nurturing your emotional health through strategies aimed at maintaining emotional stability and resilience. This holistic approach to recovery—incorporating physical, cognitive, and emotional aspects—ensures that individuals at all levels can operate at their best, making recovery a strategic element of workplace productivity and well-being.

Scott's approach integrates meditation and visualization techniques with physical exercises to combat emotional fatigue. This holistic method helps stimulate positive hormones like serotonin while reducing cortisol, the stress hormone, thereby addressing the emotional toll directly. The importance of such recovery strategies has become increasingly apparent, given the high-stress environments we navigate and the mounting research on burnout. Considering Scott's insights, integrating emotional recovery strategies is crucial for leaders who must maintain not only their cognitive sharpness but also their emotional resilience.

Recovery from fatigue is often associated primarily with the physical domain, particularly in sports and athletic activities. Reflecting on my high school days as an athlete, I recall the emphasis on physical recovery—ensuring we avoided strenuous activities before competitions to prevent injuries and allow muscle repair. This was mirrored in communal activities like pasta nights before track meets or cross-country races, and much easier workouts immediately following meets, highlighting a collective recognition of recovery's importance. Similarly, my background in dance underscored recovery's role, emphasizing proper nutrition, ample rest, and downtime, especially critical before performances. But why don't we approach recovery in the same way with our daily work? Especially if we know it can deplete us as physically, emotionally, and mentally as a sport?

It's essential that we cultivate the ability to detach from work-related tasks and thoughts. As Ariane Ollier-Malaterre, a management professor at the University of Quebec, points out, without detachment, individuals may fall into patterns of rumination. And a continuous preoccupation with work can prevent the replenishment of their "reservoir of resources," leaving them unable to return to work with energy, commitment, and creativity.[24] Such a deficit in recovery was notably linked to workplace phenomena such as the Great Resignation and "quiet quitting" following the COVID pandemic, where employees disengaged from their roles due to burnout and dissatisfaction.

The concept of liminal space and time is relevant here as we consider facilitating effective recovery. Liminality, the quality of ambiguity or disorientation that occurs in the middle stage of a process or experience, is often overlooked for its restorative powers. Days spent doing seemingly nothing can be profoundly recuperative, providing mental and emotional relief as well as a chance to reset yourself physically. These periods of intentionally disconnecting allow you to step away from your typical routines and environments to recharge.

Here are a few key ways to do that:

1. MICROBREAKS

In today's fast-paced work environments, the importance of integrating breaks throughout the day cannot be overstated. Even brief reprieves from work—microbreaks—can play a critical role in sustaining performance and enhancing well-being. The concept of "microdosing" rest offers a viable strategy for humans to rejuvenate their mental and physical stamina regularly. We may not be designed to take as many naps as the chinstrap penguin (reportedly up to six hundred micronaps in an hour!), but their commitment to taking breaks is nonetheless inspiring.

Recent research underscores the benefits and nuances of taking microbreaks, which is defined as approximately ten minutes. One study highlighted that while microbreaks are associated with improvements in well-being, their impact on performance can vary depending on the break's duration.[25] Specifically, the research indicates that longer breaks can significantly boost performance, particularly when recovering from tasks that are highly depleting. This finding suggests that while short breaks are beneficial for maintaining well-being, more extended breaks might be necessary to fully restore performance after intensive work periods.

Moreover, the effectiveness of breaks is not a one-size-fits-all solution. Try experimenting with different types of restful-to-you activities to discover what best enhances your productivity and mood. For example, maybe you start with a five-minute microbreak that includes stretching at your desk, walking a lap around the office, or even just taking time to intentionally daydream about something you're looking forward to.

2. MEETING MORATORIUMS

Meetings are one of the most significant artifacts of organizational culture. You can tell a lot about the culture of an organization by how they hold meetings: who gets to lead the meetings, the frequency of the meetings, where the meetings are held, et cetera, et cetera.

I'm a big advocate of occasional meeting moratoriums. A meeting moratorium is a decision to free up space in the calendar by removing a particular meeting or allowing it to occur with less frequency. They require a shift in the ways people think about how often they need to meet and why they need to meet. They lean into the goal of macromanagement, which is symbolized by more rest and allowing people to take breaks.

You can experiment with meeting moratoriums and approach them as prototypes. You don't need to cancel the current meeting cadence, but instead, experiment with one meeting and determine if it could happen at a lower frequency. Give space in the calendar. For example, maybe the first Wednesday of every month from 9:00 a.m. to 12:00 p.m., there will be no virtual or in-person meetings held. Start with low-hanging fruit so that it feels manageable, accessible, and not strident. Perhaps you could try it for a quarter. Collect feedback so that you understand how people are responding to it and how it's going.

3. THE SABBATICAL

Like many, my initial understanding of sabbaticals was confined to the realm of academia, particularly higher education. As a professor, I was granted a sabbatical seven years into my employment, which coincided perfectly with the deadlines for my doctoral dissertation. (Yes, I earned my PhD in four years while working full-time as a professor—a bit of naive enthusiasm on my part!) The term *sabbatical* itself is rooted in the etymology of *sabbath* or *Shabbat*, reflecting its origin in the biblical practice of resting every seventh day. This historical context underscores the sabbatical's purpose as a period for rejuvenation and reflection.

During my sabbatical, the absence of work-related duties, such as grading papers, planning lessons, and attending meetings, allowed me to immerse myself deeply in my research and writing. It was a period of profound focus and productivity—truly a gift of time.

Sabbaticals are an intentional strategy by organizations to incorporate long-term rest into the professional lives of their employees. This practice is increasingly being adopted outside academia, especially in the tech industry, where companies often offer sabbaticals after five years of service. I interviewed people who work at META, sales firms, as well as nonprofit organizations who have reaped the benefits of sabbaticals. By providing these extended breaks, companies invest in the well-being and long-term productivity of their workforces, enhancing employees' loyalty and commitment. This commitment to employee welfare fosters a culture of trust and mutual respect within the organization. However, not everyone takes advantage of this opportunity. Concerns such as fear of missing out (FOMO) or a desire to appear fully committed to the company often deter employees from taking their well-earned breaks. One effective way to counteract this hesitation is for management to lead by example, taking sabbaticals themselves to demonstrate that these breaks are neither punitive nor detrimental to one's career.

For some people, the hybrid work allowances that were a by-product of the COVID pandemic have allowed them to engineer their own sabbaticals while working far from home. And if you're not able to take a sabbatical, perhaps you can advocate for a work-from-home day here and there.

Modeling rest in the workplace is important. Employers, managers, and teams need to collaborate to foster a culture where taking breaks is normalized and encouraged. As demonstrated, this approach can lead to enhanced job satisfaction, a more positive work environment, and increased overall productivity.

~~~~~~~~~~~~~~~~~~~~~~~~~~~~~~~~

SEEDS TO CULTIVATE:
PRO TIPS TO MOVE FORWARD WITH REST

The principles we've explored throughout this chapter—from emotional recovery to liminal space, from microbreaks to sabbaticals—can be implemented at multiple levels within our work and lives. Let's explore how we can cultivate rest and recovery at the individual, team, and organizational levels.

Individual Level—Reflections and Exercises
Reflection Questions for You

1. How do you currently differentiate between anxiety-provoking and restorative ambiguity in your life?
2. When do you feel most restored? What activities or environments contribute to that feeling?
3. How might you incorporate more liminal space into your daily routines?
4. What beliefs about productivity and rest might be holding you back from fuller recovery?

Exercises for You

1. Create Recovery Rituals
   - Design a morning ritual that includes ten minutes of liminal space before checking devices.
   - Establish clear work/rest boundaries using environmental cues (e.g., specific lighting, sounds, or scents).
   - Practice intentional transitions between activities using microbreaks.
2. Implement Emotional Recovery Practices
   - Keep an emotion-awareness journal to track energy levels and emotional states.
   - Schedule regular "emotional reset" breaks during high-stress periods.
   - Develop a personal "recovery tool kit" with activities that help process different emotional states.

3. Design Your Rest Environment
   - Create a dedicated space for rest that's separate from work areas.
   - Curate a playlist of calming music or nature sounds.
   - Establish a rest routine that includes both physical and mental recovery activities.

Team Level—Reflections and Exercises
Reflection Questions for Your Team

1. How does your team currently handle emotional labor and recovery?
2. What unwritten rules exist about rest and breaks within your team?
3. How might your team better support different recovery needs and styles?
4. What impact does your team's meeting culture have on recovery time?

Exercises for Your Team

1. Establish Team Recovery Protocols
   - Create "no-meeting" blocks that are protected for individual work or rest.
   - Develop team signals for when someone needs emotional recovery time.
   - Implement regular team energy check-ins at the start of meetings.
2. Design Collaborative Rest Practices
   - Rotate team members leading short meditation or breathing exercises.
   - Create a shared recovery resource library with tools and techniques.
   - Establish buddy systems for covering work during intentional rest periods.

3. Build Recovery-Aware Communication
   - Set clear response-time expectations that allow for breaks.
   - Create team agreements about after-hours communication.
   - Develop protocols for expressing and respecting recovery needs.

Organizational Level—Reflections and Exercises
Reflection Questions for Your Organization

1. How does your organization's culture support or hinder rest and recovery?
2. What structural changes could better support emotional and cognitive recovery?
3. How might you measure the impact of rest and recovery initiatives?
4. What role does leadership play in modeling healthy rest practices?

Exercises for Your Organization

1. Implement Structural Support for Rest
   - Create dedicated quiet spaces or "recovery rooms" in the office.
   - Establish clear policies about vacation time and encourage their use.
   - Develop flexible work arrangements that accommodate different recovery needs.
2. Build Recovery-Based Leadership Development
   - Train managers in recognizing signs of emotional exhaustion.
   - Include rest and recovery metrics in performance evaluations.
   - Create leadership development programs that emphasize emotional intelligence and recovery awareness.
3. Design Organization-Wide Recovery Initiatives
   - Implement quarterly meeting moratoriums or company-wide rest days.

- Create sabbatical programs that emphasize both rest and growth.
- Develop recognition programs that celebrate healthy work-rest integration.

~~~~~~~~~~~~~~~~~~~~~~~~~~~~~~~~~~~~~~

LEAVING YOU WITH THIS THOUGHT

Remember that cultivating rest is not about doing nothing—it's about doing less, better. As you implement these ideas, start small and build gradually. Choose one action item from each level listed above that resonates most strongly with you or your organization's current needs. Monitor the impact of these changes not just on productivity but on creativity, emotional well-being, and overall satisfaction.

The journey to better rest practices is itself a form of liminal space—a transition between our current ways of working and a more sustainable future. Embrace the ambiguity of this transition, knowing that each small step toward better rest practices contributes to a more resilient and innovative work culture.

Most importantly, remember that rest is not a luxury—it's a fundamental human need and right. By cultivating rest at all levels, we create the conditions for sustainable success and meaningful work that honors our full humanity.

6

A NEW HUMAN OPERATING SYSTEM

The next level of integration is right in front of us and we can't see it. Like it's there. . . . It's actually getting yourself to pull back enough to see it to be present enough to experience it. The system is always there. You just can't see it.

—Jeff Rosenblum, investor

You may be thinking, *This MTR activity stuff sounds all fine and well, but won't this just require me to add one more thing to my to-do list?*

You ask a valid question.

And, no, not exactly.

Building in more MTR activity is really about reframing. Overwhelm won't occur if you prioritize leisure time for brain recovery.

And blurring the boundaries between work and leisure is not a bad thing—if done correctly. As I mentioned in the first chapter on cultivation, separating work from your personal life is a relatively recent development, a product of the first Industrial Revolution whose time has passed. Think about it. Our compartmentalized worlds have not reduced overwhelm but increased it.

Once upon a time in the agrarian era, people woke up in the morning, washed, ate breakfast, stepped outside of their homes, and poof—there they were at work on the farm. These days, I get up in the morning, shower, eat breakfast, step across the threshold of my kitchen, walk upstairs, and poof—there I am at work in my home office.

Now, I realize that not everyone works from home, wants to work from home, or is able to work from home. But even if you do not, technology makes it increasingly impossible to blur the line between home, your personal life, and work.

When we intentionally step away from the tasks that consume us, we allow the brain to get some of its best work done. Work in our current postindustrial era has negated this human dimension of work, our human need for movement, thought, and rest to keep our bodies and minds energized and healthy. It has resulted in calls to action from workplace experts like Erica Keswin imploring us to "bring our human to work."[1] The key to overwhelm, languishing, and burnout is to strike a new dynamic balance between work and leisure that optimizes both productivity and well-being, because truly, the two are interdependent.

Such an equilibrium is essential to cultivate a phenomenal working life. The beautiful part of moving away from a mindset of "How might I be more productive at work?" toward "How might I cultivate more in my role?" is that it can help you and your organization to make quantum leaps.

WORK, LEISURE, AND MTR

By reframing your perspective and recognizing the interconnectedness of work and leisure, you are developing your growth mindset. Prioritizing leisure activities, such as taking breaks, exercising, and exploring new places and people, will enhance your creativity, your problem-solving skills, and your overall well-being (i.e., your ability to cultivate). MTR activities position you to be in new and different environments where your growth mindset can be cultivated. And very importantly, cultivating your growth mindset by being present, open, and grateful sparks awe.

Here is an example.

I was on holiday in Spain with my husband, John. On this particular morning, I decided to spend the day away from John while he visited military and war museums, and I took a bus thirty minutes south from the bustling city of Barcelona to a small beach town called Garraf. It's a beautiful, quiet, unassuming place by the Balearic Sea. During a satisfying breakfast of fried eggs, sauteed spinach, crispy bacon, and coffee (Spanish style, so it tasted like an espresso to my American taste buds!), I found myself daydreaming out of a huge picture window facing the sea. During breakfast, the skies were shades of gray and the waves looked like undulating strokes of charcoal. Sailboats far out on the horizon became larger as they bobbed closer to shore. I took a walk along the rocky beach. Gradually, the sun emerged through the clouds, and I breathed in the shifts in color as the sky morphed from gray to an incredibly brilliant cerulean blue. The sea began to glitter with virtual diamonds along its shimmering surface. I felt very relaxed.

These shifts in natural color reminded me of the passage of time. That nothing stays the same. It was a reminder to remain expectant during hard times and to value the good times because they won't last forever. A few hours later, I returned to Barcelona and visited the Joan Miró museum in the hilly Montjuïc neighborhood. I gazed at Miró's paintings and sculptures and read about his appreciation of emptiness as reflected in his works such as *On the Dot* and *La Esperanza del Condenado a Muerte.*

Those days in Barcelona reminded me of how valuable it is to be a tourist. Because I fancy myself a world traveler (I've lived in five different countries), I relish the excitement of being out of place when everything is new, strange, and different. Every once in a while, I enjoy being the bumbling, ignorant, clumsy, and gawking tourist. One of the things that John and I have started doing when we arrive in a new city is to book a bicycle tour. These biking tours not only ease the jet lag and get us acclimated with exercise; they help us to see the city from a modified vantage point. There's also something playful and freeing about getting oriented to a new place on a bike. The streets, people, and buildings of a new city look different from the vantage point of a car versus a bus or even walking.

So being a tourist helps me to be giddy and positive about what I don't know. It helps me to accept all that I don't understand and to embrace uncertainty, ambiguity, and discovery. It helps me to reframe and shift into a growth mindset. Being a tourist gives me permission to admit ignorance. It's a relief to not be expected to know. It's okay to ask the clumsy question. And it makes me become hyper observant. For example, on our second day, walking through the tiny streets of the Gothic Quarter (full of medieval-looking architecture that was actually rebuilt in the mid-twentieth century), I came across a laminated sign on a wall full of graffiti, with the following typewritten question:

"When was the last time you were in awe, admiring your surroundings?"

What serendipity to bump into this question! On a meta level, even as I read the question, I was in total awe of my surroundings. Right there in a busy alley in Barcelona, where shopkeepers, waiters, and local residents went about their day, was a reminder to pause and be in awe and appreciation of the environment. That's the beauty of MTR activity. It is less about carving out time or adding to a to-do list. Instead, it is a lot about reorienting oneself and being completely immersed *in* time. MTR allows you to dip into the awe of your surroundings.

What would we do without awe? Think about that. There would be no delight in the ordinary. Without awe, we would never remember how important it is to pause and inhale the incredible smell of baked bread, or to be astounded at the flexibility of a baby placing its leg behind its ear, or the warmth of the fleeting sun on our forehead on an otherwise chilly spring day in Barcelona. Moments of awe allow us to return to our surroundings with depth, clarity, and delight. They help us to be grateful for all that we have, know, and are given.

And why does gratitude matter?

Well, gratitude is the foundation for building your creativity quotient, or CQ, and it is the start of your ability to become a systems designer. Here's what I mean.

When you are grateful, you recognize that you are just a tiny part of a larger system. Take, for example, a simple pen. Take thirty seconds to reflect on all that made that pen possible: the designers who conceived of it; the chemists and engineers who produced the best type of ink; the dockworkers who offloaded the container ships that transported the pen; your teachers who taught you to read and write, which affords you the usage of said pen. Being grateful for all of these inputs helps us to realize our interconnectedness.

This humble recognition of our interdependence leads us to be more boldly curious. We know that no one person can know or do everything, so there's no shame in admitting ignorance and asking questions. Asking questions and being deeply curious is the precursor to empathy. We cannot empathize with another soul unless we can first be curious about their situation. And ultimately, that empathy can lead us to take equitable action.

Put that way, there's enormous opportunity in pausing for MTR activity, sparking awe and gratitude.

But let's say a vacation in Barcelona is not currently within your plans. How do you tap into awe in your everyday life to cultivate the rejuvenation necessary for your best work?

I have a few ideas.

First, let's review the space-time continuum.

THE IN-BETWEEN

The concept of the space-time continuum has always been intriguing to me. Originating from the field of physics, the term *space-time continuum* refers to a four-dimensional framework, combining the three dimensions of space (length, width, and height) with the dimension of time. This concept was revolutionized by Albert Einstein's theory of general relativity, which posits that the threads of space and time are interwoven, are affected by matter, and can be curved.

In our daily lives, especially in work settings, we exist typically on a tension-filled tightrope, trying to navigate and negotiate both space and time. Often, we view these as rigid dimensions that we must control and manage. But what if we approached these two continuums as fluid and intrinsic elements of our existence? They are not forces to be mastered but rather dimensions to be embraced and observed more keenly.

My first profound experience with the principles of the space-time continuum came at age fifteen on an Outward Bound course during a self-directed, intentional twenty-four-hour solitude (called *Solo*) at Table Rock Mountain in Asheville, North Carolina. Equipped with just the essentials—tarp, sleeping bag, water, map (the foldable paper variety sealed in a ziplock bag for protection), compass, journal, and some food—I delved deep into both my external surroundings and my internal geography. During this experience of solitude, time seemed to expand, and the physical space around me became a canvas for introspection. It echoed the principles of the space-time continuum, where dimensions of space and time interweave and influence perception.

This introspective journey was further nurtured by my education at a Quaker high school in Philadelphia, where weekly Meeting for Worship sessions encouraged turning inward in silence, albeit communally. These practices highlighted how pausing and embracing the present moment could enrich one's internal landscape, preventing burnout and fostering a rejuvenated, optimistic outlook.

By creating the time and space to step away from the desk, we engage in two critical activities: noticing and committing. Once again, this shift is all about reframing our perspective. It's not about adding one more task to our to-do list. Instead, it's about transitioning from a focus on "doing" to a focus on "being," which is equally important to giving our work our all. When we are more conscientious of the space-time continuum in this way, we can enhance our awareness of how we occupy spaces and how we perceive time, encouraging a more thoughtful and present approach to both our personal and professional lives. This awareness can lead to greater efficiency, creativity, and well-being as we learn to move with the natural flow of time and the environments we inhabit, rather than against them.

Liminal time and space can also be experienced by organizations on a macro level during the in-between times of courting new clients, pitching business, and waiting for the deal to close. To this end, it matters how physical space and environment is designed. I learned this when I interviewed Bastien Baumann, the founding partner at Le Truc, an internal creativity catalyst at Publicis, where Bastien is the chief design officer. Their goal was that Le Truc be an internal catalyst for Publicis's client work and experimentation. He knew intuitively that the space would need to be designed in a way that sparked creativity, which is why he hired A+I (as described in Chapter 2). The variety of space design allows people to find their own recipe for work according to the project goals, intended outcomes, and questions the team may be pondering. And what's interesting is that the space is also attractive for other Publicis staffers who work on different floors in the same building, but whose space is designed in a more predictable office floor layout.

> So, at first, we wanted to protect the space. You know, it's very territorial. But the purpose of that space was to be shared. Some rooms are just for certain teams, but everybody inside the building is allowed to be in [a wide range of] areas. So the orange area where you were and some other areas over there is where they love to come . . . especially for lunchtime!

I saw this for myself during my visit as people had lunch or took calls there. It made me wonder, *What if every floor was designed in this way? How might that affect the work product?* Because there is definitely a business ROI that the space has delivered. Bastien shared that, within the first year, the firm won two major accounts after pitching business in the Le Truc space:

> The truth is that every single new business that we've run in this space, I could see on the face of the potential new clients, just, like, their amazement, their feeling of being in the future [through this] space. The experience made a big impact on them beyond just the work itself. So I think

that the bet that [Publicis] took was the right one because we won [a pharmaceutical firm] in the same year, which is a massive account; and [a luxury fashion brand] just followed—so, from pharma to fashion—two completely different clients—but every time they come in that space, they feel like, "Wow! We like this." There is a sense of pride as if to say, "I want to be working with that group." And I think the space generates that. The space also helps with hiring new talent.

The design of the Le Truc space not only elevated the client experience but also became a magnet for talent, making both employees and clients feel inspired and connected to their work. When spaces are crafted to spark creativity and collaboration, the potential for innovation and business success grows exponentially.

START MICRO

So much MTR activity is happening when we are experiencing these in-between times. For example, when we are putting away the clean dishes (or washing the dirty ones); when we settle in to read a book; or when we decide in the car to listen to our favorite playlist—or to drive in silence. Don't think of those moments as wasted time. They are highly desirable moments that allow your brain to do new activity.

One great way to intentionally create in-between time is by micro-retreating. These aren't just escapes during longer vacations but short, regular intervals of solitude embedded into your routine. Years ago, my friend Holly was influenced by the Dalai Lama's teachings on the necessity of solitude for spiritual growth to find pauses amid the chaos of being a new mother in New York City. In partnership with her husband, she figured out ways to schedule in one-night personal hotel retreats in the same city where she lived—and came back home the next day totally refreshed and attuned. Picking up on her example has taught me the value of intentional, regular solitude—not as an unattainable luxury but as a critical element for sustaining mental health and cultivating my creativity.

Here are inexpensive and accessible ways to integrate such micro-retreats into your life:

1. A Noticing Retreat: Dedicate a morning or afternoon to explore a new area in your city, absorbing the environment as a detached observer, reveling in its novelty.
2. A Walking Retreat: Commit to a weekly walk, whether urban or nature-bound, and use this time to keenly observe your surroundings and your responses to them, embodying the role of an anthropologist.
3. A Quarterly Reflection Retreat: Consider booking a local hotel for a night or two, bringing along reflection prompts that challenge and engage your mind—for example, you could generate a list of questions for yourself or conjure up gratitude statements.

These micro-retreats aren't just about self-care; they're a strategic recognition of the importance of liminal space and time in our lives. By allowing ourselves these pauses, we both rest and rejuvenate our minds. We allow space for the invisible work of cultivation to occur on its own human terms. And we set ourselves up to reap the benefits when we return to our daily lives.

EQUITY CONSIDERATIONS FOR MTR

We must consider the socioeconomic inequities that exist when discussing these concepts of movement, thought, and rest in the context of work for all people. What if you don't have a sedentary, white-collar type of job? How is MTR activity relevant or even feasible in those contexts? Not everyone has the privilege of occupying a job where they can easily incorporate these elements into their daily routines. In fact, for many people in physically demanding roles that support white-collar work (e.g., delivery truck drivers and delivery bike riders; food service workers; janitorial staff in institutions), these ideas may seem like luxuries or even irrelevant to their lived experiences.

Consider the following example of Lisa.

Lisa is a single mom raising two middle school–aged children. She is dependent on public transportation to get to two part-time jobs. One of Lisa's jobs is working in a fast-food restaurant three days a week, and the other job is working as a home health care aid four days a week. The *movement* portion of MTR may seem obvious because she's standing all day and moving a lot while serving food and also tending to people's health care needs. But often that motion is very repetitive, and it doesn't spark the diversity of movement that the body requires to really achieve the full advantages of MTR activity. Also, the movement is not on Lisa's own terms. Perhaps *thinking* also seems null and void in Lisa's case, because the work does not inspire Lisa and her managers are not curious about her intellectual contributions. Lisa's boss rarely asks Lisa's opinion about much. Maybe Lisa's thinking skills are more valued through the emotional intelligence and on-the-spot problem-solving she utilizes in how she cares for her elderly clients. And finally, these two jobs, combined with parenting two tweens, are incredibly exhausting. Making time for *rest* feels sporadic at best. So how might Lisa apply MTR?

This is where redesigning work to better support movement, thought, and rest for *everyone* is crucial to enhance humanity and our collective well-being. Without equitable access to MTR, we risk creating an increasingly stratified society where only privileged workers have opportunities for creative thinking, physical restoration, and mental renewal. Those in physically demanding or service roles may become further marginalized, treated as mere instruments of labor rather than full human beings deserving of intellectual engagement and rest.

When we fail to design work that incorporates MTR across all job types, we perpetuate systems that exhaust people physically while starving them intellectually. The truth is that some of the best innovations come from the people who work in direct contact with the final client and consumer. They are privy to the complaints and praise, and they also must be able to improvise solutions on a moment's notice. Home health care workers, for instance, often possess deep insights about improving patient care but may lack forums to share their thoughts. Restaurant workers who are on the front lines with customers develop efficient systems through daily experience but rarely have channels to implement their innovations. The full innovation of business solutions is mediocre at best if we do not allow for MTR activity for the people on the front line and the ground floor—not just for the people who are decision-makers in the corner offices. Otherwise, we risk a massive loss of human potential and wisdom.

Moreover, chronic fatigue and repetitive strain without adequate rest can lead to increased workplace injuries, higher health care costs, and shortened working lifespans. The lack of mental engagement can result in decreased job satisfaction, higher turnover, and lost organizational knowledge. These add up to huge business costs that are difficult to recuperate in the short term. Beyond these practical impacts lies a deeper moral concern: Treating any segment of people as purely physical laborers rather than whole human beings with needs for varied movement, intellectual stimulation, and genuine rest undermines our collective humanity and social fabric. And it means that we have failed to learn lessons from the mistakes of the first Industrial Revolution, which reduced people on the factory lines to cogs in the wheel. By failing to design work equitably with MTR principles, we not only harm individual workers but also diminish our society's creative and innovative potential. Every person denied opportunities for meaningful thought and rest represents lost possibilities for problem-solving, innovation, and human flourishing. The stakes are not just economic but deeply human—it's about recognizing and nurturing the full humanity of every person, regardless of their job role or socioeconomic status.

The challenge then becomes identifying practical strategies that people can initiate on their own as well as MTR tactics that managers can implement to meaningfully integrate MTR activity into the daily lives of all their employees, including those in non-sedentary, non-white-collar positions. Ultimately, people like Lisa can claim the agency and well-being they deserve, while also unlocking productivity benefits for both the individual and the organization.

Lisa could self-initiate MTR activity by finding small pockets of opportunity throughout her day. During her public transit commute, she could use this time for both thought and rest—perhaps journaling in the notes app on her phone or in a physical book, or reading during some rides. She could also spend time during her commute briefly meditating or simply closing her eyes for mental restoration. While performing repetitive tasks at the restaurant, she might engage her mind by creating mental challenges like practicing math with food orders or imagining process improvements. Her physical movement, though abundant, could be diversified through simple stretching exercises during bathroom breaks or by connecting with her children when walking with them to the bus stop.

A thoughtful and inspired manager could support and enhance these MTR efforts by implementing structural changes. In the restaurant, they could rotate staff between different stations to vary physical movement patterns and reduce repetitive strain. For home health care work, a manager could build in short stretch breaks between patients and create "idea boards" where staff can post suggestions for improving care processes. Most importantly, managers could protect designated break times, ensuring workers can take uninterrupted rest periods in quiet spaces rather than feeling pressured to remain "on call." They might also implement flexible scheduling whenever possible, to accommodate the complex demands of working multiple jobs while raising children.

The key is recognizing that even within tight constraints, there are opportunities to integrate more intentional movement, focused thought, and genuine rest. By combining individual initiative with institutional support, Lisa can access the benefits of MTR despite her challenging schedule and physically demanding work.

With this context in mind, here are some key strategies managers can consider to achieve this new operating system by actively involving their teams, understanding their unique needs, and ultimately redesigning work practices for their well-being and productivity:

1. Actively seek input and feedback from employees. Lisa's example emphasizes the importance of valuing the opinions of those who are on their feet all day and whose opinions are rarely asked. Make concerted efforts to listen to their experiences and ideas. Promote opportunities for reflective thought:
   - Schedule regular "daydream breaks," where employees are encouraged to step away from their tasks and engage in open-ended thinking.
   - Facilitate collaborative huddles, where employees can discuss ideas, problem-solve, and connect with one another.
   - Encourage employees to share their insights and perspectives, even if their roles are not traditionally seen as intellectually demanding.

2. Implement hacks and exercises that enhance movement, thought, and rest throughout the workday.
   - Invite and ask for ideas and suggestions from staff like Lisa.
   - Implement scheduled movement breaks throughout the workday, such as standing stretches, walking meetings, or brief exercise sessions.
   - Provide standing desks, treadmill desks, or other equipment to enable more movement during work.
   - Organize group activities like team walks or exercise classes during breaks.

3. Reconfigure work schedules and practices to provide more opportunities for diverse movement, inspired thought, and adequate rest.
   - Adjust schedules to provide more frequent and longer breaks, especially for employees in physically demanding roles.
   - Encourage employees to take their full lunch breaks and step away from their workstations.

- Consider implementing flexible work arrangements, such as compressed workweeks or remote work options, to allow for better work-life balance.

4. Recognize the physical and mental demands of non-sedentary jobs and design interventions accordingly. Acknowledging the embedded stressors can go a long way and allow managers to lead by example.

   - Demonstrate the value of movement, thought, and rest by modeling these behaviors yourself as a manager.
   - Communicate the importance of these practices and their benefits for productivity, well-being, and job satisfaction.
   - Recognize and celebrate employees who actively incorporate movement, thought, and rest into their daily routines.
   - Regularly solicit feedback from employees on the effectiveness of the implemented strategies.
   - Be open to adjusting and refining the approaches based on employee needs and preferences.
   - Encourage a culture of continuous improvement and inclusive experimentation around work design.

The key is to *cocreate* a work environment that empowers and enables employees, regardless of their job type, to prioritize movement, thought, and rest as integral parts of their daily routines.

SEEDS TO CULTIVATE:
PRO TIPS FOR YOUR NEW MTR OPERATING SYSTEM

In reflecting on the power of MTR as a human-centered operating system for productivity, it's important to remember that this approach isn't about simply adding more to your plate but about reimagining how you engage with your work and life. If you want to flourish, then MTR isn't just an option; it's a new operating system that can transform the way you approach work and life. Whether you have a full day or just five minutes, work solo or are part of a large organization, there are bite-size ways to practice MTR and integrate it into your daily routine. Organizations like Le Truc, as evidenced by Bastien's reflections, have embraced diverse physical and virtual spaces that foster creativity and support these practices for teams and individuals alike. And there are positive business outcomes to boot.

The question is: How might you start cultivating MTR in your own work environment? Can you carve out a few moments of stillness, or take a walking break to reset your mind? And what would it feel like if your team embraced rest and reflection as a core part of yielding productivity rather than something that needs to be "earned"?

Here are some expanded questions and tips to help guide your journey toward adopting MTR as a sustainable operating system for working and living.

1. What bite-size ways could you integrate movement, thought, and rest into your workday?

   Tip: Even on your busiest days, there are small windows of opportunity to incorporate MTR practices. For example, take a two-minute stretch between meetings, or walk while brainstorming ideas. You might also set a timer for deep thought or reflection, allowing yourself just five minutes to sit quietly and ponder a challenge or idea. And when it comes to rest, don't underestimate the power of a ten-minute break or a short nap—both can do wonders for clarity and focus.

   Example: Many professionals use the Pomodoro technique, working in twenty-five-minute bursts followed by five-minute breaks, which naturally incorporates movement and rest throughout the day. By adding a quick walk or stretch during these breaks, you can weave MTR into your routine effortlessly.

2. How might your organization or team create more space for MTR during the workday?

Tip: Advocate for diversity in workspaces that support movement, thought, and rest. Suggest walking meetings for brainstorming sessions or standing desks to keep energy high. Encourage leadership to prioritize "deep work" periods, where team members can focus on complex tasks without distractions. By setting boundaries for when emails or notifications can be sent, you'll protect focused thought time. Also, explore options for communal spaces that encourage both social interaction and moments of solitude for reflective work.

Example: Companies like Slack and Salesforce offer flexible schedules and encourage rest through mental health days and designated "no-meeting" afternoons. You could suggest similar initiatives at your workplace, such as starting a pilot program with "focus hours" or creating quiet zones where deep work and reflection can happen uninterrupted.

3. What is the current relationship between work and leisure in your life, and how would you like it to evolve?

Tip: Assess how much of your time is spent in a cycle of constant work versus rejuvenation. Is your downtime truly restful, or is it spent worrying about the next task? Strive for a balance where work energizes you and leisure restores you. Incorporating MTR principles means acknowledging that both work and rest are essential for long-term productivity.

Example: Think about how you spend your breaks—are you scrolling through your phone, or are you engaging in activities that bring you joy and peace? Consider replacing passive activities with something more restorative, like a brief meditation, a walk outside, or even daydreaming, which has been proven to boost creativity.

4. When is movement, thought, or rest most needed for you, and how can you prioritize them?

   Tip: Pay attention to the natural rhythms of your body and mind. Some people find they do their best thinking in the morning, while others peak in the afternoon. Build your day around these natural cycles. If you find yourself feeling stuck or drained, it might be time for a movement break, while moments of high energy may be perfect for diving into deep thought. Rest isn't just for recovery—it's a tool for preventing burnout and maintaining peak performance.

   Example: To boost energy and creativity, take movement breaks after periods of intense focus. These breaks can be as simple as stepping outside for fresh air, or practicing a short stretch routine at your desk. By understanding your own needs, you can tailor your workday to include strategic moments of movement, thought, and rest.

5. How would your experience of work change if you allowed yourself to just *be*, rather than always striving for control?

   Tip: The idea of *being* at work—of allowing moments of stillness and reflection—goes against the grain of hustle culture, but it's crucial for tapping into your full potential. Allow yourself to experience liminal spaces, the moments in between tasks when creativity often emerges. Let go of the need to always be "doing" and trust that sometimes, simply being present can lead to breakthroughs. This requires a mindset shift from micromanagement to macroman-agement, where you trust yourself and your team to find innovative solutions when given the space to explore.

Example: Reflect on a time when you were so intensely (and tensely) focused on finishing a task that you didn't allow space for a fresh perspective to come to light. Now, imagine letting go of that pres-sure, taking a break, and returning to the work with renewed energy. It's likely that not only would your work improve, but you would also feel more connected to the process, rather than just the outcome.

LEAVING YOU WITH THIS THOUGHT

By intentionally cultivating movement, thought, and rest, you're embrac-ing a more human-centric operating system that values creativity, well-being, and sustainable productivity. Whether it's through the physi-cal design of workspaces, daily rituals, or creating a culture of rest, MTR can help individuals and teams thrive in the modern workplace, inclusive of people who work behind desks and people who work on their feet all day. Instead of chasing endless productivity, this new system asks us to slow down, reflect, and cultivate more meaningful and impactful work.

The key takeaway? Work doesn't have to be a grind. It can be a place where movement, thought, and rest come together to unlock deeper cre-ativity and satisfaction for *everyone*.

7

START WHERE YOU ARE

Every great dream begins with a dreamer.

—Harriet Tubman

Start where you are.

In fact, you've probably already begun doing MTR activity.

I can almost guarantee it.

If you go for a walk when you need to puzzle out a tricky concept, that's *movement*.

If you've noticed that your best ideas come in the shower, or while washing dishes, or after a jog, that's *thinking*.

If you relish the ritual of steeping tea in your favorite ceramic mug because you know you'll return to your desk revitalized, that's *rest*.

Even if you've taken a two-minute break to stare into space while composing an email, that's MTR activity.

You're doing MTR activity whenever you set about solving a problem or tackling a question using a process or activity that seems tangential, or even totally unrelated, to the nature of the problem. That MTR activity allows you to live your own life on your own terms. It allows you to flourish.

Let me tell you about how I used MTR (in the form of dance) to become a better person—specifically, a better life partner.

Around eighteen years ago, when I was still single, I had a realization: "I think I'd like to be married one day." This was quickly followed by a sobering realization: "But marriage means I won't always be in charge!" I loved being the leader (and still do), but realistically, I knew marriage would require me to be the follower every now and then.

For about three months, I was stuck on the question: What would be a fun way for me to get better at following? The usual suspects like self-help books and personal development classes felt too obvious. I didn't want to take the chance that I'd get bored or give up halfway through—or both.

Then a light bulb went off: *Tango!*

To be clear, I knew next to nothing about tango. But I knew I loved dance, and I knew that in dancing the tango, the woman was usually the follower. Maybe it was a bit of a stretch to assume that literally following a dance partner would be the same as sharing the shot-calling with a future spouse, but that tenuous connection was good enough for me.

So, I signed up for ballroom dance classes.

Step by step, I began to learn the basics of Argentinian tango. Gradually, I developed an instinct for when to move, when to respond, when to share the dance with someone else as we sank into the music. Before I knew it, I'd fallen in love with tango . . . and eventually salsa, and rumba, and West Coast swing, and the hustle . . . and the man I'd end up marrying.

The point of this story isn't that I went on to become a champion ballroom dancer, because I didn't. The point isn't even that I went on to meet my husband, because that was just a fortuitous blind date—no tango involved! If I'd gone into that dance class wanting to chase dreams of tango superstardom or hoping I'd meet an eligible bachelor, tango wouldn't have been MTR—the connection between my actions and my desired outcome would have been super obvious.

The point here is that being a good life partner and learning to tango are not obviously connected. When I used one to learn how to do the other, I did MTR.

But here's what else evolved because of my initial self-query "How might I become a better follower?" Because of that, I am now a steadfast student of ballroom dance. I take regular lessons with my private instructor and a group class now and then. Which means that I have inadvertently integrated ample opportunity into my life to do more generative work because dance sparks movement *and* thought *and* requires me to rest afterward. It has had a resounding effect on my daily work, helping me to incorporate more fearlessness to experiment, deeper curiosity, and the courage to follow my intuition.

Granted, not all MTR activity is rooted in such an intentional question. The process of the MTR activity you're already doing might be subconscious—like "randomly" getting great ideas after going for a run, or taking a nap or staring at a tree for five minutes.

But there are ways to intentionally reflect upon and discover the existing MTR in your life. You need to think about *how* you think. When you practice this superpowered self-awareness—a.k.a. metacognition—you'll not only reveal some starter practices for your MTR but also strengthen a vital skill for all-around growth.

Let's explore a few of those ways.

BUILDING IN MOMENTUM AND FLEXIBILITY

Moving through ambiguous liminal space requires momentum and flexibility.

Let's look at each in turn: Liminality is the medium; momentum is how you get through the medium of liminal space; and flexibility maintains your momentum.

Liminality is the ambiguous space where you've got to figure out stuff. For example, completing a marketing strategy, accessing new clients, or understanding how to integrate a new technology into your team's work process. The only way you get through liminal space is by gathering and maintaining the momentum to take the next step, and then the next, and push through. Flexibility is what gives you traction to maintain the momentum of moving through liminal space.

Let me explore this concept further with another personal example.

I've always had an eye out for that perfect app. You know, the one that will finally get me drinking eight glasses of water a day, meditating before bed, or keeping up with a regular stretching practice. *Especially* that last one. For whatever reason, I can start all these things gung ho, but eventually, no amount of beeping notifications will keep me on track. I stray.

So when Alicia Archer, a fitness and flexibility expert I follow on Instagram, mentioned an app called STRETCHIT, I was hesitant to try it at first. I figured that their ninety-day splits challenge would mean stretching every day, and that's been my exact problem—stretching every day. However, this app *doesn't* expect you to stretch every day. In fact, it barely asks you to do the same thing twice, *ever*. The session times are manageable—some as short as nine minutes, and others as long as forty-five minutes—and you can jump in whenever you want (so long as you're wearing comfy pants). It has built-in recovery days, and it celebrates milestones along the way—not just at that big ninety-day mark.

My forward splits are still a long way off. The results are barely perceptible and feel incremental at best. But not only has this app helped me stick with this habit to stretch, but I also feel those tinier results along the way to the splits. I'm standing taller, I'm walking with improved balance, I feel more elongated and present in myself.

Keeping up any habit is often framed as a matter of momentum versus friction, of trying to sustain forward motion even as life crowds in and forces you to pump the brakes. When it comes to cultivating a flourishing life, having the skills to maintain momentum and reduce friction are key. Momentum is like roller-skating along a flat street. Once you start pushing into the asphalt and rolling along (representing a flexible, supportive environment or positive habits), you coast naturally. Each push you give (consistently practicing flexibility) doesn't just propel you forward but makes the next push easier as you pick up speed. Similarly, initial efforts to form MTR activity habits can become easier over time, and you will more efficiently maintain them.

But friction is another thing entirely. In the context of habit formation, friction is anything that makes it harder to perform positive habits consistently. It's like trying to roller-skate over a gravelly parking lot with a few potholes. The gravel and potholes represent obstacles, negative influences, or unsupportive environments. The rougher the path, the more energy you must exert to skate forward, and the harder it is to maintain any momentum you've built.

Friction is not necessarily a bad thing. Outside forces—such as our environment, our sensory input, even physical sensations from our own bodies—not only can't be entirely avoided, but they are preconditions for us to think creatively. None of us work or live in a vacuum. There will be unexpected variables that stop us from perfectly executing our new habit. I might dismiss my notification to stretch on a day when I'm tired. That's okay.

If friction is an outside force that drives you *back* (like a crazy travel day that prevents me from stretching), momentum is an outside force that propels you *forward* (like the badges that STRETCHIT awards me as I progressively show up and commit to doing the stretching exercises). Whether it's stretching or incorporating MTR activity into our daily lives, what sustains a long-term habit of doing anything is identifying what builds the *momentum* in our lives.

Stretching is the literal embodiment of the power of momentum. That's why I use my stretching journey as an example for talking about cultivating long-term MTR habits to flourish. For one thing, when you stretch yourself, you are, at some level, working against an opposing force—tight muscles. You gently, patiently, and gradually, but nevertheless doggedly, loosen those muscles up over time. But for another, the approach of the STRETCHIT app follows principles of flexibility that I see as key to cultivating MTR activity in your life:

- Keep the barriers to entry—time and resources—low.
- Warn yourself that moments of friction will happen; therefore, build in recovery days.
- Set a goal, but celebrate those incremental moments of teeny-weeny successes.
- And always give yourself permission to mix it up, to make whatever you're doing a little more pleasant for yourself.

MTR activity helps you to be flexible about your work because it affords you the space and time to step away and zoom out. When you get fixated on a problem and get tunnel vision, you become more myopic and inflexible.

Flexibility requires three main things: stretching, commitment, and reframing. First, stretching. The only way you get more flexible is by extending yourself. This usually feels uncomfortable at first, but the more you stretch, the more limber and agile you become. Second, commitment. For most of us, our default over time is to get more rooted into our own points of view and ways of doing things. Flexibility is not the default. To become more flexible (so that we can maintain momentum), we must practice the effort of extending and stretching ourselves into discomfort (i.e., the gray) in all sorts of small ways. Third, flexibility requires us to reframe our perspective. For example, say you are on a flight that you expect will land you in Philadelphia by 4:00 p.m. Midway through the flight, the pilot announces there is bad weather in Philadelphia, the airport has been closed, and so the flight will have to be rerouted to Allentown. You have a couple of options. You can get grouchy or alarmed at the inevitable change in plans and tardiness of your schedule. Or you can reframe. You can consider how great it is that there's technology for the pilot and aircraft to spot the storm so that you and your fellow fliers can be safely grounded. Once you land, you'll just have to rearrange some appointments. That sort of flexible thinking becomes easier the more you commit to zooming out and the more evidence you get that it helps to maintain momentum—instead of stopping you in your tracks and stagnating a process.

TAKE A MTR INVENTORY

Just as you can compile an inventory of courage (recall Chapter 2, "What Is MTR?"), you can also compile an inventory of MTR activity. Start by acknowledging all the ways that you have already begun to integrate movement and exercise, breaks and pauses, and energizing ways to think more deeply and reflect upon your work. Think of taking stock of MTR inventory as a systematic approach to sourcing and storing your energy levels.

When I worked in global sourcing in the fashion apparel industry, inventory management consisted of demand forecasting, stock replenishment, inventory ordering, warehouse organization, inventory tracking, and stock control. Similar principles reign for maintaining your personal MTR inventory. If warehouse organizing involves creating a systematic layout for efficiency and prioritization, the human equivalent for integrating more movement, thought, and rest (MTR) into your life would be:

1. Design Your "Life Floor Plan"
   - Forecast what lies ahead and prioritize tasks or personal resources, such as energy, time, and skills—soft skills or technical skills. Create a personal schedule or routine that systematically incorporates time for movement, deep thinking, and intentional rest. This could mean allocating specific blocks of time during your day for walking meetings, reflective journaling, and short breaks to relax and recharge.

2. Strategically Label Activities
   - Label your tasks based on their cognitive or physical demands and align them with the times when you're most productive. For example, tackle deep-thought work during your peak focus hours and use low-demand times for movement or restful activities.

3. Utilize "Storage Solutions"
    - Organize your physical environment to support your MTR goals. For movement, keep a yoga mat or weights nearby; for thought, have notebooks or whiteboards ready; and for rest, ensure access to calming spaces, such as a quiet room or a comfortable chair for short naps.

4. Apply the "80/20 Rule"
    - Avoid overcommitment or underutilization of your time and other life resources. This is similar to stock control in inventory management. Focus 80 percent of your effort on the 20 percent of activities that deliver the greatest value to your physical and mental well-being. For example, if walking clears your mind and energizes you, prioritize it over less impactful activities like scrolling through Instagram.

5. Optimize Space for Efficiency
    - Just as warehouses maximize their physical space, optimize your mental and emotional "space" in the ways that Le Truc has done. Use practices like mindfulness to clear mental clutter and enhance the design of your physical environment to focus, reflect, and generate ideas.

6. Review and Reward
    - Regularly analyze, review, and reflect upon the progress you make toward personal and professional goals. Similar to recording three wins every day in a journal, as advocated by Dan Sullivan and Ben Hardy in *The Gap and the Gain*, or a short reflection—write down three ways you *did* do MTR today. Also collect observations of how people are doing MTR differently from you that is inspiring to you.

By systematically organizing your day to integrate MTR, you create your own personal framework to work smarter, not harder—maximizing energy, creativity, and productivity. Taking inventory of the ways that MTR activity shows up in your life has several effects. First, you collect evidence of some of the ways that you have already been doing it. Second, by unpacking it and laying it out all in front of you, the positive evidence is a contagion. It helps you to build the confidence, flexibility, and momentum to continue doing it. Third, once this is all unpacked, you can identify small tweaks and variations you might do to make it more real and consistent in your life.

HOW DO YOU DO WHAT YOU DO, WHEN YOU DO WHAT YOU DO?

Perhaps you're thinking, *This is all well and good, but I just want to go with the flow! I just want to engage in deep thought, or reflection, or get that eureka moment, or shake my body, or take a nap as the spirit moves me. This feels way too calculated.*

Well, MTR activity is calculated. You're correct.

You must be intentional about MTR. Disrupting the staid and out-dated ways of working that we've normalized over the past two centuries is not going to happen by chance. It's going to require you, your team, your managers—heck, the entire cultural system of your organization—to choose to work very differently.

Here's the thing. The boundaries between work and leisure have already become irrevocably blurred. Technology is a big contributor to this enmeshment. But I'm not suggesting that we make more work of our leisure time or make our leisure activities feel more like work. Quite the opposite. What I am advocating for is bringing more leisure into work (via MTR) to cultivate greater yields from our work.

This is the shift we must make. From productivity to cultivation. From work and leisure to what I like to call *weisure*. I thought I had made up the phrase *weisure*. Nope! It turns out that NYU sociologist Dalton Conley first coined and introduced the term in 2009.[1] But Conley and I describe weisure in totally different ways. While I mark weisure as an opportunity we should seek, Conley used weisure to characterize the work creep that increasingly happens in a world where the boundaries blurred between work and home because of the digital leash that is your smartphone. He was exploring the term to caution us about the ways that "activities and social spaces are becoming more work-play ambiguous."[2] Conley was warning us about bringing work into our leisure time. I am encouraging us to bring more leisure into our work lives for all the reasons I've outlined—health benefits, efficiency advances, and better collaboration—in the previous chapters.

I first started using the term *weisure*—work + leisure—when traveling for business. I would always make sure I got in some time to visit a museum, or go to a spa, or walk through an interesting park and then sit and people-watch. For example, on a business trip to Cleveland, Ohio, to deliver a keynote to a global insurance company, I got in some weisure time when I arrived a day early. I visited the main branch of the Cleveland Public Library and meandered through an incredible art installation of sixty thousand dried flowers by English artist Rebecca Louise Law. It was absolutely magical. As I departed, I decided to briefly turn off my Google Maps, followed the scent of the lake shoreline, and got a little lost driving through the large boulevard streets—huge in scale compared to my East Coast acclimatization to the narrow one-way streets of Philadelphia. However, as a result of my circumnavigation, I stumbled upon a cool Mexican restaurant where I had a delectable late lunch, seated in front of a large floor-to-ceiling glass wall with a full view of Lake Erie. My lunch was delicious not only because of the amazing recipe mash-up between Mexican and Korean cuisine but also because it's rare for me to have a leisurely, slow, and delicious lunch, by myself, in the middle of the late afternoon in a new environment. I then took an invigorating twenty-minute walk in the bitterly cold wind along the Lake Erie shoreline before hopping into my rental car and driving thirty minutes south to my hotel in Westfield.

That day of weisure was a win!

Habits require repetition, incentives, and rewards. You will find that the incentive is that your work becomes more fun, juicy, and energizing. Remember the "sexy bits of productivity" that I advocated for in the Introduction? Well, now you can access them! MTR's reward is that your work feels less arduous. You'll tweak ways to practice MTR individually, as a team, and within your organization, and you'll consequently discover many more ways to spark inspiration through restorative and generative MTR practices.

When I put it that way, doesn't MTR feel like something worth getting intentional about?

SEEDS TO CULTIVATE:
PRO TIPS FOR BEING INTENTIONAL ABOUT MTR

Metacognition, or thinking about one's own thinking, can be greatly enhanced after activities like exercise, deep reflection, and naps because such MTR activity clears the mind, reduces stress, and increases brain function. Here are some exercises, question prompts, and "What if . . . ?" questions you can pose to yourself and to your team to practice metacognition in these contexts.

Individual Level—Reflections and Exercises
Reflection Questions for You

1. How much time do you have? MTR activity is scalable from micro amounts of time to macro amounts of time. So whether you have five minutes, five hours, or five days, you can dedicate time to move, think, and rest.
2. Where will you be? At work, home, or somewhere else? Indoors or outdoors? What are your space constraints?
3. With whom will you be? By yourself? With people you know or with strangers?

4. What's your energy level? Are you feeling tired or energized?

5. What's your mood? Feeling happy? Feeling sad? Feeling angry? Feeling indifferent?

6. Are you in this moment gravitating more toward movement, toward thought, toward rest, or perhaps a combination?

Exercises for You

Solo Activity: Compare and contrast pre- and postexercise thought patterns or ideas related to a specific topic or project.

- **Prompt:** In what ways has your perspective on this current project or problem changed after exercising?
- **What-if question:** What if you tackled your most challenging problems immediately after exercising? Would the solutions be different?

Team Level—Reflections and Exercises
Exercises for Your Team

After Taking a Break (or Rest)

Team Activity: Engage in a reflective journaling session. Ask your team members to write about how the break affected their thought process or mental clarity.

- **Prompt:** How has your thinking changed before and after the break? Are you viewing your challenges or tasks differently now?
- **What-if question:** What if you structured your breaks differently? How might it impact your productivity or creativity?

Team Activity: Mind mapping. Encourage your teammates to create a mind map about a current project or problem, noting any new perspectives or ideas that come post-break.

- **Prompt:** Identify new connections or insights about this project that emerged after this break. How do these affect your approach?

- **What-if question:** What if you integrated these new insights into your project? What potential outcomes could arise?

After Exercise or Movement

Team Activity: Have a group discussion or personal reflection on the impact of exercise on mental processes.

- **Prompt:** How does physical activity influence your cognitive functions, problem-solving abilities, or creativity?
- **What-if question:** What if you increased the frequency of your exercise during the workday? How might that affect your work or thought processes?

After Engaging in Deep Reflection

Team Activity: Facilitate a session where team members share insights gained during a reflection and explore how these insights can be applied.

- **Prompt:** What did you discover about your thought processes during this reflection? How can you apply this understanding to enhance your work or personal growth?
- **What-if question:** What if you applied these insights consistently? How might your decision-making or creativity be influenced?

Team Activity: Encourage people to set specific, actionable goals based on their reflections.

- **Prompt:** Based on your deep reflection, what specific changes or actions would you like to implement in your thinking or work approach?
- **What-if question:** What if you successfully implemented one of these changes? How might it transform your approach to challenges?

These exercises and questions can help you become more aware of your thinking patterns, potentially leading to enhanced problem-solving skills, increased creativity, and better decision-making.

Organizational Level—Reflections and Exercises
Reflection Question for Your Organization

1. Where in your current workflows are employees *most likely to feel depleted*, and how might integrating movement, thought, or rest there improve not only how people feel but how they perform?

This question invites leadership to tie well-being directly to performance—and see rest and movement not as time lost but value gained.

Exercise for Your Organization: Tracing the MTR Effect: A Metrics Map
Instructions:

1. Select three metrics your organization already tracks (e.g., engagement, innovation, and absenteeism).
2. List recent initiatives tied to movement, thought, and rest. For example:
   - Movement: Introduced walking meetings.
   - Thought: Added quiet focus time blocks on calendars.
   - Rest: Encouraged midday screen-free breaks or implemented No Meeting Fridays.
3. Compare before-and-after data over a three- to six-month period. Look for shifts in those metrics. Did engagement scores rise? Did absenteeism drop?
   - Bonus Step: Add qualitative data. Ask teams: "What effect, if any, did the new walking meetings or rest breaks have on your ability to stay focused, be creative, or collaborate?"

8

CULTIVATING THE
IMAGINATION ERA

The problem with the race to the bottom
is that you might win. The alternative is
to be the sort of organization that races
to the top instead—one that's based on
dignity, delight, and human innovation.[1]

—Seth Godin, author, *This Is Strategy*

The Information Age is behind us. So is hyper-hustling micro-productivity. Our workplaces require a reinvention focused on long-term cultivation driven by deeper self-awareness and broader collaboration with others.

We're perched at the edge of something new: the Imagination Era.

Earlier in Chapter 3, "Move: It's How We're Designed," I shared about my open-water swimming adventures in Greece and the ways that experience helped me to get out of my head and into my body. A year later, I gained a new perspective through open-water swimming in northern Vermont—movement that rewired my brain and sparked pattern interruption. That phenomenon helped me zoom out to gain perspective. And then *that* shift further rewired my brain for the work that awaited me upon my return.

I decided to give Charlotte Brynn's swim clinic at Lake Memphremagog, which straddles Vermont and Quebec, a try after it was recommended by fellow open-water swimmer Lisa, even though I had a lot of trepidation about swimming in cooler temperatures. My open-water swimming so far was limited to warmer climates with shimmering turquoise water. I wasn't certain Charlotte's swim clinic would be for me. Charlotte has mastered open-water swims through decades of triathlons and competitions. She recently crossed the English Channel after her third attempt. She's a badass. But I had no desire to prove myself by swimming faster or longer. As I shared with Charlotte on our introductory Zoom call, my goals for this clinic were "to get more comfortable, confident, and joyous in the water." She beamed back at me: "Excellent! It's all about working on our relationship with the water and energy and flow."

Well, then. *Now* she was speaking my language. So I showed up.

Three of us attended this particular clinic: Lisa, Alva (a Vermonter), and me. The morning of the first day consisted of an overview from Charlotte, a wonderful stretching session, and drills followed by laps around buoys to practice working on the techniques we'd just learned. After a nice break, we were invited to swim a half mile to tiny Horseneck Island plus the half mile back to Charlotte's dock.

I started off on this Horseneck Island swim feeling nervous. I typically do. But Charlotte kayaked right beside me, serving as my line of sight. With every breath stroke I took, pivoting my head out of the water to breathe in air, she smiled at me, encouraging me with a thumbs-up or a nod. By the time I reached the little island, I felt triumphant. I was happy to have made it that far. But then came time to swim the half mile back to the dock. I wasn't looking forward to it. It was nice to chill out a bit by the rocky edge of Horseneck Island with my new swim pal Alva. But I set out anyway.

Five minutes into this leg, my shoulder began to bother me—no doubt due to my subpar technique. And I felt so tired, like it would be great to just . . . stop! Every time I caught a glimpse of the dock, it never seemed to get any closer. I felt exhausted and frustrated. I was the slowest swimmer and way behind Alva (Lisa sat this one out, as she had swum 4K the day prior and wanted to rest). This time, Vera, Charlotte's assistant, was sighting me with her kayak. At a low point when I was beginning to feel quite discouraged, I took a breath and glanced at Vera. She shouted to me, "You're doing great!" For the remainder of the swim, I kept repeating those words to myself. With each stroke, I said to myself, "I. Am. Doing. Great! I. Am. Doing. Great!" Over and over again, even though I didn't feel great. I said those words silently to myself until they reverberated throughout my body. Eventually, I made it to the dock, tired, smiling, and proud.

A week after I returned home from the swim clinic, I received a text from Charlotte, with a photo of me swimming that first leg. It captured me taking a breath, with lake weed strewn all over the side of my face and forehead. Charlotte texted, "Mental fortitude and focus right there." I recalled that it was really in the return leg of the swim that my focus and fortitude kicked in. When I was tired, with my aching shoulder, I kept telling myself over and over, "I. Am. Doing. Great!" despite my skepticism. The physical exertion helped me to immerse myself into my senses.

Since that swim, there have been numerous times that I've scrolled through my "Lake Memphremagog Vermont Swim" photos folder on my phone and zoomed into that photo to remind myself of Charlotte's words. I do indeed have the mental fortitude and focus to take on new, challenging pursuits *and* to see them through until the end. That photo is just the reminder I need to complete a client project, or to remain hopeful about the keynote contract I want to close, or to finish writing the article that's full of disjointed ideas. If I just stay the course, continue to move forward stroke by stroke, and apply that same mental fortitude and focus that I had while swimming to and from Horseneck Island, I'll get there. Wherever I am on my journey, I. Am. Doing. Great!

When we persevere through challenging physical movement, we receive in return rich metaphors that we can apply to our daily, more mundane experiences. The activity rewires not just our bodies but our hearts, emotions, senses, and minds. This is the power of MTR activity. It catalyzes a cellular rewiring that allows us to imagine more for ourselves. We can then transfer that rewiring into the organizations where we work.

That rewiring is essential during this time of rapid technological advancements—AI, automation, and robotics—that make it easy to feel overwhelmed, as if the future belongs only to machines. But that's not the case. The opportunity before us is to tap into our uniquely human capacity to imagine: our one truly infinite resource. We can imagine our way into a new, exciting future that requires different ways of being and doing to flourish.

And the way we cultivate our imaginations is through movement, thought, and rest.

Back in 1993, Charlie Magee, an illustrator and designer, predicted this shift, declaring that the human imagination would control the information tools of the industrial age.[2] Decades later, Rita J. King, the executive vice president of Science House, revisited the concept by writing and speaking about the "Imagination Age," positioning it as the bridge between the industrial era and what she calls the Intelligence Era.[3] She even redefined AI as "applied imagination," a copilot for human creativity.[4]

Today, data and information have become easily accessible commodities. Information processing can be done by AI and LLMs. The old productivity models, built on mechanistic, reductionist ideas, don't fit anymore. Those models that prioritize efficiency and consequently treat humans like machines, requiring people to churn out tasks on a rigid, step-by-step assembly line, are not only unethical, they're not very pragmatic in the long run because humans are *not* machines. In addition, increasingly what humans produce of value is intangible (new ideas) and digitized (alternative processes) as much as it is physical and analog. And that's why the Imagination Era is so timely and prescient; it makes space for curiosity, creativity, and inspiration to become the new currencies and means to the end. As explored in Chapter 6, "A New Human Operating

System," we actually thrive in the liminal, ambiguous, uncertain, and gray spaces where these currencies live—because it is only when we are at the edge, on the verge, and in the in-between spaces that we discover something new.

This was the MO of Grace Hopper, the mother of computer science. Early on in her career, when she taught math at her alma mater, Vassar College, she required her students to communicate their answers to calculations and observations about nature through stories. Her biographer Kurt Beyer wrote: "In her probability course, she began with a lecture on one of her favorite mathematical formulas and asked her students to write an essay about it. These she would mark for clarity of writing and style."[5] She caught a lot of flak for this unconventional—yet imaginative— method that encouraged students to use language, story, and metaphor to explain mathematical problem-solving. That distinctive way of thinking through ambiguous areas was something that she carried forward in her career.

Hopper continued to embrace experimentation while working for the US Navy during World War II. Amid a lot of uncertainty and high stakes whose outcomes required immense precision, she improvised code that enabled the Mark I computer to generate reliable ballistic calculations to detect torpedoes. Later, Hopper pioneered new ways to develop code so that computers talked to one another. This meant that instead of computers functioning as isolated machines, they became part of interconnected systems that allowed for seamless data exchange. As a result, workflows improved dramatically and made for more efficient human-machine interaction. We can thank Hopper for this underlying premise of AI: that computers are interactive copilots for our thinking. Her work later led her to codevelop COBOL (common business-oriented language), a business computing language, which enabled computers to respond to words as well as to numbers. This meant that nontechnical business professionals could more easily understand and participate in programming tasks. COBOL was adopted early on as a game changer by Wall Street banks and is used to this day to process financial transactions. And Hopper was able to do this principally because she was a great translator, open to applying her imagination in the hard sciences and mathematics.

I define the imagination as the integration of memory, awareness, analysis, and visual thinking that enables us to see new possibilities. And like Hopper, I believe our ability to cultivate our imaginations will drive future business success, team accomplishments, and community fulfillment.

Jane McGonigal, author of the incredible book *Imaginable*, writes that the key to exercising our imaginations is to "unstick our minds."[6] Without fully deploying the imagination, we are stuck—disconnected from ourselves and from others. MTR activity acts like the WD-40 to get our brains cranking and moving in new ways. When we make time to intentionally embrace playing, daydreaming, traveling, napping, reflecting, exercising, and so on, it's then that our work improves. Moving, thinking, and resting combine to spark our imagination, leading to new idea generation and an expanded creative capacity.

THE BUSINESS ROI OF MTR: LIMITLESS

The Imagination Era loves the liminal space that opens up when we say, "I don't know." And you should, too.

These three words are the key to curiosity, the bridge to innovation, and the catalyst for exploration. The acknowledgment of "I don't know" thrives in ambiguous, liminal spaces—the gray areas—where we wrestle with ideas, explore new possibilities, and prepare ourselves for action. James Hewitt, a human performance scientist, explained to me that our evolutionary history demonstrates that pausing to ponder and make sense of ambiguity yields the best results for problem-solving. Think about it: Our migratory ancestors, when faced with new terrain for hunting and gathering, needed to get comfortable with pausing to work through ambiguity ("Is that a lion's den up ahead or just a dense grove of trees?") for survival.

Currently, there's a significant gap between recognizing the value of "I don't know" and providing the resources to cultivate the curiosity and creativity to find new answers. But in the Imagination Era, it's a chasm that we can bridge if we embrace MTR activity at home and at work. By strategically cultivating our movement, thought, and rest through activities such as reading fiction, playing, daydreaming, traveling, and actively collaborating in new environments, we can unlock our creative potential and harness the power of our imagination for unlimited personal growth, professional fulfillment, and collective innovation. But not, perhaps, the type of upward, straight-line trajectory growth the business world has erroneously come to expect.

The way we have been thinking about growth is simplistic and frankly wrong.

The typical visual depicting growth is a straight-line arrow projecting from the origin of the X and Y axes on a 2 × 2 graph, sloping up from left to right into infinity. One of my favorite apps, the Noun Project, populates variations of that visual when you search for icons that depict "growth." And heck, there have been so many times when I have doodled that same representation to connote growth. If we attempt to be slightly more realistic, then the arrow line may have a few indentations downward to indicate some rough spots. But generally speaking, the line is always pointed upward.

The challenge is that an eternally upward trajectory of growth is unrealistic.

As we face environmental challenges and social inequities, we must confront the reality that growth in its traditional depiction comes with a price. The degrowth movement, for example, questions the notion of infinite expansion on a finite planet. In 2013, Sir David Attenborough, a renowned natural historian, stated at an event organized by conservation group Fauna & Flora International at the Royal Geographical Society: "Anyone who thinks that you can have infinite growth in a finite environment is either a madman or an economist."[7] This sentiment is echoed by environmental activists like Greta Thunberg, who famously challenged the assumptions of world leaders about unchecked economic expansion at the September 2019 United Nations Climate Action Summit when she proclaimed, "People are suffering. People are dying. Entire ecosystems are collapsing. We are in the beginning of a mass extinction, and all you can talk about is money and fairy tales of eternal economic growth. How dare you!"

The call for degrowth compels us to rethink how we measure success and progress. It's a fair and desperate plea given how much of our natural environment has been devastated. But it assumes that all resources are finite.

An alternative view comes from economist Daniel Susskind. He points out that the benefits of growth are not only reflected in salaries or physical output but also in intangible resources like innovation, creativity, and the discovery of new ideas.[8] *Those* resources are truly infinite. In fact, that's one of the reasons I named my company *Figure 8 Thinking*: There are an infinite number of ways to think creatively and innovatively.

Economic growth today comes from technological progress, which, in turn, is driven by the discovery of new ideas. The shift from the material to the intangible in our productive output opens up vast opportunities for us to rethink growth. The old, first Industrial Revolution view of economic activity—focused solely on the tangible world of objects—has its limits, because tangible resources eventually run out. Susskind argues that in a world of infinite ideas that can drive the technological innovations that propel our economy, growth can also be infinite.[9] He uses the metaphor of a well-stocked pantry to illustrate this perspective: the number of ways to recombine the ingredients in the pantry is nearly endless.

The question, then, is not whether infinite growth is possible on a finite planet but rather how might we redefine growth in a way that supports sustainability, creativity, and human flourishing. As Susskind and others suggest, growth can be fueled by an "idea economy," which, instead of exhausting resources, finds better ways to use them. Creativity and collaboration, which fuel technological progress, are key to this new growth model and are the hallmarks of our incoming Imagination Era.

Imagination leads to better ideas. Ideas are the currency of the future and lead to new combinations for improved technologies. When we lean into our imagination to spark curiosity, collaborate effectively, and lead with the heart, then our work initiatives, coupled with the technology we can leverage, will result in higher efficiencies, new strategic partnerships, and greater market value.

In other words, MTR activity sparks a limitless business ROI.

As we build our creative capacity and lean into the infinite potential of human imagination, we will find new ways to navigate our world's challenges. And as I've hopefully made clear by now, our best ideas will come from strategically engaging in movement, thought, and rest as individuals and as teams. MTR activity is the way to sustainably grow your business because that's the best way to tap into the limitless imagination of the people in your organization.

A DIFFERENT WAY TO THINK ABOUT GROWTH

Think of a bicycle.

Consider how the wheels of that bicycle work to propel you forward. They cycle through from top, to bottom, then backward and up again to gain traction. That's how growth actually works. We propel forward only when we move through cycles of momentum, slowdown, and rest.

In this alternate scenario, my doodled straight-line arrow in a 2 × 2 graph depiction of growth over time would be replaced with a series of overlapping circles that propel us forward—but not without some backcasting and borrowing from the past and some dips downward in time. These slowdowns and pauses are not obstacles to growth but essential phases of growth. They allow us to regroup and reassess to push ahead. Growth is not only upward but is also generated by lateral traction and by making the time to go deep. The visual of bicycle wheels in motion is a more accurate metaphor for *cultivating* growth, especially in today's rapidly evolving world where creativity, technological innovation, and sustainability are at the heart of progress.

In the Imagination Era, cultivating growth doesn't just happen through expansion—it also happens through nurturing, resting, and allowing for renewal. Ultimately, we need to embrace *cycles* of growth, recognizing that the pauses and resets are just as critical as the forward motion. This cyclical view of growth aligns with Susskind's assertion to invest in research and development, reform intellectual property regimes, and encourage a range of people in industries responsible for generating new ideas.[10] Sustainable progress is enhanced by cultivating cycles of movement, thought, and rest.

What happens when we return to our desks after engaging in movement, thought, and rest activities? We're not just physically coming back to the same space; we are returning with a transformed mindset because we've activated the DMN in the brain. For me, whether it's after a five-minute daydream break or after spending three days at Charlotte's northern Vermont swim clinic, I return to my work with a renewed clarity and sense of empowerment. Swimming through the murky waters of Lake Memphremagog wasn't just a physical challenge—it allowed my DMN to do its thing, rewiring the neural pathways in my brain. When I came back to my desk, the challenges that had once seemed insurmountable now appeared more manageable. The focus, emotion, and mental fortitude I built in those waters (I. Am. Doing. Great!) boosted my creative capacity and carried over into my work.

Companies like A+I and Le Truc (discussed in Chapters 2 and 5) have taught us the importance of spatial interruption, where the design of the physical layout promotes movement and dynamic interaction. That's because the physical environment and design of our workspaces plays a significant role in how we work, either enhancing or stifling creativity. Whether it's open spaces for brainstorming; quiet, cozy corners for reflection; or adaptable workstations, space can support movement, thought, and rest for greater creativity.

And this sense of the value of MTR activities isn't only anecdotal.

According to the World Economic Forum's *Future of Jobs Report 2023*, creativity is the second most critical skill for the workforce, outranking resilience, flexibility, agility, and curiosity.[11] We are in a time when the ability to think creatively is essential, not just in artistic fields but in problem-solving and innovation for health care, transportation, finance, and education. New idea generation (i.e., creativity) is the fruit of MTR activity, and when we intentionally set aside time to move, think, and rest throughout our day, the ripple effects touch every corner of our professional lives.

MTR AT THE TEAM LEVEL

I just shared the effects of MTR on the individual level. But what happens when we bring the benefits of MTR back to our teams? First, it builds community. After time away to recharge and reflect, we naturally want to share our experiences and insights. Instead of quiet quitting, MTR sparks collective persistence.

This could take many forms. Imagine a series of corporate show-and-tells where employees present new ideas or discoveries from their MTR activities. The in-person element, post-MTR, becomes rich with high-touch interaction. The desire to connect increases because colleagues want to share what they've learned or have been reflecting on. I heard this over and over again in my interviews with people who opted into company-sanctioned sabbaticals. For example, Becca Foy, who's taken three sabbaticals during her fifteen-year tenure at META, values the ways that intentionally disconnecting helps her to collaborate better: "I come back, and without even realizing it, I'm fresher. I have different ideas. I show up differently for my meetings."

The feedback collected on new ideas you've shared can amplify the learning and takeaways even further. Collaboration is no longer just a buzzword but becomes an organic part of the work culture—all sparked by MTR activity. Building on this point, Peter Knutson, chief strategy officer at the architectural firm A+I, reflected back to me on the Le Truc team's usage of the diamond model of work (a series of work processes that require divergent thinking and convergent thinking) as well as Leigh Thompson's *Harvard Business Review* article "Give Workers the Power to Choose: Caves or Commons." Knutson recognizes how necessary it is to flow between being a "solo operator" and a "collective operator" when cultivating work—not just producing output—is the norm:

> The solitary operator and collective operator is that diamond shape, that rich production of a large group of people brainstorming . . . coming together and being a piece of a thinking organism, and then that reduction back to the cave . . . where you take yourself back to the solitary operator. There's a value of the solitary operator even in brainstorming. You know, for years now people have said it's not just throwing people in a room to be creative. You need a moment where you're thinking as a unit, and you [also] need a moment where you're thinking alone. And that's how you actually create meaningful progress.

This cyclical dance between solitary and collective thinking isn't just a process—it's a rhythm that shapes how meaningful work emerges. As Knutson suggests, this balance is not only foundational for creativity but also for cultivating deeper, more intentional outcomes in our work. An ebb-and-flow model of working also creates an opportunity to embed rituals into our work culture, reinforcing the rhythm of MTR activities.

By framing these MTR practices as rituals or ceremonies, we can elevate everyday habits into intentional acts that fuel both imagination and productivity. Whether individual or collective—a morning team walk, a creative lunch break, or a post-work reflection session—these rituals anchor us in purpose and connection, creating space for the innovation and reflection that modern work demands. Here are three examples that illustrate how MTR activity will level up the way we work in an Imagination Era: (1) creative breaks, (2) work share, and (3) and apprenticeships.

CREATIVE BREAKS

First, let's examine creative breaks. Traditionally, workplace breaks have been viewed as simple pauses in productivity—quick trips to the coffee machine, scrolling through phones in the break room, or eating lunch while catching up on emails. These conventional breaks often leave us more drained than refreshed, trapped in what Linda Stone termed *continuous partial attention* in 1998 during her time at Microsoft: a state where we're neither fully working nor fully resting but constantly scanning for new information and opportunities without deep focus.[12]

The Imagination Era demands a different approach to breaks—one that intentionally integrates movement, thought, and rest to spark creativity and innovation. Creative breaks transform these pause points from mere interruptions into opportunities for renewal and inspiration. Instead of reaching for our phones during downtime, we can engage in activities that energize our bodies, stimulate our minds, and provide genuine restoration. For example, FLOWN, discussed earlier in Chapter 4, demonstrates how structured breaks can be integrated into workplace culture. The platform combines movement (walking desk sessions), thought (facilitated deep work periods), and rest (timed breaks) into a cohesive system for taking breaks. What makes FLOWN unique is how it transforms breaks into engaging experiences—participants can play quick brain games, listen to curated Spotify playlists, or gaze at inspiring scenes from nature. These intentionally designed break activities help reset the mind while maintaining a sense of community through shared virtual spaces. By weaving MTR activities into our break times, we transform these pauses into essential components of innovation and creative thinking. Here are some examples of how teams can integrate creative breaks into their workday:

1. Walking Book Club

- Movement: Gather a small group of coworkers and take a walk around the office neighborhood or a nearby park.
- Thought: During the walk, discuss a book or article that's relevant to your field—or choose something inspiring and outside of work. This sparks fresh thinking and invites different perspectives.
- Rest: The natural movement combined with conversation and fresh air gives your mind a break from the usual stressors of the

day. Walking outside also provides mental rest from screens and indoor environments.

2. Lunchtime Stretch and Reflect

- Movement: Start the lunch break with a ten- to fifteen-minute stretching session. Apps like STRETCHIT can guide you with accessible and simple stretches, or you can do elementary yoga poses to loosen up stiff muscles from sitting too long.
- Thought: After stretching, spend a few minutes reflecting on a thought-provoking question, riddle, or challenge. Journaling during this time can also help clarify ideas and get creative juices flowing.
- Rest: End the break by sitting quietly for five minutes, either daydreaming, meditating, or listening to relaxing music to reset minds before heading back to work.

3. Team "Walk and Wonder" Sessions

- Movement: Set up a rotating schedule where team members take turns leading short walking routes near the office.
- Thought: The person leading the walk presents a "wonder" question for the group to discuss afterward. It could be something creative, like "What's something you observe on our walk that we could incorporate to improve our project?" or "Consider sharing a what-if question that occurs to you during our walk that could help us think differently about our work project."
- Rest: Let the final five minutes be reflective silence where everyone simply takes in their surroundings, unwinding and letting ideas sink in.

4. Park Picnic with "Mindful Eating"

- Movement: Bring lunch to a nearby park or outdoor space. The walk to the park is your physical movement.

- Thought: Practice mindful eating. Encourage each person to focus on each bite, savor the flavors, and notice how their body responds. Discuss with coworkers or reflect silently on how this simple practice increases awareness and appreciation for your food.
- Rest: After eating, spend a few minutes lying or sitting in the grass, simply enjoying the outdoors, watching the clouds, or even taking a short nap to rejuvenate.

5. Desk Dance Break

- Movement: If you're in the mood to stay indoors, take five to ten minutes to turn on a popular favorite upbeat song and dance by your desks or in a shared open space. Consider creating a team playlist with a favorite song from each colleague.
- Thought: Allow your minds to wander. Many times, the most creative solutions arise when we're moving and thinking in an unstructured way (see Chapter 3).
- Rest: After the mini dance session, take a short pause to sit and relax, allowing each person to soak in the creative energy you've collectively unleashed.

6. Creative Coworking Cafés

- Movement: Walk or bike to a nearby café or workspace that has an artistic vibe, with interesting artwork or design elements.
- Thought: Bring a work of fiction to spark reflective thinking. You can also use this time to brainstorm ideas or draw inspiration from your surroundings. Consider creating a team fiction library that consists of one shelf with everyone's favorite works of fiction.
- Rest: Before heading back, let everyone take a quiet moment with their drinks to simply observe the environment, absorb the atmosphere, and rest their minds. Consider creating a

post-break whiteboard or chalkboard where colleagues are encouraged to share reflections.

Each of these breaks blend movement, thought, and rest, creating opportunities to return to work refreshed, inspired, and more connected to one's teammates. The key is to break away from the desk and introduce activity that nourishes both body and mind. In the same way that Lake Memphremagog rewired my neural pathways, these daily or weekly rituals can creatively disrupt your team's thinking and rewire how they approach tasks, making space for creativity and new ideas to flourish.

NEW WORK-SHARE MODELS

Second, we can start considering new work-share models. Historically, work-sharing has been viewed primarily as a cost-saving measure or a way to preserve jobs during economic downturns. Companies split full-time positions between multiple workers, each person working reduced hours. While this approach helps maintain employment levels, it often treats workers as interchangeable parts in a machine, focusing solely on output rather than growth and innovation.

The Imagination Era demands a fundamental revision of work-sharing. New work-share models propel the distribution of ideas, tasks, and responsibilities and don't only take place during a time of crisis. Teams can take turns leading different aspects of a project, fostering a culture of collaborative cultivation rather than one where a few people bear all the weight. The focus shifts from individual output to collective growth. Instead of simply dividing labor, modern work-share models create purposeful spaces for collaboration, creativity, and collective growth. By incorporating MTR activities, these new models recognize that the best ideas often emerge when people have time to move (physically collaborate), think (cross-pollinate ideas), and rest (reflect and integrate learnings). This approach transforms work-sharing from a purely economic tool into a catalyst for innovation and community building. Here are some examples of how organizations can implement work-share approaches:

1. Project Rotation Pods

- Movement: Teams physically rotate between different work areas or "pods" designed for specific project phases.
- Thought: Each pod focuses on different aspects of work (ideation, development, testing) with dedicated time for knowledge sharing.
- Rest: Built-in buffer periods between rotations allow for reflection and integration of learning.

2. Skill-Share Workshops

- Movement: Skill-sharing can be brought to life through movement by hosting monthly interactive workshops where team members teach one another a range of skills—from professional strengths, like presentation delivery, design thinking, and facilitation techniques, to wellness practices, such as stretching routines, mindfulness walks, or expressive movement—fostering both personal growth and workplace connection.
- Thought: To emphasize deeper thinking, monthly skill-sharing workshops can include peer-led sessions on reflective practices like journaling for clarity, structured ideation techniques such as mind mapping or question-storming, or methods for strategic foresight and scenario planning—helping teams sharpen intellectual agility and make space for creative problem-solving. Cross-disciplinary learning expands everyone's capabilities and perspective.
- Rest: To foster rest, workshops can feature team members guiding one another in restorative activities, such as guided breathing exercises, creative visualization, or even shared storytelling circles—offering time to pause, reconnect with self and others, and normalize rest as a source of clarity and energy

in the workday. Learning happens in relaxed, low-pressure environments with time for practice and questions.

3. Collaborative Sprints

- Movement: Teams work together intensively for short periods (two to three days) on specific challenges.
- Thought: Mix different expertise levels and backgrounds to spark fresh thinking.
- Rest: Follow sprints with dedicated recovery days for processing and integration.

For example, Spotify's squad model demonstrates how work-sharing can foster innovation. Small, cross-functional teams work autonomously on specific features while sharing knowledge across the organization. This approach has helped them maintain agility and creativity even as they've grown.

REINVENTING APPRENTICESHIPS

Third, apprenticeships should be revived. And not the apprenticeships of medieval times but apprenticeships befitting an Imagination Era. Bringing back apprenticeships not only is a form of collaborative learning by thinking and doing together, it helps to resolve the learning curve gap made vacant for younger people and new hires because of hybrid, remote work. Apprenticeships date back to medieval times when master craftsmen would take on young learners, teaching them specific trades through years of hands-on training. This model persisted through the Industrial Revolution, evolving into more formalized programs in manufacturing, construction, and technical fields. While effective for transferring specific skills, traditional apprenticeships often emphasized rote learning and rigid hierarchies, with knowledge flowing in one direction from master to apprentice.

The Imagination Era calls for a complete reinvention of apprenticeships. Rather than focusing solely on technical skill transfer, modern apprenticeships must become incubators for creative thinking and innovation. By integrating MTR activities, these new apprenticeships create dynamic learning environments where both mentor and apprentice grow together. Movement activities facilitate hands-on learning and experimentation, thought activities encourage questioning and creative problem-solving, and rest activities provide space for reflection and integration. This approach transforms apprenticeships from a simple skills-transfer model into a collaborative journey of discovery and innovation, and it propels more companies to become the learning organizations discussed in Chapter 4. It also means that in a world of remote work, the times when we come together in person will be premium experiences for learning, connecting, and growing collaboratively. Here's how organizations could structure Imagination Era apprenticeships:

1. Creative Mentorship Pairs

- Movement: Mentors and apprentices work side by side on projects, physically collaborating in shared space.
- Thought: Regular reflection sessions explore not just what was done but why and how decisions were made.
- Rest: Design time for mentors and apprentices to independently explore creative experimentation.

2. Innovation Labs

- Movement: Apprentices rotate through different departments or project teams.
- Thought: Focus is on problem-finding as much as problem-solving.
- Rest: Dedicated time is reserved or personal projects and skill development.

3. Community Learning Circles

- Movement: Regular gatherings where apprentices from different teams or companies meet.

- Thought: Convenings allow apprentices to learn from mentors' shared experiences, challenges, and insights.
- Rest: Social time for informal networking and relationship building.

Google's Associate Product Manager (APM) program offers an excellent example of an Imagination Era apprenticeship. APMs rotate through different products and teams, gaining hands-on experience while being mentored by experienced product managers. The program emphasizes learning through doing, creative problem-solving, and building a strong peer network.

IMPLEMENTATION TIPS FOR ALL THREE MODELS OF CREATIVE BREAKS, WORK-SHARE, AND APPRENTICESHIPS:

1. Start small: Begin with pilot programs in one department or team.
2. Build in flexibility: Allow for adaptation based on feedback and results.
3. Measure impact: Track both traditional metrics and creative outcomes.
4. Create support systems: Ensure resources and time for learning and sharing.
5. Celebrate progress: Recognize and share success stories across the organization.

These approaches help organizations move from traditional hierarchical structures to more fluid, creative environments where learning and innovation naturally flow. They create spaces where people can grow together, share knowledge freely, and build the collaborative skills needed for the Imagination Era.

Ultimately, MTR activities are not just about stepping away from work; they're about coming back transformed, with new perspectives, ideas, and a deeper connection within teams.

CHAORDIC COMPETENCY: STRIKING THE BALANCE BETWEEN WONDER AND RIGOR

Having explored how teams can implement MTR practices, let's examine the theoretical underpinning that makes these approaches so powerful in the Imagination Era. The interplay between wonder and rigor—between expansive possibility and focused execution—lies at the heart of how organizations can use MTR to thrive amid uncertainty.

The give-and-take between wonder and rigor mirrors what Dee Hock, the first president of Visa credit card company, called *chaordic systems* in his book *One from Many*—systems that harmoniously blend characteristics of chaos and order. Chaos is not anarchy—it's randomness; and order is not control—it's structure. Just as I explored in *The Creativity Leap*, chaordic systems thrive not by eliminating uncertainty and ambiguity but by finding rhythm within those liminal spaces. And just as true growth mirrors the forces of a bicycle wheel turning, chaordic systems maintain forward momentum through continuous cycles of divergence and convergence.

This chaordic framework helps explain why traditional linear models of growth fall short in the Imagination Era. When we try to force creativity and innovation into straight-line trajectories, we ignore the natural oscillation between exploration (wonder) and refinement (rigor). Instead, like the overlapping circles of our bicycle wheel metaphor, growth in the Imagination Era requires us to embrace both the expansive phases, where we dream and imagine, and the focusing phases, where we analyze and execute. Creativity is the engine for innovation: An innovation is an invention converted into scalable value, and creativity is that conversion factor. MTR activities support this rhythm—movement energizes divergent thinking, thought enables convergent analysis, and rest creates space for integration.

The chaordic nature of innovation work becomes particularly evident in how successful teams operate in the Imagination Era. Rather than trying to eliminate uncertainty through rigid processes, they develop what I call a *chaordic competency*—the ability to remain grounded while navigating ambiguity. Consider how Pixar's animation teams embraced this chaordic competency. Their Brain Trust meetings[13] intentionally created space for both wonder and rigor. During these sessions, Pixar directors, animators, and writers shared unfinished work—rough storyboards, incomplete animations, early character designs—knowing they were entering an uncertain space of critique and possibility. Rather than rushing to perfect solutions, they used movement (often standing and gesturing at storyboards), thought (focused discussion and feedback), and rest (breaks for private reflection) to navigate through the messy middle of the creative process.

Similarly, IDEO's design teams demonstrated chaordic competency through their "Yes, and . . . " approach to ideation.[14] When developing new products or services, they began with expansive brainstorming where all ideas, no matter how seemingly impractical, were welcomed. This created psychological safety for wonder. Then, through structured prototyping phases, they applied rigor to test and refine these ideas. The process wasn't linear—teams cycled between divergent and convergent thinking, using physical movement (prototyping), collaborative thought (feedback sessions), and intentional rest (reflection time) to maintain momentum.

The Mayo Clinic offers yet another powerful example. Their health care innovation teams regularly practiced what they called *structured serendipity*[15]— intentionally designing the physical space and organizational practices so that different specialists and staff will have helpful encounters. They might have cardiologists observe orthopedic surgeries or bring in artists to reimagine patient experiences. These encounters were carefully designed to balance wonder (cross-disciplinary inspiration) with rigor (practical medical constraints). The teams used movement (walking the hospital floors), thought (facilitated ideation sessions), and rest (dedicated processing time) to transform these creative tensions into breakthrough innovations in patient care.

And even in highly regulated industries like financial services, we see chaordic competency at work. Capital One's innovation lab Capital One Lab exemplified this through their approach to developing new financial products.[16] Their teams practiced what they called *regulated experimentation*—using design thinking methods within the strict constraints of banking regulations. For example, when developing new mobile banking features, they brought together compliance officers, UX designers, and customers in early ideation sessions. The teams used movement (interactive prototyping sessions), thought (compliance-aware brainstorming), and rest (reflection periods) to find creative solutions that satisfied both regulatory requirements and user needs. This approach led to innovations like their award-winning mobile app features while maintaining strict security and regulatory compliance.

A chaordic competency emerges through the intentional practice of MTR activities, which helps teams build comfort with the transference between wonder and rigor. When we embrace this chaordic perspective, we can better appreciate how periods of apparent slowdown or "nonproductive" time actually fuel our forward progress, just like the backward rotation of a bicycle wheel contributes to its overall forward motion.

MINIMUM VIABLE EXPERIENCES: NEW KPIs FOR THE IMAGINATION ERA

In the new Imagination Era, we have the opportunity to dream up a very different sort of workplace. This is inevitable if we embrace a novel, human-centered approach to growth. The best path toward that future state is to incorporate movement, thought, and rest in an integrative fashion in the workplace. And that means we will need some new KPIs. As James Hewitt told me,

> I think that we'd need to look at economic models very differently, both kind of at a high level, but also even at a micro level as well. It's kind of at a whole scale. I think it means looking at KPIs in a very different way for individuals, where we actually start to really understand what value creation means for knowledge workers in particular. Because the work is so abstract, it's (currently) very difficult to define what productivity means.

In Chapter 4, "Think: The Inside-Out Work of Cultivation," I mentioned how learning organizations were all the rage in the 1990s. The concept comes from Peter Senge's *The Fifth Dimension*, a book that explored organizational management from a systems thinking approach. A 2008 *Harvard Business Review* article explains that a learning organization is "an organization made up of employees skilled at creating, acquiring, and transferring knowledge. These people could help their firms cultivate tolerance, foster open discussion, and think holistically and systemically. Such learning organizations would be able to adapt to the unpredictable more quickly than their competitors could."[17] The article emphasized values such as "openness to new ideas" and "time for reflection" as key to building a learning organization.

We need to revive those values if we are going to spark and leverage imagination. MTR activity is a great way to build a learning organization because it ensures that learning will seed and blossom in a multitude of places beyond the physical confines of the company's org chart or office building. This is a modification of the learning organization of the past in that the boundaries for where learning takes place are greatly expanded. Angela Val, CEO of Visit Philadelphia, told me,

> I would rather be a company that does a few things really well than one hundred things kind of so-so. [That] means we have to make room for other new projects, new ideas. The only way to do that is to evaluate both the new ideas that people are suggesting, and also evaluate the work that we currently do every so often to ask, "Does the effort that we're putting into this particular project give us the benefit that we want as it pertains to our goals or KPI's [goals]?" Because if it's not, we're going to have to look at phasing it out.

Currently, your organization or team's KPIs may be tied to markers such as inventory turnover, cost per lead, retention rates, market share, and customer conversion or churn rates. I'm not saying those benchmarks don't matter. What I am suggesting is that we can *add* to this list, especially given that a lot of what contributes to productivity happens in realms that we cannot see or tangibly monitor—namely, through MTR activity.

When I conducted interviews for this book, the final questions I asked each person were: "Imagine a future state where MTR activity was a reality. What new KPIs would you want to be included? What else would you want considered for your performance review and promotion?"

What follows are suggestions for new KPIs for the Imagination Era. They reflect the range of activity that actually goes into a future state of work that leverages both complementary and substitutive technology. Think of these new KPIs as additional components to a dashboard with levers that you could dial up or down according to your company's goals. These KPIs would cultivate holistic growth and emphasize how workplaces can integrate the human elements of creativity, rest, and movement to foster innovation, collaboration, and well-being. The following KPIs are not all measurable in the traditional sense—after all, imagination blooms in the ambiguous spaces—but they are indicators of ways we can produce what I call *minimal viable experiences* that cultivate more dynamic work and innovative output:

1. **Meaning**—How connected employees feel to the significance of their work and its impact beyond profits—this could be gauged via surveys on a pre-activity/project and post-activity/project basis.
2. **Time to think and ponder**—The number of minutes per week dedicated to deep reflection and unstructured thinking.
3. **Value creation in terms of new ideas**—Measuring success through idea generation instead of only through sheer output (such as number of hours or widgets produced).
4. **Experimentation and prototyping**—The number of small-scale experiments and prototypes created to test and refine new concepts.

5. **Big, audacious ideas in service to the organization**—The number of bold ideas generated that have the potential to propel the company forward in a transformative way.

6. **Big, audacious ideas in service to people's community**—The number of bold ideas generated that have the potential to benefit society and create positive social impact.

7. **Number of sabbaticals taken per person in an organization**—Tracking the number of extended breaks taken to recharge and reflect.

8. **Impact of sabbaticals on the team in terms of new idea creation**—Measuring individual and team effectiveness (in terms of ideas generated and executed, team collaboration, and traditional productivity) before and after sabbaticals.

9. **Autonomy given**—Assessing the level of independence employees have in managing their time, projects, and decisions.

10. **Group learning**—How often teams engage in collective learning experiences that lead to growth in terms of new valuable products or services generated and shared knowledge.

11. **Time for play**—Time allocated for creative play and unstructured activities that enhance well-being and creative thinking.

12. **New connections at work generated because of recess/playtime**—Tracking the relationships and collaborations that form as a result of informal play and movement breaks.

13. **Effective collaboration**—Measuring the quality of teamwork and how well diverse perspectives are integrated to produce better outcomes.

14. **Number of walking meetings**—Number of meetings held while walking, promoting movement, relaxation, and creative thought.

15. **New stakeholders invited into a process because of time away to rethink**—How time spent away from routine enables fresh stakeholders and perspectives to be introduced into projects.

16. **Emotional well-being**—Programs and initiatives that prioritize mental health, emotional balance, and stress reduction.

17. **Impact in terms of costs of burnout**—Measuring the impact of integrating MTR activities into the workplace on employee turnover and sentiment.

18. **Diversity of thought to cultivate the best ideas**—Tracking the variety of perspectives and ideas that contribute to more innovative and adaptive solutions.

19. **Social business skills**—The number of opportunities provided to employees to develop interpersonal skills that support collaboration, communication, and relationship-building.

20. **Incentivized to share new learnings at multiple touchpoints**—Tracking the sharing of insights and learnings across the organization for collective improvement.

21. **Creative downtime**—Time spent away from screens for creative reflection and mind-wandering.

22. **Cross-departmental collaboration**—Number of new ideas or projects initiated by different departments coming together.

23. **Apprenticeship engagement**—Number of mentoring relationships formed and the impact on both mentor and mentee.

24. **Resilience building**—Number of initiatives or programs that foster emotional and psychological resilience in teams.

25. **Work-life integration**—The ability to maintain balance between personal life and work, measured by employee satisfaction surveys.

26. **Mindfulness sessions attended**—The number of and participation in mindfulness, meditation, or yoga sessions as part of workplace wellness programs.

27. **Innovation sprints**—Number of time-boxed sessions where teams focus on developing innovative solutions to problems.

28. **Post-recess productivity boost**—Tracking the difference in focus and creativity following regular outdoor or movement-based

breaks as measured by new ideas generated and traditional productivity metrics.

29. **Time spent in nature**—The number of minutes spent in natural environments per week, whether through outdoor meetings or nature-based retreats.

30. **Idea incubation time**—The amount of time allocated to let ideas "simmer" before final decisions are made, allowing for more thoughtful reflection.

31. **Interdisciplinary learning**—The number of opportunities for team members to learn from unrelated fields, leading to new insights and approaches.

32. **Reduced stress metrics**—Reduction in stress levels, measured through regular employee health and wellness assessments.

33. **Active listening**—The number of workshops or sessions aimed at developing better listening skills to enhance communication and understanding.

34. **Emotional intelligence development**—Tracking progress in emotional intelligence through training programs and peer feedback.

35. **Celebrating small wins**—Measuring small wins and tracking when they are celebrated, boosting morale and team cohesion.

36. **Reflective journaling**—The amount of time per week allocated to reflecting on personal and professional growth through journaling or self-assessment.

37. **Curiosity-driven projects**—The number of projects or initiatives driven purely by curiosity and exploration, not immediate business needs.

38. **Collective well-being activities**—The number of group activities offered and participated in that focus on collective mental and emotional health, such as gratitude circles or group breathing exercises.

39. **Team rituals**—The number of shared rituals (e.g., end-of-week reflections) that build trust and camaraderie within teams.

40. **Community impact projects**—The number of initiatives that extend beyond the workplace to positively impact the broader community.

MTR IS YOUR COMPASS TO FUTURE-PROOF WORK

Productivity is about extraction.

Production is mechanical: 1 + 1 = 2.

You follow the directions exactly and you ideally get to the same desired result every time.

But cultivation is about seeding new ideas, new human collaborations, and new processes. Cultivation leaves room for more insights to evolve as they may. It embraces those liminal spaces in which creativity develops. It leans into our humility and into our humanity. This is why we need to approach our modern work from the perspective of cultivation.

Cultivation, in the form of sustainable innovation and human flourishing, is the result of a work life that makes room for movement, thought, and rest. It is what happens when all three overlap. In other words, we are our most productive when we are free to move, think, and rest in ways that honor our natural rhythms.

Meanwhile, our current productivity model disconnects us from our senses and our well-being. Take my friend Tanya. She's a high-powered attorney who spends a lot of her days sitting at a desk, plugged into the digital grind, putting out lots of little fires for clients. She believes that over time, the lack of movement and perpetual digital connection left her with swollen legs and chronic gastric issues. Disconnection like this occurs for all of us when we ignore our essential needs for movement, thought, and rest in the name of productivity. This is why we need to redefine *productivity* and redesign work.

When we shift away from a rigid, outdated productivity model and move toward a more holistic approach that incorporates movement, thought, and rest, work becomes less of a series of tasks and more of a progression of cultivated learning experiences. This seasonal approach to work means that there are times for intense focus as well as times for rest and renewal. In this way, we pace ourselves.

With MTR, we make work sustainable, more generative, and future-proof.

We're standing at the threshold of the Imagination Era, a time when we have the opportunity to redesign not only how we work and what it means to be productive but also our relationship with time.

The world is changing rapidly, and MTR activity is the perfect compass to navigate this transformative period. Orienteering is a process where hikers and explorers use a compass to navigate unfamiliar terrain. It's a skill I learned during my teenage excursion with Outward Bound. It showed me how to identify my true north, stay alert to signals, and constantly reassess and adjust my course. My appeal to you is that you use MTR activity like a compass to spot new ways forward, stay open to possibilities, and adapt to change.

Whether you're embarking on a literal journey or taking on a metaphorical one—such as a career shift or launching a new business strategy for your team—imagination is the catalyst that sets everything in motion, and MTR activity is the nourishment that will keep you on a flourishing path.

MTR activity is fluid, iterative, and adaptable. It requires self-awareness on both an individual and organizational level. For individuals, it means moving regularly, thinking deeply, and resting fully. For organizations, it's about designing biodiverse spaces that encourage movement, incentivizing collective wisdom through both solitary reflection and collaborative ideation, and embracing rest and seasonality.

Cultivation takes time.

If we fail to reimagine work through a MTR lens, we risk stagnation. But if we embrace this new way of working, we will unlock untapped talent, increase engagement, and transform workplaces into dynamic communities where ideas—and humans—thrive. Work will become a place to cultivate, not simply replicate, and the possibilities for growth and creativity become endless.

It's time to dream bigger, reimagine what's possible, essential, and transformative so that we move forward with intention, guided by the true north of our MTR activity. The Imagination Era is here, and there's an infinite bounty to gain.

THE 66-DAY MTR CHALLENGE

The 66-Day MTR Challenge is an opportunity to cultivate new habits that ensure you are intentionally making time for movement, thought, and rest. Approach it as a game and involve people in your family. Invite friends to participate or engage team members on your job. It's a great way to activate and actualize the principles and information in this book.

The reason you should do this 66-Day MTR Challenge is to build muscle memory and habits so that movement, deep thought, and rest become a regular part of your workday. A 2024 article in *Scientific American* reported 2009 research showing that it can take anywhere from 18 days to 254 days[1] to truly create a habit. On average, it takes 66 days for people to develop a habit. So these 66 prompts should get you off to a healthy and great start.[2]

These prompts are also inclusive of people who are living with physical disabilities or who have ADHD or dyslexia. I learned years ago from the universal design community that when we design for those of us who are, so to speak, on the margins and not often considered in the mainstream—then we design better services and experiences for all of us!

INSTRUCTIONS: Over 66 days, do one movement, thinking, or resting prompt a day. Think of the 66-Day MTR Challenge as an experiment. Record how you (and your team) are feeling before the challenge and directly after. Do your ideas feel more generative, interesting, or practical? Are you approaching your work in more energized and energizing ways? What has 66 days of MTR yielded in your life—professionally and personally? Most exercises can be done within a fifteen-minute window.

Some have suggested time frames of sixty minutes. I suggest you read the prompt the evening before so that you can be sure to carve out the requisite time window. There are some questions that ask you to do the prompt with a team. If you don't have a team, then do the exercise solo and share with a friend for feedback.

Have fun, enjoy, and share with friends, colleagues, your social media community . . . and me: natalie@figure8thinking.com. And tag me on LinkedIn (linkedin.com/in/natalienixonphd/) or Instagram (@natwnixon). After you integrate these activities, you can also challenge yourself to think up your own MTR prompts and send them to me at natalie@figure8thinking.com. I'd love to hear from you!

1. Move: Take a seven-minute walking break sometime today. Use your timer. It's more beneficial to walk outside in the fresh air and sunshine, but if you can't, simply walking the halls of your office will work.

2. Think: Participate for fifteen to thirty minutes in a brief virtual discussion forum (for example, a LinkedIn Live) or a webinar on a topic about which you know very little.

3. Rest: Take a five-minute "sensory break" in a space with calming textures or visual elements to decompress and refocus today.

4. Move: Use a fidget tool like a stress ball, hand spinner, or resistance band while working on a task today. Alternatively, stand at a standing desk converter for a portion of your day.

5. Think: Identify your dream thought partner. Spend fifteen minutes journaling about what you admire about their work or development process. This person could be someone outside your professional sector.

6. Rest: Take a two-minute daydream break sometime today. Get up from your desk and stare out a window. Use your timer.

7. Move: Create your own row or column of movements for a bingo card to use during breaks today. (See the MTR Bingo card on page 228 for examples.)

8. Think: Read one article today about your field that challenges you. Share one takeaway with a colleague or friend.

9. Move: Collect your team members' favorite dance songs and create a short playlist to use for an end-of-the-day-dance celebration.

10. Rest: Think about what one aspect of your dream/ideal resting space at work would look like. Doodle the space or jot down a few words describing it, then share with one colleague or friend for feedback.

11. Move: Try a short chair yoga session using an accessible online video today.

12. Think: Reflect on where you do your best thinking. Journal for five minutes about how this space looks, sounds, and smells. Use a timer and write descriptively; feel free to doodle!

13. Rest: For twenty minutes today, consciously try to step away from tasks and reduce stimulation by focusing on one of your senses (e.g., noticing the temperature on your skin).

14. Move: Convert one of your shorter video meetings today into a phone meeting and take it on a walk. Reflect/journal briefly on how this meeting felt different.

15. Think: Listen to a short podcast or audiobook today that gives inspired advice about your work or an area of interest.

16. Rest: Identify a one-hour time slot within the next seven days when you or your team can pilot a moratorium on email. Do something non-work-related during this hour.

17. Move/Play: Here's a short scavenger hunt idea: Find and photograph three specific items (like "something blue," "something round," and "something unexpected") within your individual/shared workspace. Keep it simple, immediate, and playful without any advance coordination needed. Share at the start of the next meeting.

18. Move: Request that your next in-person thirty-minute meeting be a standing meeting (if the person is able to stand). Afterward, briefly ask for one piece of feedback about how meeting that way felt.

19. Think: Today, watch a short webinar/video/vodcast clip (under fifteen minutes) *outside* of your field and note one thing you learned.

20. Move/Think: Here's a prompt for you to journal about for five minutes: *How might I move more in the next hour?* Then do that movement.

21. Rest: Designate a quiet zone in your workspace (even a temporary one) for a few minutes today where visual and auditory stimuli are minimized.

22. Move/Think: Here's a question for a quick team discussion today: *How might our team create an opportunity to move physically within the next twenty-four hours?* Then practice doing that movement as a team for a few minutes.

23. Think: Journal prompt: *What if I identified a deep thought partner and sent them one question I'd like to explore with them? Who would that person be, and what question would I ask them?*

24. Move: Implement one short team-building activity today that focuses on physical movement rather than reading or writing, such as a quick stretch break or a walk around the office.

25. Think: For discussion with your team today: *For which small upcoming work project might we identify a thought partner or strategic thinking buddy?* Ask each person for one suggestion. Encourage them to identify people outside your sector.

26. Move: Take a solo dance break to your favorite song today.

27. Rest/Think: Journal prompt, five minutes: *Where might I insert one short pause into my day in the next hour?*

28. Move: Fill in the blank: *My favorite way to move is* _____. Share with one teammate or friend.

29. Think: Fill in the blank: *I do my best thinking when I am* _____. Share with one teammate or friend.

30. Rest: Fill in the blank: *I feel rested when or after I* _____. Share with one teammate or friend.

31. Move/Play: If feasible, play a quick game of water pong (nonalcoholic) with a colleague or another team over lunch today.

32. Move: Explore a short virtual reality experience that simulates movement or travel for a few minutes today, if you have access to VR technology. If you do not have access to this technology, then research a VR technology that you could use.

33. Rest/Think: Discussion prompt for a fifteen-minute team discussion today: *How might our team find one opportunity to integrate a brief pause into our day tomorrow?*

34. Move: Invite team members to set a personal movement intention for the day—such as taking three walking breaks, stretching between meetings, or using stairs instead of the elevator. At the end of the day, host a quick "movement moment" where everyone shares what they did, how it felt, and any surprising insights from being more physically engaged during the workday.

35. Think: Start a virtual book club discussion by suggesting one book outside your industry that you find interesting, and invite teammates to do the same.

36. Rest: Participate in a short, guided relaxation or meditation session that is verbally led and does not require any physical movement today.

37. Move: Try one new form of physical activity (e.g., jumping rope) for at least five minutes today and reflect on the experience.

38. Think: Invite colleagues to share their favorite book that they read as a child or teenager. Have a discussion about why those books were meaningful. If you meet in a physical place, perhaps start a shelf featuring those books.

39. Rest: Create a temporary "virtual relaxation sonic room" by putting on calming music for yourself during a break today.

40. Move: Introduce a "fitness snack" break today—share a five-minute exercise routine that can be done between meetings or tasks.

41. Think: Take a "learning lunch" today by watching a short TED Talk or similar educational content (under twenty minutes).

42. Rest: Listen to an audiobook or podcast clip for fifteen minutes in a rest area or during a break today.

43. Move: Implement a short (e.g., one song) dance break where team members can briefly join a video call to enjoy a fun, energizing dance together today.

44. Think: Identify a current task or challenge (the "subject") and doodle a mind map (circle ideas and connect them with lines) on paper to organize your thoughts. Do this within fifteen to thirty minutes, and use a timer.

45. Rest: Use a mindfulness app for a short mindfulness or meditation break today.

46. Move: Transform your mundane tasks into movement opportunities! Challenge yourself to "task dance"—complete a small project while incorporating three different physical postures or movements. Whether it's sorting papers with synchronized shoulder rolls, filing documents with a side lunge between cabinets, or brainstorming while walking figure eights around your space—let your body lead the process, and notice how changing your physical approach might spark unexpected mental insights. Bonus: Create a playful point system to reward yourself when you successfully integrate movement into activities that would typically keep you stationary.

47. Think: Set up a small, temporary inspiration corner in your workspace today with one or two stimulating items like a puzzle or a volume of poetry. Begin the puzzle or read one poem.

48. Rest: Observe a silent hour sometime today where you avoid meetings and try to minimize interruptions.

49. Move/Think: Engage in a brief movement and brainstorming session (e.g., walking around while discussing) with one colleague for fifteen minutes today.

50. Think: Dedicate one hour today to tinker on a small project outside your usual responsibilities, or collaborate with one colleague over a coffee on a quick challenge.

51. Rest: Implement a "virtual commute" today by using the first fifteen minutes of your day to read or engage in a nonwork activity and then transition into work mode.

52. Move/Think: Create a fifteen-minute movement and brainstorming session for yourself today by walking or stretching while thinking about a problem/challenge/opportunity.

53. Think: Connect with one colleague from another department today for a fifteen- to thirty-minute chat to gain a fresh perspective on a topic.

54. Rest: Take a five-minute visual art break today by doodling on blank paper. Whatever materializes is great!

55. Move/Think: Fill in the blank: *I feel most connected with my team/colleagues when we* _____. Share your response within your team.

56. Think: Introduce a short, timed brainstorming session (e.g., five minutes) with a brief break afterward to think about a specific question today.

57. Rest: Promote nature time today by taking a fifteen-minute break spending time outdoors. Share a photo of a cool moment and a brief description with your team or social media community.

58. Move/Think/Rest: Fill in the blank: *I feel most inspired when I* _____. Share with one colleague or friend.

59. Move/Play: Take a "surprise stretch break" by randomly selecting five everyday objects in your immediate environment and creating a simple movement inspired by each one. A coffee mug might mean arm circles, a bookshelf could inspire reaching stretches, or a doorway could become a frame for gentle side bends—no planning required, just spontaneous movement play for ten minutes.

60. Think: Ask a younger or newer colleague for their insights or fresh ideas on a current project today.

61. Rest: Take a fifteen-minute nap today if possible.

62. Move: Wander—take a different route during one of your regular walks today, or try navigating without a map for a short distance.

63. Think: Give yourself a "curiosity pause" by looking out a window or at an ordinary object in your space for three uninterrupted minutes. Ask yourself, *What small detail haven't I noticed before?*

or *What might someone from a completely different profession observe here?* Let your mind wander without judgment or pressure.

64. Move: Play a five-minute "Object Obstacle Course" using items in your immediate environment. Choose four or five objects around your workspace or room (chair, trash bin, doorway, desk, etc.), then create a simple circuit where you move between them in different ways—sidestep to the chair, do three gentle squats, weave around the trash bin, stretch in the doorway, and so on. Complete the circuit three times at your own pace for a quick, playful movement break that requires zero preparation.

65. Think: Set a ten-minute timer and use your phone's voice memo feature to record yourself talking through a current challenge. Ask yourself three specific questions: *What's working well?*, *What's the biggest barrier?*, and *What's one small solution I haven't tried?* Listen back immediately for insights.

66. Rest: Take fifteen minutes to improve your primary sitting area with whatever's available—roll up a jacket for lumbar support, place a book under your feet if they don't reach the floor, or move your chair to access natural light. Make three small adjustments that immediately enhance your physical comfort and senses.

THE MTR SOUNDSCAPE

Here are just a *few* musical tunes that I enjoy and that help jump-start movement, thought, and rest in my life. With a nod to the name of my company, Figure 8 Thinking, I've limited these lists to eight tunes per category—what a challenge! Tune into these playlists on Spotify (find them via @natwnixon) and also create your own MTR playlist.

MOVE (on Spotify go to the "Move. Think. Rest: MOVE" playlist by @natwnixon)

1. "Happy" by Pharrell Williams
2. "Centuries" by Fall Out Boy
3. *The Four Seasons*, "Summer," III: Presto, by Antonio Vivaldi
4. "Money" by Leikeli47
5. "Fly Me to the Moon" by Frank Sinatra
6. "La Bachata" by Manuel Turizo
7. "I Love Rock 'n' Roll" by Joan Jett and the Blackhearts
8. "Only Girl (in the World)" by Rihanna

THINK (on Spotify go to the "Move. Think. Rest: THINK" playlist by @natwnixon)

1. "Stardust" by Wynton Marsalis
2. "Try" by Madison McFerrin
3. "Daydreamin'" by Lupe Fiasco (featuring Jill Scott)

4. "C'est Magnifique" by Melody Gardot
5. Sarabande, Cello Suite No. 1 in G Major, by Johann Sebastian Bach
6. "Strange Fruit" by Billie Holiday
7. "Alone" by Garth Stevenson
8. "Throw It Away" by Abbey Lincoln

REST (on Spotify go to the "Move. Think. Rest: REST" playlist by @natwnixon)

1. "Lazy Afternoon" by Wynton Marsalis
2. "Your Love Is King" by Sade
3. "On the Nature of Daylight" by Max Richter
4. "Oxalá" by MARO
5. "Beyond This Moment" by Patrick O'Hearn
6. "Junto Al Mar" by Schwarz & Funk
7. "I'll See You in My Dreams" by Sue Raney
8. "Lonely Woman" by Horace Silver

MTR BINGO

This MTR Bingo game offers specific, actionable, integrative, and time-conscious activities to ensure that you are practicing MTR throughout your day!

HOW TO MTR BINGO:

1. Review the MTR Bingo card at the start of your day.
2. Throughout the day, aim to complete the activities in the squares.
3. Mark off each square as you finish the corresponding activity.
4. Your goal is to achieve five squares in a row (horizontally, vertically, or diagonally) *or* to try to complete the whole card.

B Move	I Think	N Rest	G Move + Think	O Think + Rest
Take a **7-minute walking break**.	**Journal** for 5 minutes about your ideal thinking space.	Take a **2-minute daydream break**.	**Journal** for 5 minutes after a short walk about one idea that came to mind.	**Reflect** for 5 minutes on where you might insert more rest into your day.
Do a **quick dance break** to one song.	Read **one article** in your field and note two takeaways.	Listen to **calming music** for 10 minutes.	Have a brief **walking meeting** (under 15 minutes) to brainstorm ideas.	Take **5 minutes of silence** to clear your mind and consider a work challenge.
Try a **5-minute stretch**.	**Identify** one way your team could have more physical movement today.	Practice a **3-minute mindfulness exercise**.	**Discuss** with a teammate how your team might have more opportunities to move physically, and then do that movement together briefly.	**Journal** for 5 minutes about how a moment of rest made you feel or shifted your perspective
FREE SPACE —Integrate one **move, think, or rest** activity today.	**Reflect** on who your dream thought partner would be and one question you'd ask them.	Observe a **5-minute quiet period** with no distractions.	Engage in a **movement and brainstorming session** for 10 minutes on a specific problem.	Listen to a short **audiobook or podcast** for 10 minutes in a rest area.
Use a **fidget tool** for 5 minutes while focusing on a task.	**Share** with a teammate when you do your best thinking.	Take a **10-minute break** away from your screen.	Take a **5-minute walk and think** about a current challenge.	**Brainstorm** for 5 minutes how your team could integrate more pauses into the day.

ACKNOWLEDGMENTS

A few weeks ago I pulled into a parking spot behind an old mill building in the Manayunk neighborhood of Philadelphia. I sat briefly in a daydream, facing the Schuylkill River, enjoying the moment on a beautifully sunny and chilly afternoon. Then, my eyes focused on a poster in front of me, nailed to a fence, separating the parking lot from the Manayunk Canal. It was an illustration of a man, 1940s WPA style, the sleeves of his work shirt rolled up, wearing a large leather apron and the words Never forget . . . WORK is a privilege emblazoned across the top of the poster. I was at the back of the old Lincoln Mill—formerly one of the hundreds of textile mills and dye houses that used to populate Philadelphia. The Lincoln Mill is now home to office suites accommodating a very different type of worker and economy. But that phrase *"WORK is a privilege"* stuck with me because it's been the underpinning value while writing this entire book. The reminder is equally parts aspirational and humbling.

The work that I've been privileged to do is to write this book by channeling reflection, connection, vulnerability, and curiosity. All of it has linked me with others in new ways. I used to think that writing is a solo pursuit. And many times it is—that was certainly my experience when I wrote *The Creativity Leap*, with the occasional exceptions of conducting interviews for the book. But in writing *Move. Think. Rest.* I learned something new about the writing process. As in individual sports such as track or swimming, there are a legion of other people—coaches, guides, accountability partners, and encouragers—who work tirelessly with the athlete so that they can do the reps and show up brilliantly, seemingly solo. This writing project was cultivated through the wisdom, generosity, and championing of a phenomenal circle of collaborators.

First, deep thanks to Meghan Stevenson and Blair Thornburg of Meghan Stevenson Books who helped me build the foundation to communicate the nuggets of this book before a single chapter was ever written. Their early insights and strategic scaffolding helped to shape its core message. Knowing Meghan led me to my literary agents, Steve Troja and Jan Baumer at Folio Literary. Steve and Jan have been true and dependable navigators for me: steadfast advocates who helped me venture through the winding terrain of the publishing industry. I'm grateful to the entire team at Hachette/Balance. I first worked with Dan Ambrosio as my editor, who got me off to a terrific start. And then for the final stretch of the book's writing I worked with the wonderful Diana Ventimiglia, whose sharp editorial instincts and warm enthusiasm for my topic helped polish and shape the final manuscript. And a big thanks to Nzinga Temu for her attention to the details.

Then, I was gifted with a second round of partnership with Danielle Goodman, my developmental editor. Danielle also worked with me during the final stages of *The Creativity Leap*. It was through that collaborative experience that I learned that Danielle is a true writer's sherpa and thus hired her at the *beginning* stages of writing *Move. Think. Rest.*! This time around she bore the compass to help me suss out ideas and planted constructive questions that brought care, clarity, and curiosity to every page. Danielle asked me questions to help reorient my thinking, and to translate my ideas into content that was both personal and practical.

I met my clever and efficient research assistant, Marie Edland, through my friend Lisa Herzog (huge thanks!). Marie's thorough pouring through secondary research brought both nuance and robust grounding to my ideas. I also greatly appreciate Ivy Silver, who generously leased to me her beachside condo in Miami—a serene, light-filled space that housed my personal writing retreat and allowed me to embody the very principles of *Move. Think. Rest.* As a result, I experienced a proper solo writing retreat to stitch together the plethora of ideas swimming in my head. Equally crucial was Ali Caravella, my former business coach, who served as a supportive and strategic sounding board and cheerleader as I clumsily unpacked the early stage ideas for this book. And a very enthusiastic thanks goes to my awesome team, who help me stay focused, organized, and energized: Tracie Douglas, Jessy Dorsett, Blair Nichols, and Michelle Anderson.

I interviewed a wide range of people for this book, to understand the varied ways that movement, thought, and rest show up in life and work around the world—from psychologists to a residential electrician; from marketers to designers; and from a professional ballerina to an elite sky-jumper. As is always the case, not every gem of a quote from these interviews made it into the final version of the book. However, our conversations always left me with a new insight, a fresh question to follow up on, or a sparkly example to integrate into the body of this book. The following people made time to be interviewed for this book and I am very grateful for their time: Alex Simon, Alicia Archer, Alicia Navarro, Angela Val, Ani Schug, Anna Braun, Anna Marley, Annie Dean, Ariane Van de Ven, Ashley Simpson, Barbara Oakley, Bastien Baumann, Becca Foy, Bhushan Sethi, Bob Moroni, Brendan Boyle, Brynn Harrington, Cal Thompson, Carla Silver, Chris Barton, Christine Trodella, Dag Folger, Dan Brodnitz, David Bentley, Hannah Perry, Heidi Hamilton, Ivy Ross, James Hewitt, Jeff Maggioncalda, Jeff Rosenblum, Jen Mazi, Jocelyn Miller, Josep Alcover, Josh de Leeuw, Kerri Hall, Kyoko Minehishi, Leah Sutton, Luke Bloom, Michelle Tugade, Muriel Kreske, Nick Begley, Paula Intravia, Peter Knutson, Samantha Flores, Samantha Skey, Scott Peltin, Shalinee Sharma, Shelley Zalis, Shirin Etessam, Snigdha Ganesh, Stacey Boston, Susan Kyles, Susan Magsamen, Tim Adams, Tim Miner, Tom Begley, Tyler Blaetz, and Tyler Turner.

I am connected to a number of communities that, probably unbeknownst to them, were truly timely sources of rejuvenation and inspiration: DanceFit Entertainment, The Fitler Club, Impact Eleven, Luminary, SHE Media, Society Hill Dance Academy, SwimTrek, Swim with Brynn (Charlotte Brynn), The List, and The What Alliance.

Jessi Hempel at LinkedIn interviewed me very early on for an episode of her podcast *Hello Monday*—that conversation helped me to oxygenate my ideas at prototype phase. Seth Godin had me over for lunch and conversation—that afternoon and his cheerful emails replenished me in multiple dimensions. The spaces, convenings, retreats, and Zoom calls that all these folks offered always happened exactly when I needed them.

And most especially, I thank my husband John—my partner in every sense. His unwavering curiosity, presence, and belief in me and my work—even when my ideas were still fragile doodles—made this journey possible, and a lot more fun!

Writing a book is its own form of privileged orienteering. You move forward, you pause to think, you rest and recalibrate. Then, with the help of others, you keep going.

To every single person who contributed time, talent, insight, a question or encouragement: thank you. This book is yours, too.

NOTES

Chapter 1: Cultivation over Productivity

1. Susan Magsamen and Ivy Ross, *Your Brain on Art: How the Arts Transform Us* (Random House, 2023).

2. Elizabeth Gilbert (@GilbertLiz), Facebook, January 13, 2016, https://www.facebook.com/GilbertLiz/posts/question-of-the-day-what-are-you-doing-with-your-lifedear-ones-i-get-a-lot-of-qu/948792035202912/?_rdr.

3. "Statistics and Data Directorate," OECD, https://www.oecd.org/en/about/directorates/statistics-and-data-directorate.html.

4. Paul R. Krugman, *The Age of Diminished Expectations* (MIT Press, 1997).

5. "How to Be Productive in Life," Tony Robbins, https://www.tonyrobbins.com/blog/what-is-productivity-really?srsltid=AfmBOopenTjoz_dBFzvXheRKzXLt0P4x69LuOEpB-OOlwtPhmmOuZ9l0.

6. Matt Plummer, "How to Be More Productive Without Burning Out," *Harvard Business Review*, December 11, 2017, https://hbr.org/2017/12/how-to-be-more-productive-without-burning-out.

7. Jordan Turner, "3 Ways to Monitor Employee Productivity," Gartner, June 9, 2022, https://www.gartner.com/en/articles/the-right-way-to-monitor-your-employee-productivity.

8. Nola Taylor Tillman, Meghan Bartels, and Scott Dutfield, "Einstein's Theory of General Relativity," Space.com, May 14, 2023, https://www.space.com/17661-theory-general-relativity.html.

9. Mihaly Csikszentmihalyi, *Flow: The Psychology of Optimal Experience* (Harper and Row, 1990).

10. Brad Olson, "Why You Need to Take a Break from Work in Order to Be Successful," *Fast Company*, December 13, 2022, https://www.fastcompany.com/90823185/why-you-need-to-take-a-break-from-work-in-order-to-be-successful.

11. Ryan Wong, "'Productivity Theater' Is Officially Out of Control at Work. Here's How to Prevent It," *Fast Company*, April 21, 2023, https://www.fastcompany.com/90884412/productivity-theater-is-officially-out-of-control-at-work-heres-how-to-prevent-it.

12. "New Survey: Performative Work and Productivity Theater," Visier, https://www.visier.com/blog/productivity-survey-shows-performative-work/.

13. "The Anatomy of Work Global Index," Asana, 2023, https://asana.com/resources/anatomy-of-work.

14. Erika Watts, "10-Minute 'Micro-Breaks' May Help Prevent Worker Burnout, Study Finds," Medical News Today, August 31, 2022, https://www.medicalnewstoday.com/articles/10-minute-micro-breaks-may-help-prevent-worker-burnout-study-finds?utm_medium=organic&utm_source=blog&utm_campaign=micro-breaks.

15. Danielle Boyd, "Workplace Stress," American Institute of Stress, https://www.stress.org/workplace-stress/.

16. "Burn-out an 'Occupational Phenomenon': International Classification of Diseases," World Health Organization, May 28, 2019, https://www.who.int/news/item/28-05-2019-burn-out-an-occupational-phenomenon-international-classification-of-diseases.

17. Ben Wigert and Sangeeta Agrawal, "Employee Burnout, Part 1: The 5 Main Causes," Gallup, July 12, 2018, https://www.gallup.com/workplace/237059/employee-burnout-part-main-causes.aspx.

18. Stuart Crainer, *The Management Century: A Critical Review of 20th Century Thought and Practice* (Jossey-Bass, 2000).

Chapter 2: What Is MTR?

1. Jill Bolte Taylor, *My Stroke of Insight: A Brain Scientist's Personal Journey* (Penguin, 2016).

2. Gary G. Berntson, John T. Cacioppo, Karen S. Quigley, and Vincent T. Fabro, "Autonomic Space and Psychophysiological Response," *Psychophysiology* 31, no. 1 (1994): 44–61, https://doi.org/10.1111/j.1469-8986.1994.tb01024.x.

3. Dale Purves, George J. Augustine, David Fitzpatrick, Lawrence C. Katz, et al., "Physiological Changes Associated with Emotion," in *Neuroscience*, 2nd ed., ed. D. Purves, G. J. Augustine, D. Fitzpatrick, et al. (Sinauer Associates, 2011), https://www.ncbi.nlm.nih.gov/books/NBK10829/.

4. John Medina, *Brain Rules: 12 Principles for Surviving and Thriving at Work, Home, and School* (Pear Press, 2008).

5. Medina, *Brain Rules*.

6. Susan Magsamen and Ivy Ross, *Your Brain on Art: How the Arts Transform Us* (Random House, 2023).

7. Girija Kaimal and Kendra Ray, "Free Art-Making in an Art Therapy Open Studio: Changes in Affect and Self-Efficacy," *Arts & Health* 9, no. 2 (2016): 154–66, https://doi.org/10.1080/17533015.2016.1217248.

8. Adam Grant, "Post-Covid Happiness Comes in Groups," Opinion, *New York Times*, July 10, 2021, https://www.nytimes.com/2021/07/10/opinion/sunday/covid-group-emotions-happiness.html?unlocked_article_code=1.qE0.KHlI.nfiF-2wno-SU&smid=url-share.

9. Samuel E. West, Eva Hoff, and Ingegerd Carlsson, "Play and Productivity: Enhancing the Creative Climate at Workplace Meetings with Play Cues," *American Journal of Play* 9, no. 1 (2016): 71–86, https://files.eric.ed.gov/fulltext/EJ1123863.pdf.

10. Stephen M. Siviy, "A Brain Motivated to Play: Insights into the Neurobiology of Playfulness," *Behaviour* 153, nos. 6–7 (2016): 819–44, https://doi.org/10.2307/43955737.

11. Jennifer Lynn Aaker and Naomi Bagdonas, *Humor, Seriously* (Currency, 2020).

12. West, Hoff, and Carlsson, "Play and Productivity."

13. Grant, "Post-Covid Happiness."

14. Adam "Smiley" Poswolsky, "The Great Reconnection: How to Build Human Connection in a Hybrid Workforce," *Friends with Smiley*, February 14, 2023, http://friendswithsmiley.substack.com/p/the-great-reconnection-how-to-build?utm_source=substack&utm_medium=email.

15. Poswolsky, "The Great Reconnection."

16. Brenna Hassinger-Das and Katelyn Fletcher, *The Benefits of Playful Learning: Key Insights from Research and Analysis of Playful Learning Landscapes* (Center for Universal Education, 2023), accessed January 5, 2025, http://files.eric.ed.gov/fulltext/ED640394.pdf.

17. Museum of Failure, accessed December 15, 2024, https://museumoffailure.com/.

18. Adam Piore, "Do You Play Enough? Science Says It's Critical to Your Health and Well-Being," *Newsweek*, July 19, 2023, http://www.newsweek.com/2023/07/28/do-you-play-enough-science-says-its-critical-your-health-well-being-1813808.html.

19. Piore, "Do You Play Enough?"

20. Ann Charlotte Thorsted, "Communities of Play—a Collective Unfolding," *International Journal of Play* 5, no. 1 (2016): 28–46, https://doi.org/10.1080/21594937.2016.1147292.

21. Thorsted, "Communities of Play."

22. Thorsted, "Communities of Play."

23. Thorsted, "Communities of Play."

24. Adam Piore, "Do You Play Enough?"

25. Hassinger-Das and Fletcher, *The Benefits of Playful Learning*.

26. Piore, "Do You Play Enough?"

27. Piore, "Do You Play Enough?"

Chapter 3: Move: It's How We're Designed

1. This anecdote is adapted from an article I wrote in 2023: Natalie Nixon, "At 53, I Went on an Open-Water Swimming Vacation—Here's What It Taught Me," Katie Couric Media, December 8, 2023, https://katiecouric.com/lifestyle/travel/what-is-an-open-water-swimming-trip-like/.

2. Bonnie Hayden Cheng and Yolanda Na Li, "To Improve Your Work Performance, Get Some Exercise," *Harvard Business Review*, May 30, 2023, https://hbr.org/2023/05/to-improve-your-work-performance-get-some-exercise.

3. "Exercising to Relax," Harvard Health, July 7, 2020, https://www.health.harvard.edu/staying-healthy/exercising-to-relax.

4. Raed Mualem, Gerry Leisman, Yusra Zbedat, et al., "The Effect of Movement on Cognitive Performance," *Frontiers in Public Health* 6 (April 2018), https://doi.org/10.3389/fpubh.2018.00100.

5. Lieke L. ten Brummelhuis, Charles Calderwood, Christopher C. Rosen, and Allison S. Gabriel, "Is Physical Activity Before the End of the Workday a Drain or a Gain? Daily Implications on Work Focus in Regular Exercisers," *Journal of Applied Psychology* 107, no. 10 (2022), https://doi.org/10.1037/apl0000976.

6. Allie Volpe, "How to Microdose Movement," *Vox*, January 25, 2024, https://www.vox.com/even-better/24048120/microdose-movement-sitting-sedentary-posture.

7. "Global Action Plan on Physical Activity 2018–2030: More Active People for a Healthier World," World Health Organization, 2018, https://www.who.int/publications/i/item/9789241514187.

8. "Global Action Plan," World Health Organization.

9. Daniel Lieberman, *Exercised: The Science of Physical Activity, Rest and Health* (Penguin, 2021).

10. Annie Murphy Paul, *The Extended Mind: The Power of Thinking Outside the Brain* (Mariner, 2022).

11. Peter Lovatt (@drpeterlovatt), "Discovering the Mind-Body Connection," Instagram, September 13, 2024, https://www.instagram.com/reel/C_2qGq2o5EG/?utm_source=ig_web_copy_link&igsh=MzRlODBiNWFlZA==.

12. "4 Reasons to Laugh out Loud," Cleveland Clinic, November 10, 2022, https://health.clevelandclinic.org/is-laughing-good-for-you.

13. Sam Jayanti, "We Should Start Recess in the Workplace," Ideamix, May 8, 2023, http://www.theideamix.com/library/global-trends/recess-in-the-workplace.

14. "Standing Desk Research Proves Benefits of Standing at Work," Steelcase, July 24, 2018, https://www.steelcase.com/research/articles/topics/wellbeing/year-long-study-reinforces-benefits-standing-desks/.

15. Susan A. Abookire, Sujata G. Ayala, and Nancy A. Shadick, "Supporting Wellness, Resilience, and Community with Forest Therapy," *Global Advances in Integrative Medicine and Health* 13 (January 2024), https://doi.org/10.1177/27536130241246503.

16. Abookire, Ayala, and Shadick. "Supporting Wellness."

17. "Increasing Physical Activity Among Adults with Disabilities," CDC, December 16, 2024, https://www.cdc.gov/disability-and-health/conditions/physical-activity.html?CDC_AAref_Val=https://www.cdc.gov/ncbddd/disabilityandhealth/pa.html.

18. "Physical Activity for People with Disability," CDC, December 12, 2024, https://www.cdc.gov/disability-and-health/articles-documents/physical-activity-for-people-with-disability.html?CDC_AAref_Val=https://www.cdc.gov/ncbddd/disabilityandhealth/features/physical-activity-for-all.html.

19. "Increasing Physical Activity," CDC.

20. "The Mental Health of People with Disabilities," CDC, December 16, 2024. https://www.cdc.gov/disability-and-health/articles-documents/mental-health-of-people-with-disabilities.html?CDC_AAref_Val=https://www.cdc.gov/ncbddd/disabilityandhealth/features/mental-health-for-all.html.

21. "How to Exercise with Limited Mobility," UNC Health Talk, January 10, 2024, https://healthtalk.unchealthcare.org/how-to-exercise-with-limited-mobility/.

22. "Physical Activity for Adults: An Overview," CDC, February 21, 2024, https://www.cdc.gov/physical-activity-basics/guidelines/adults.html?CDC_AAref _Val=https://www.cdc.gov/physicalactivity/basics/adults/index.htm.

23. Antronette K. Yancey, *Instant Recess: Building a Fit Nation 10 Minutes at a Time* (University of California Press, 2010).

24. "Instant Recess—a 10-Minute Fitness Break—Takes Off Around Campus," UCLA, March 20, 2014, https://newsroom.ucla.edu/stories/instant-recess-takes -off-around-271708.

25. Héctor J. Tricás-Vidal, Maria O. Lucha-López, César Hidalgo-García, Maria C. Vidal-Peracho, Sofia Monti-Ballano, and José M. Tricás-Moreno, "Health Habits and Wearable Activity Tracker Devices: Analytical Cross-Sectional Study 2022," *Sensors (Basel)* 22, no. 8 (2022): 2960, doi: 10.3390/s22082960, PMID: 35458945, PMCID: PMC9031391.

26. Sam Glick, "How Gen Z Are Reshaping the Healthcare Industry," World Economic Forum, September 26, 2023, https://doi.org/10.3390/s22082960.

27. "Fitness Trackers—Worldwide," Statista, https://www.statista.com/outlook /hmo/digital-health/digital-fitness-well-being/fitness-trackers/worldwide.

28. Rasmus T. Larsen, Vibeke Wagner, Christoffer B. Korfitsen, et al., "Effectiveness of Physical Activity Monitors in Adults: Systematic Review and Meta-Analysis," *BMJ* 376 (January 26, 2022), https://doi.org/10.1136/bmj-2021-068047.

29. "Why Do Some People Seem to Be Obsessed with Fitness Trackers?," NPR, December 21, 2023, http://www.npr.org/2023/12/21/1220850731/why-do-some -people-seem-to-be-obsessed-with-fitness-trackers.

Chapter 4: Think: The Inside-Out Work of Cultivation

1. John Dewey, *Experience and Education* (Touchstone, 1938).

2. Victoria Masterson, "Future of Jobs: These Are the Most In-Demand Core Skills in 2023," World Economic Forum, May 1, 2023, https://www.weforum.org /stories/2023/05/future-of-jobs-2023-skills/.

3. Monique Solomons, "70 Creativity Statistics: Work, School, and More," Linearity, November 24, 2023, https://www.linearity.io/blog/creativity-statistics/.

4. Georgi Todorov, "16 Top Creativity Stats to Discover How Common Creativity Is," Thrivemyway, March 12, 2024, https://thrivemyway.com/creativity-stats/.

5. "Life with 3M," 3M, https://www.3m.com/3M/en_US/careers-us/working-at-3m /life-with-3m/.

6. Ellie Huizenga, "A Week with No Meetings," Zapier, October 25, 2022, https:// zapier.com/blog/no-meetings/.

7. "How to Be Less Distracted," *Psychology Today*, January 8, 2022, https://www .psychologytoday.com/us/blog/automatic-you/202201/how-to-be-less-distracted.

8. Johann Hari, *Stolen Focus: Why You Can't Pay Attention* (Bloomsbury, 2023).

9. Gloria Mark, *Attention Span: A Groundbreaking Way to Restore Balance, Happiness and Productivity* (Harlequin, 2023).

10. Mark, *Attention Span*.

11. David Gelles, *Mindful Work: How Meditation Is Changing Business from the Inside Out* (Houghton Mifflin Harcourt, 2015).

12. *The Battle Against Workplace Stress: How Smart Organizations Are Creating Healthier Environments* (Harvard Business Review, 2023), https://hbr.org/resources/pdfs/comm/calmbusiness/TheBattleAgainstWorkplaceStress.pdf.

13. "Meditation: A Simple, Fast Way to Reduce Stress," Mayo Clinic, December 14, 2023, https://www.mayoclinic.org/tests-procedures/meditation/in-depth/meditation/art-20045858.

14. David S. Black and George M. Slavich, "Mindfulness Meditation and the Immune System: A Systematic Review of Randomized Controlled Trials," *Annals of the New York Academy of Sciences* 1373, no. 1 (2016): 13–24, https://doi.org/10.1111/nyas.12998.

15. Warren Berger, *A More Beautiful Question: The Power of Inquiry to Spark Break-through Ideas* (Bloomsbury, 2014).

16. F. Diane Barth, *Daydreaming: Unlock the Creative Power of Your Mind* (Viking Adult, 1997).

17. Markus Baer, Erik Dane, and Héctor Madrid, "Zoning Out or Breaking Through? Linking Daydreaming to Creativity in the Workplace," *Academy of Management Journal* 64, no. 5 (2020), https://doi.org/10.5465/amj.2017.1283.

18. Danah Henriksen, Carmen Richardson, and Kyle Shack, "Mindfulness and Creativity: Implications for Thinking and Learning," *Thinking Skills and Creativity* 37 (September 2020), https://doi.org/10.1016/j.tsc.2020.100689.

19. Jill Suttie, "What Daydreaming Does to Your Mind," Greater Good, July 5, 2021, https://greatergood.berkeley.edu/article/item/what_daydreaming_does_to_your_mind.

20. Suttie, "What Daydreaming Does."

21. Claire M. Zedelius and Jonathan W. Schooler, "Mind Wandering 'Ahas' Versus Mindful Reasoning: Alternative Routes to Creative Solutions," *Frontiers in Psychology* 6 (June 2015), https://doi.org/10.3389/fpsyg.2015.00834.

22. Hao-Ting Wang, Giulia Poerio, Charlotte Murphy, Danilo Bzdok, Elizabeth Jefferies, and Jonathan Smallwood, "Dimensions of Experience: Exploring the Heterogeneity of the Wandering Mind," *Psychological Science* 29, no. 1 (2017): 56–71, https://doi.org/10.1177/0956797617728727.

23. Steve Bradt, "Wandering Mind Not a Happy Mind," *Harvard Gazette*, November 11, 2010, https://news.harvard.edu/gazette/story/2010/11/wandering-mind-not-a-happy-mind/.

24. "How Memory Works," Harvard University, https://bokcenter.harvard.edu/how-memory-works.

25. "How Memory Works," Harvard University.

26. David Perkins, *Smart Schools: Better Thinking and Learning for Every Child* (Free Press, 1992).

27. Deborah L. Butler and Philip H. Winne, "Feedback and Self-Regulated Learning: A Theoretical Synthesis," *Review of Educational Research* 65, no. 3 (1995): 245, https://www.proquest.com/scholarly-journals/feedback-self-regulated-learning-theoretical/docview/214113160/se-2.

28. Ethan Bernstein, Jesse Shore, and David Lazer, "How Intermittent Breaks in Interaction Improve Collective Intelligence," *Proceedings of the National Academy of Sciences* 115, no. 35 (2018): 8734–39, https://doi.org/10.1073/pnas.1802407115.

29. Bernstein, Shore, and Lazer, "How Intermittent Breaks."

30. "Newborn-Senses," Children's Hospital of Philadelphia, https://www.chop.edu/pages/newborn-senses.

31. Ketaki Bapat, "Why Do We Get Our Most Creative Ideas In The Shower?," ScienceABC, updated October 19, 2023, https://www.scienceabc.com/humans/why-do-we-get-our-most-creative-ideas-in-the-shower.html#google_vignette.

32. Diana Valenzuela, "Trust Your Gut: What to Know About the Stomach-Brain Connection," Katie Couric Media, April 19, 2024, https://katiecouric.com/health/mental-health/micrombiome-mental-health-gut-brain-axis/?utm_source=Sailthru&utm_medium=email&utm_campaign=WUC_Tuesday&utm_term=all_users.

33. Natalie S. Werner, Katharina Jung, Stefan Duschek, and Rainer Schandry, "Enhanced Cardiac Perception Is Associated with Benefits in Decision-Making," *Psychophysiology* 46, no. 6 (2009): 1123–29, https://doi.org/10.1111/j.1469-8986.2009.00855.x.

34. Antoine Bechara, Antonio R. Damasio, Hannah Damasio, and Steven W. Anderson, "Insensitivity to Future Consequences Following Damage to Human Prefrontal Cortex," *Cognition* 50, nos. 1–3 (1994): 7–15, https://doi.org/10.1016/0010-0277(94)90018-3.

35. Barnaby D. Dunn, Tim Dalgleish, and Andrew D. Lawrence, "The Somatic Marker Hypothesis: A Critical Evaluation," *Neuroscience & Biobehavioral Reviews* 30, no. 2 (2006): 239–71, https://doi.org/10.1016/j.neubiorev.2005.07.001.

36. Giulia Calabretta, Gerda Gemser, and Nachoem M. Wijnberg, "The Interplay Between Intuition and Rationality in Strategic Decision Making: A Paradox Perspective," *Organization Studies* 38, nos. 3–4 (2017): 365–401, https://doi.org/10.1177/0170840616655483.

37. Galang Lufityanto, Chris Donkin, and Joel Pearson, "Measuring Intuition," *Psychological Science* 27, no. 5 (2016): 622–34, https://doi.org/10.1177/0956797616629403.

38. Carol S. Dweck, *Mindset: The New Psychology of Success* (Random House, 2006).

39. Seth Godin, "Patterns, Culture and Theft," *Seth's Blog*, January 6, 2023, https://seths.blog/2023/01/patterns-culture-and-theft/.

40. "Joshua R. de Leeuw," Vassar, https://www.vassar.edu/faculty/jdeleeuw.

41. Dacher Keltner, *Awe: The New Science of Everyday Wonder and How It Can Transform Your Life* (Penguin, 2023).

42. Adam Bulley and Muireann Irish, "The Functions of Prospection—Variations in Health and Disease," *Frontiers in Psychology* 9 (2018), https://doi.org/10.3389/fpsyg.2018.02328.

43. Lisa Feldman Barrett, *How Emotions Are Made: The Secret Life of the Brain* (Picador, 2020).

Chapter 5: Rest: Doing Less Better

1. Tricia Hersey, "Rest Is Anything That Connects Your Mind and Body," Nap Ministry, February 21, 2022, https://thenapministry.wordpress.com/2022/02/21/rest-is-anything-that-connects-your-mind-and-body/.

2. Katherine May, *Wintering: The Power of Rest and Retreat in Difficult Times* (Rider, 2021).

3. Bonnie Tsui, "You Are Doing Something Important When You Aren't Doing Anything," Opinion, *New York Times*, June 21, 2019, https://www.nytimes.com/2019/06/21/opinion/summer-lying-fallow.html?smid=nytcore-ios-share&referringSource=articleShare.

4. Yoshida Kenkō, *Essays in Idleness: The Tsurezuregusa of Kenkō*, trans. Donald Keene (Columbia University Press, 1998).

5. Kimberly Dawn Neumann, "Liminal Space: What Is It and How Does It Affect Your Mental Health?," *Forbes*, September 6, 2022, https://www.forbes.com/health/mind/what-is-liminal-space/.

6. Edward Traversa, "How to Induce the Hypnagogic State," LinkedIn, January 4, 2022, https://www.linkedin.com/pulse/how-induce-hypnogogic-state-edward-traversa/.

7. Brett Stetka, "Spark Creativity with Thomas Edison's Napping Technique," *Scientific American*, December 9, 2021, https://www.scientificamerican.com/article/thomas-edisons-naps-inspire-a-way-to-spark-your-own-creativity/.

8. Célia Lacaux, Thomas Andrillon, Céleste Bastoul, et al., "Sleep Onset Is a Creative Sweet Spot," *Science Advances* 7, no. 50 (2021), https://doi.org/10.1126/sciadv.abj5866.

9. Susan Steinbrecher, "Jumpstart Your Creativity with This Secret Early-Morning Hack," *Inc.*, October 28, 2016, https://www.inc.com/susan-steinbrecher/jumpstart-your-creativity-with-this-secret-early-morning-hack.html.

10. Adam Haar Horowitz, Kathleen Esfahany, Tomás Vega Gálvez, Pattie Maes, and Robert Stickgold, "Targeted Dream Incubation at Sleep Onset Increases Post-Sleep Creative Performance," *Scientific Reports* 13, no. 1 (2023): 7319, https://doi.org/10.1038/s41598-023-31361-w.

11. Robert Fulghum, *All I Really Need to Know I Learned in Kindergarten* (Villard Books, 1988).

12. "What's a Nappuccino?—It's as Simple as a Coffee Nap!," Restworks, August 8, 2024, https://rest.works/en/article/what-is-a-nappuccino/.

13. "Employees Are Still Skipping Lunch Despite Working from Home, New Tork Survey Finds," PR Newswire, https://www.prnewswire.com/news-releases/employees-are-still-skipping-lunch-despite-working-from-home-new-tork-survey-finds-301311085.html.

14. "Employees Are Still Skipping Lunch," PR Newswire.

15. Adam Waytz, "Beware a Culture of Busyness," *Harvard Business Review*, March 1, 2023, https://hbr.org/2023/03/beware-a-culture-of-busyness.

16. "Employees Are Still Skipping Lunch," PR Newswire.

17. Waytz, "Beware a Culture."

18. Katie Jgln, "Why America's Hustle Culture Might Kill Us Before Anything Else Does," Medium, August 30, 2023, https://medium.com/the-no%C3%B6spher/why-americas-hustle-culture-might-kill-us-before-anything-else-does-c0a0710deb48.

19. Jgln, "Why America's Hustle Culture."

20. Pete Grieve, "Americans Work Hundreds of Hours More a Year than Europeans: Report," *Money*, January 6, 2023, https://money.com/americans-work-hours-vs-europe-china/.

21. "Long Working Hours Increasing Deaths from Heart Disease and Stroke: WHO, ILO," World Health Organization, May 17, 2021, https://www.who.int/news/item/17-05-2021-long-working-hours-increasing-deaths-from-heart-disease-and-stroke-who-ilo.

22. Michelle Braden, "Busyness Is Our Worst Addiction," *Forbes*, December 6, 2018, https://www.forbes.com/councils/forbescoachescouncil/2018/12/06/busyness-is-our-worst-addiction/.

23. Erin Shrimpton, LinkedIn, August 5, 2022, https://www.linkedin.com/posts/erinshrimpton_workfromanywhere-culture-autonomy-activity-69612701312052 75648-DQ1z/.

24. Niha Masih, "Tired of After-Work Emails and Calls? In These Countries, They're Outlawed," *Washington Post*, February 1, 2023, http://www.washingtonpost.com/business/2023/02/01/right-to-disconnect-laws.

25. Patricia Albulescu, Irina Macsinga, Andrei Rusu, Coralia Sulea, Alexandra Bodnaru, and Bogdan Tudor Tulbure, "'Give Me a Break!': A Systematic Review and Meta-Analysis on the Efficacy of Micro-Breaks for Increasing Well-Being and Performance," *PLOS One* 17, no. 8 (2022), https://doi.org/10.1371/journal.pone.0272460.

Chapter 6: A New Human Operating System

1. Erica Keswin, *Bring Your Human to Work: 10 Surefire Ways to Design a Workplace That Is Good for People, Great for Business, and Just Might Change the World* (McGraw-Hill, 2019).

Chapter 7: Start Where You Are

1. Dalton Conley, *Elsewhere, U.S.A.* (Vintage Books, 2009).

2. Stephanie Thomas, "'Weisure' or Work-Life Balance? One Big Take Away from 'Lean In,'" ERE, April 10, 2013, https://www.ere.net/articles/weisure-or-work-life-balance-one-big-lesson-from-lean-in.

Chapter 8: Cultivating the Imagination Era

1. Seth Godin, "The Race to the Bottom," *Seth's Blog*, August 20, 2012, https://seths.blog/2012/08/the-race-to-the-bottom/.

2. Charlie Magee, "The Age of Imagination: Coming Soon to a Civilization Near You," Internet Archive, https://archive.org/details/the-age-of-imagination-coming-soon-to-a-civilization-near-you.

3. Rita J. King, "The Origin of the Imagination Age," LinkedIn, June 21, 2016, https://www.linkedin.com/pulse/origin-imagination-age-rita-j-king/.

4. King, "The Origin of the Imagination Age."

5. Kurt Beyer, *Grace Hopper and the Invention of the Information Age* (MIT Press, 2012).

6. Jane McGonigal, *Imaginable: How to See the Future Coming and Feel Ready for Anything—Even Things That Seem Impossible Today* (Spiegel and Grau, 2022).

7. Mark Riley Cardwell, "Attenborough: Poorer Countries Are Just as Concerned About the Environment," *The Guardian*, October 16, 2013, https://www.theguardian.com/environment/2013/oct/16/attenborough-poorer-countries-concerned-environment.

8. Daniel Susskind, *Growth* (Random House, 2024).

9. Susskind, *Growth*.

10. Susskind, *Growth*.

11. Victoria Masterson, "Future of Jobs: These Are the Most In-Demand Core Skills in 2023," World Economic Forum, May 1, 2023, https://www.weforum.org/stories/2023/05/future-of-jobs-2023-skills/.

12. Linda Stone, "Beyond Simple Multi-Tasking: Continuous Partial Attention," *Linda Stone* (blog), November 30, 2009, https://lindastone.net/2009/11/30/beyond-simple-multi-tasking-continuous-partial-attention/.

13. Ed Catmull and Amy Wallace, *Creativity, Inc.: Overcoming the Unseen Forces That Stand in the Way of True Inspiration* (Random House, 2014), 86.

14. Tom Kelly and David Kelly, *Creative Confidence: Unleashing the Creative Potential Within Us All* (Crown Business, 2013).

15. Leonard Berry and Kent D. Seltman, *Management Lessons from Mayo Clinic: Inside One of the World's Most Admired Service Organizations* (McGraw-Hill, 2017).

16. Clint Boulton, "Capital One Innovation Lab Banks on Emerging Tech," *CIO*, April 2019, https://www.cio.com/article/capital-one-innovation-lab-emerging-tech.html.

17. David A. Garvin, Amy C. Edmondson, and Francesca Gino, "Is Yours a Learning Organization?," *Harvard Business Review*, March 2008, https://hbr.org/2008/03/is-yours-a-learning-organization.

The 66-Day MTR Challenge

1. Jocelyn Solis-Moreira, "How Long Does It Really Take to Form a Habit?," *Scientific American*, January 24, 2024, https://www.scientificamerican.com/article/how-long-does-it-really-take-to-form-a-habit/.

2. Solis-Moreira, "How Long Does It Really Take?"

INDEX

ABOUT THE AUTHOR

Dr. Natalie Nixon is "the creativity whisperer to the C-Suite." As a creativity strategist and the CEO of Figure 8 Thinking, she helps leaders unlock creativity's ROI for inspired business results. She's the author of the award-winning *The Creativity Leap*, is the editor of *Strategic Design Thinking*, and is ranked in the 2024 Thinkers50 Radar. Real Leaders named Dr. Nixon one of the top 50 keynote speakers globally, and she's been featured in *Forbes*, *INC*, and *Fast Company*.

A hybrid thinker with a background in cultural anthropology, Dr. Nixon worked in the fashion industry in Sri Lanka and Portugal for a division of the Limited Brands in global sourcing. She was then a professor for sixteen years and the founding director of the strategic design executive MBA program at Thomas Jefferson University.

Dr. Nixon received her BA from Vassar College and her PhD from the University of Westminster. She's a trustee of the Smithsonian's Cooper Hewitt Design Museum and is a lifelong dancer, doodler, and novice open water swimmer. She's the proud stepmother of Sydney and lives with her husband, John, in her hometown of Philadelphia.

RAISING READERS
Books Build Bright Futures

ﺍank you for reading this book and for being a reader of books in general. As an ﺍuthor, I am so grateful to share being part of a community of readers with you, ﺍd I hope you will join me in passing our love of books on to the next generation ﺍ readers.

ﺍd you know that reading for enjoyment is the single biggest predictor of a ﺍild's future happiness and success?

ﺍore than family circumstances, parents' educational background, or income, ﺍading impacts a child's future academic performance, emotional well-being, ﺍmmunication skills, economic security, ambition, and happiness.

ﺍudies show that kids reading for enjoyment in the US is in rapid decline:

- In 2012, 53% of 9-year-olds read almost every day. Just 10 years later, in 2022, the number had fallen to 39%.
- In 2012, 27% of 13-year-olds read for fun daily. By 2023, that number was just 14%.

Together, we can commit to **Raising Readers** and change this trend. How?

- Read to children in your life daily.
- Model reading as a fun activity.
- Reduce screen time.
- Start a family, school, or community book club.
- Visit bookstores and libraries regularly.
- Listen to audiobooks.
- Read the book before you see the movie.
- Encourage your child to read aloud to a pet or stuffed animal.
- Give books as gifts.
- Donate books to families and communities in need.

BOB1217

Books build bright futures, and **Raising Readers** is our shared responsibility.

For more information, visit **JoinRaisingReaders.com**

Sources: National Endowment for the Arts, National Assessment of Educational Progress, WorldBookDay.org, Nielsen BookData's 2023 "Understanding the Children's Book Consumer"